## A YOUNG PARATROOPER LEAPS
## INTO THE ARMS OF A CRUEL DESTINY.

Our eyes close. Our legs fold. Then the opening, the incredibly brutal wrench to the whole suffering body. The gigantic cupola fills the whole sky. No wind at all. And immense joy flows through every vein, like liquid gold.

The earth is now rushing toward us at constantly increasing speed. Only when I am down to fifty yards from the ground do I remember that today I am landing in foreign, unfamiliar country. Then the air is rent with terrifying uproar. To our right, to our left, in front of us and behind us, the machine guns are suddenly blazing away, and the air between us is vibrating with hundreds and hundreds of invisible bullets. The descent is nearing its end, and I recognize some of my comrades around me. They are gliding slowly down, apparently very relaxed. Again fear disappears, and a strange joy comes over me. This war. Real war, at last....

# THE WAR IN ALGERIA
## Memoirs of a Paratrooper

### PIERRE LEULLIETTE

*(Formerly published as* ST. MICHAEL
AND THE DRAGON*)*

BANTAM BOOKS
TORONTO · NEW YORK · LONDON · SYDNEY · AUCKLAND

*This low-priced Bantam Book
has been completely reset in a typeface
designed for easy reading, and was printed
from new plates. It contains the complete
text of the original hard-cover edition.*
NOT ONE WORD HAS BEEN OMITTED.

THE WAR IN ALGERIA

*A Bantam Book / published by arrangement with
Les Editions de Minuit*

*PRINTING HISTORY*

*Originally published in the French language under the title*
Saint Michel et le dragon

*Les Editions de Minuit published in 1961
Houghton Mifflin edition published 1964
Bantam edition / July 1987*

*Illustrations by Greg Beecham and Tom Beecham.*

*Maps by Alan McKnight.*

*All rights reserved.
Copyright © 1961 by Les Editions de Minuit.
Copyright © 1964 by Houghton Mifflin Company.
Library of Congress Catalog Card Number: 64-18330.
This book may not be reproduced in whole or in part, by
mimeograph or any other means, without permission.
For information address: Bantam Books, Inc.*

ISBN 0-553-26480-X

*Published simultaneously in the United States and Canada*

PRINTED IN THE UNITED STATES OF AMERICA

O      0 9 8 7 6 5 4 3 2 1

*"Je n'aime pas que l'on abîme les hommes."*

SAINT-EXUPÉRY

# FOREWORD

"O Iago, the pity of it; the pity of it, Iago." No words express better than Othello's the sense of compassion in which this remarkable war book is bathed. There have been many accounts of the Algerian war, in at least a half-dozen languages. Some have been political polemics, on one side or another; some have argued the pros and cons of the rebellion, some have described the tortures, some have dealt with the terrorism and counter-terrorism, or with the guerilla tactics, or with the economic or ethnic aspects of Algeria. SAINT MICHAEL AND THE DRAGON has the boldness to brush aside these marginal matters in order to get at the monstrous Thing itself—what war as such is like, what happens to human beings when they play at war and find that it strips them not only of comfort and pleasure and decency, but of feeling and of humanity itself.

Pierre Leulliette wrote about the Algerian war because he happened to enlist in it as a volunteer paratrooper. Like the other 18-, 19-, and 20-year old boys who volunteered he was hopeful of finding a chance for "adventure, excitement, service." He fancied himself in the green uniform, the red beret, and the paratrooper boots with the commando knife stuck inside. He turned out to be more sensitive than most of the others, sharing few of their tastes as they shared few of his distastes. It was a lucky chance for us that made him keep a soldier's journal out of which these pages were shaped. I cannot decide whether he was a soldier-turned-writer or a writer-turned-soldier. Perhaps it was the same impulse that led him to both soldiering and writing—some wild impulse toward a joy or ideal to which he could surrender his being. But whatever it was, it has led to a rare book, vivid, precise, deeply felt, unflinchingly depicted, which I am confident will become a classic not only of the Algerian war but of all war experience.

If you are looking for a history of the Algerian war, you will not find it here. The soldier slogging away over impassable trails or lying in a foxhole shivering from the rain and cold knows little about the larger outlines of a war of which he and his company form a tiny segment. He has a worm's-eye view of the war. Leulliette has not been false to this psychological truth by pretending to know more than he or his comrades could know of the grand arc, rising and falling, of the war's fortunes—or even to be interested in that grand arc. He and they had a job to do from day to day, combing a particular bit of terrain, making contact with an enemy that was constantly disappearing and re-appearing when you least expected him, having to catch him before you could fight him, flushing him out of caves and from behind and under boulders, carrying a heavy submachine gun or an even heavier mortar, bumping along through the night in trucks, having to search villages and market-places for disguised fellaghas with their telltale weapons.

What is authentic about this book is the detail, the pitiless detail, piled up against any denial, and all in the service of a brooding compassion and a sense of absurdity. There is the thirst and exhaustion, the broiling sun, the bitter cold, the sleeping on watch, the sleeping while marching. There is the sense of futility, the discipline of having to obey orders when they make no sense, the constant need to be alert against an enemy you cannot see, the dysentery, the killing and the dying and the burying of the dead, the everlasting waiting, the fear and the hate, and the sheer unalloyed boredom.

Leulliette makes the boredom and futility live, for he has an observant mind. But he also has a devouring eye, and he makes something else live too: the valleys and mountains and ravines, the brush, the burning sands, the clouds of yellow dust, the skies, the rocks, the caves, the silent mechtas in the abandoned Arab villages, the torturous casbahs, the fruits, the fields of wheat in which an army could hide, the dogs, the flowers, the little donkeys (so like the soldiers), the whole world of sight and sound and color. He tells of a soldier companion of his, Marc R., who could sit and recite from Rimbaud and Valéry and from Baudelaire's "Invitation au Voyage" ("luxe, calme, volupté" where there was none of any);

but there is more than a touch of the poet in the author himself, otherwise this book would not be what it is.

The landscape and manscape Leulliette describes are those of Algeria in the first three years of the war, from November 1954 to late 1957. The war went on for four years more, in a senseless confusion of cross-purposes. It might have gone on even longer if de Gaulle had not come to power in France, largely with the help of the generals who thought he would carry it on. But de Gaulle was the only man with the strength to end it, and with larger purposes in his mind for France that demanded an end of it. As it happened, I was over much of the terrain the author describes, as a correspondent accompanying de Gaulle in a three- or four-day tour he made of the army posts in the summer of 1959. I saw enough for Leulliette's pages to give me a powerful shock of recognition. But nothing that I saw, and nothing seen by the correspondents who covered the whole war could approach what the reader will find here. For war cannot be observed; it must be experienced.

It is this existential quality, more than any other, that permeates and makes memorable this book. Long after laying it down the reader will be haunted by some of its tableaux: the eyes of the dead as they stare at those who come upon them or who leave them behind; an Arab who lies wounded and dying, but who cannot be left until he is dead and seems to take forever to die; the brothels, where the currency is cartridges and to which the soldiers are drawn despite the hatred and the danger of death; the young fellagha whom Leulliette suddenly meets on the path up the mountain, almost exactly his own age, height, build, and the split second of their astonished gaze at each other before Leulliette's bullets cut him down; the group of Arab women surprised in their bath; the grove full of bodies hanging feet upward from trees, the faces purple and swollen; the soldiers coming on a store of wedding dresses and decking themselves out in them.

"I don't like men to be degraded," the author quotes from Saint-Exupéry. And it is the degrading and dehumanizing of men wrought by war that forms the nub of the indictment of it here. War does it to both camps in the fighting, to the paratroopers and the fellaghas, to the terrorists and counter-terrorists, and to the hapless Arab workers and hill-dwellers caught between them. They are all caught in a deadly spiral: violence breeds hatred, which doubles the violence, which in turn redoubles the hatred. Leulliette recoils from the abyss it opens. Others do not. It may well have been the six or seven pages describing the torture of Arab prisoners by electrical devices which brought about the book's banning when it was published in Paris just before the end of the war. The mutilations which the F.L.N. performed, on Europeans and on Arab collaborators alike, were more primitive, and were meant as vengeance and to strike terror, but I found them none the less debasing. If the author seems to take them more in his stride while he dwells on the electric torture, it may be because he was helpless before what the enemy did but felt a shame at what his own people did. It was this shame, widespread through Paris and most of France, which formed the crisis of the French conscience. However others may have arrived at their sense of complicity in the guilt, Leulliette reached his by direct experience.

It is well not to forget, however, that there were aspects of the war that he liked, along with his fellows. It is part of the book's authenticity that these aspects are not denied. There was a certain joy in the long awaited first engagement with the enemy. There was pleasure in the "pitiless hardships" of the campaigning, and the more brutal the hardship the prouder the capacity to endure it. There was admiration for the endurance and courage of the fellaghas in Algeria, just as there was a scarce-concealed scorn (in the memorable pages devoted to the Suez campaign in Egypt) for the haste with which the Egyptian soldiers threw down their weapons and ran. There was excitement about the parachute jumps, including the "jump of fear" and the jump under fighting conditions at Port Said. There is a hint of awe at the sturdy professionalism of the Foreign Legion mercenaries. On the part of many of his companions, if not Leulliette, there was a secret joy in the violence; and even he to some extent came to love the danger itself.

One of the disquieting things we learn is how thin is the line that separates killing as routine obedience to orders from killing as perverse pleasure and a wild sense of power. Leulliette was troubled when he found that many of his comrades were eager for "security" duty in Algiers itself, where their job was to search anyone for weapons and where there was almost no curb on their mastery of the fate of the man or woman they searched. After he has refused to re-enlist and as—returning to France a civilian—he sees a boatload of recruits leaving Marseilles for the war, he sadly remarks: "they risk more than death: they risk the loss of everything that could make them men." He had seen this loss take place in many. It had not taken place in him. With all that had happened, he had still retained the capacity to reflect on the risks he had run. That may be the final way to define the human condition.

What Leulliette had, and what some of the others lacked, was imagination—the imaginative capacity to see himself in his enemy. The emblem of the paratroopers was the dragon against whom St. Michael fought. It is a deep truth that the hero becomes the animal or enemy whom he kills. It is also true that a man will sometimes recognize his own lineaments in his victim. Early in the campaign Leulliette sees a dead fellagha and ponders "how this abandoned corpse might well be mine." As the war went on he had an increasing sense of kinship with the men he had to flush out of their hiding places, the men he had to kill because otherwise they would kill him. It was this sense of human connection between himself and the rest of humanity which finally saved him.

That and the celebration of life itself. Despite the pervasiveness of death in its pages, there is always in this book the reassertion of a life-force even more powerful than death. After every combing of the countryside in an effort to destroy every sign of life that may show itself, the soldiers return—for a fitfully snatched rest, for the longed-for leaves. They catch fish by detonating a grenade, they forage for fowl and savor its delights, they sleep between clean sheets, they sit down for meals with families in the still friendly fishing villages, they stroll with the girls under blossoming trees, they dream of marriage and children and a peaceful land.

You can read SAINT MICHAEL AND THE DRAGON as the story of the dehumanizing wrought by war. But in that case don't forget the important corollary—the affirmation of life which is all the more triumphant when set beside the idiocy of war.

MAX LERNER

# 1

November 8th, 1954. Two battalions of paratroops parade quietly through Algiers. A lyrical reporter writes: "The colonial paratroops, silent and redoubtable, are here!"

These redoubtable paratroops, to whom I have the honor to belong, are mostly very young men, between eighteen and nineteen. Their cheeks are still rosy, many without a sign of a beard. They don't know what they're here for! Some haven't even fired the five "Mas 36"[1] bullets that turn a civilian into a soldier. Not one has completed the eight jumps that make a soldier a paratrooper... Well, what's the difference? Are they going to need all that for what they have to do? "Just a hike," they were told when they left France. "You're here for six months at most," they heard when they landed. A holiday...

November 11th. Another parade, the third since our arrival. Even the youngest can now put on a serenely fierce expression when marching: we're learning.

A volunteer paratrooper is never at the start anything but a grown-up little boy, at best an enthusiastic boy scout, dreaming of cuts and bruises, of bursts of machine-gun fire, of his parachute spread in the wind, and of the glamorous uniform, red beret, jungle-green combat suit, and commando dagger slipped into the boot. He lives in a world of marvels which our modern recruiting sergeants skillfully exploit: "Mon domaine la gloire, mon rêve la bagarre."[2] How resist such an appeal at eighteen? He leaves everything, parents, friends, school, work, for "adventure." It's his first free act. It will be his last, too, for a long time: the enlistment is for three years...

---

[1] Rifle.
[2] "My domain glory, my dream fighting."

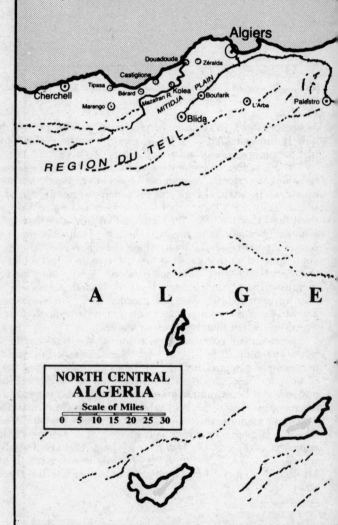

MEDITERRANEAN

Algiers

Douadouda
Castiglione
Zéralda
Tipasa
Bérard
Kolea
Mazafran R.
PLAIN
Boufarik
Cherchell
Marengo
MITIDJA
L'Arba
Palestro
Blida

REGION DU TELL

A L G E E

NORTH CENTRAL
ALGERIA
Scale of Miles
0  5  10  15  20  25  30

After Algiers comes a parade on the 13th in Boufarik. The colonials think we're back from Indochina and give us frantic, wholehearted applause. With fingers tensed and eyes on the neck of the man ahead, I march on, just glancing now and then to right or left to make sure I am in line. The sun beats down with full force on our heads. Our jump boots crush our feet at every step. Much could be said about this misshapen footwear issued to every paratrooper at the start of his career; did the bilious old general who claimed to have designed them ever wear them?

End of the parade. "Right face!" The battalion faces the colonel. He's slowly parading all by himself now, every now and then trying out on one or another of us the pale glance of his ice-cold eyes. "At ease! Parade rest! Attention! At ease! Right shoulder...arms! Present...arms!" We stand there sweaty and cramped. Military ritual.

## 2

Two days later, we begin our first operation. This is a "ratissage,"[1] a kind of operation new to us now, but one that we shall soon have to carry out so often we'll even stop counting.

We set out at night. No one has had much sleep. We are billeted in straw shacks where tobacco is dried, with our packs for pillows and a few big rotten leaves for bedding—not enough to prevent our feeling the hard cold ground. This is our first night in Kabylia, a short and chilling prelude to what through the next three years will torment us most: lack of sleep, and the cold—the great unexpected cold, the dry, subtle cold of Africa which, as soon as autumn begins, will beset us every night from the instant the sun goes down, and make us writhe under our blankets, no matter how tight we draw them round us. Fortunately, everybody thinks this first

---

[1] "Combing of the terrain."

night exceptional; nobody, except a few old soldiers among us, knows this will last three years.

Dog-tired and staggering clumsily under the packs and weapons hung from the straw roof, we drink the bitter army coffee and without the least appetite swallow a chunk of the traditional "boule"[2] before getting into the trucks that have arrived during the night. The war has begun.

First objective: Tigzirt-sur-Mer, where the first fellaghas[3] had been reported to us the day before. We are after no less a person than the rebel leader himself (was it Krim Belkacem?) and his personal guard. Only about fifty men, we are told, but resolved to fight to the death if necessary.

"We're not taking prisoners," says a sergeant. "These men aren't soldiers. They don't take any, either." And everyone thinks: This is adventure, at last. We solemnly load the magazines of our "Mas 36's" with five of the sixty bullets we drew yesterday. Not the chambers, mind you. Some among us are doing this for the first time, and the old-timers are even more wary of them than of the fellaghas.

A fierce, cold wind keeps the canvas snapping and slapping over our heads, and the lurching and pitching of the truck is making us sick. Every now and then, a particularly hard jolt slams us against each other amid a great din of falling weapons. A pale dawn appears, and, beneath the helmets we are all wearing also for the first time, it reveals the faces of children grown old. There is general silence. "Visit Algeria, land of sunlight," sadly remarks Bernard, who knows his classics. He is a Parisian like myself, but from Charonne.

A light rain has set in, and all we can see is fog. Across from me, someone is vomiting, politely, quietly, very sadly. In the back of the truck, another does the same, also without a word. And I feel so sick myself that I have a hard time not giving in, too.

Cold and tired though we are as we get off the trucks, we nevertheless feel a secret joy, mixed with fear, at the thought we are about to know that game that, ever since childhood, we have been told is the greatest: war . . . It's also a joy at last to be able to stretch our legs. But above all it is a

---

[2] A round loaf of bread.
[3] Rebels.

joy to think yourself become a man, because you are carrying a gun.

The joy is brief: the rain keeps on. The landscape may be very fine, but, shrouded in wet and fog, it is oppressively sad. An hour goes by, and we are still standing motionless under the rain, ten yards apart, a hundred yards from the trucks, waiting for we know not what. So this is war: standing like a stake and waiting, without knowing why or for how long? In our three years' campaigning over the length and breadth of Algeria, we shall find that often it is just that: standing up, lying down, crouching, in all positions, in all weather, waiting, endlessly waiting...

Three hours. Not a shot fired. Bernard, who in all his life has never kept quiet so long, mutters, "This is too much! What do they think they're doing?" Choking with rage, he lays his gun on the wet stones and sits down.

Sergeant L. sees him. He's a gigantic Alsatian, with a face hollowed and sharpened by years of war just about everywhere, in various armies. In silence he walks up to him. "Where do you think you are?" No more. But in his voice there is so much scorn for this little volunteer who can't endure three hours of rain and fatigue without moving that Bernard understands at once and stands up without a word.

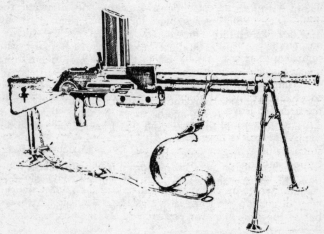

Chatellerault 7.5 mm 1924 M29 L.M.G.

Three more hours go by. Nothing has happened. No one has eaten, or drunk, or moved. We have never been so wet in our lives. Will this rain ever end? I look around at my comrades. Under their big helmets, they all look as miserable as wet cats. So must I! Adventure!... Only the sergeant has kept his cold, grave expression, apparently untouched by what goes on around him. That, I cannot help admiring.

Finally, toward evening, an automatic rifle crackles, then another. With a start, everyone snaps out of his ill-tempered drowse. At last!

We have forgotten that we are tired and cold. All our attention is concentrated on what is going on in front of us, in Makouda. The bursts of F.M.[4] fire are nearer now, and the only response is a few shots that seem to come from the houses. My curiosity is stronger than my fear, and I am restless at having to stand idle while this dramatic game is being played, eight hundred yards ahead of me. All we can see is a few puffs of smoke here and there, punctuating the shots.

Soon the light begins to fade. An hour later, the last volleys die out and night invades the valley. The engagement has ended without us. "You can eat," says the sergeant. By now we can't see a thing. My fingers tremble with cold as I open the can of rations that I have kept in my pocket since morning. No one eats much. We are too cold and tired to have any appetite. A futile day. "We've been robbed, refund our money!" shouts one incorrigible, who all through the campaign imagines himself playing a Western, to the day he meets his death, at Tebessa, before the blazing caves.

Time passes. Several more hours. Not a sound. Darkness covers everything. At about eleven o'clock, suddenly, we get the order to leave.

There is no question, though, of going back the way we came. The trucks have gone. We have to do it on foot, over steep paths that ten hours of rain (it's still pouring) have turned into muddy ditches. The night is pitch-black.

The battalion stumbles along, an interminable, winding column. We go up and then down, up and then down. But in what direction? We learn later that the colonel lost his way; but at the time it never occurred to anyone that a colonel

---

[4] Fusil mitrailleur, automatic rifle.

could get lost . . . Absolute silence has been ordered. All we can hear is the rain and now and then the cries of jackals on the mountaintops. The distance between men, five yards at the start, is reduced till we can touch the back of the man ahead. I am an automatic rifleman, and the weight of my weapon saws my shoulder till I could cry with rage. But I am too busy keeping on my feet to think of my weariness.

After several unsuccessful attempts at shortcuts, we finally decide to follow the bed of a narrow, winding oued.[5] We now are marching to our knees in icy water that paralyzes our legs with cold, while all the rest of us is in a sweat. This rushing, eddying flood is carrying off quantities of earth washed from the slopes. As we stumble along over the hidden stones and boulders, men fall into the stream, weapons, pack and all, and are soaked from head to foot. I fall in too, but some reflex causes me to brandish my F.M. above the surface, despite its weight . . .

At two in the morning, we finally see moving lights in front of us. "The trucks, the trucks!" Great rejoicing . . . "Quiet," shout the platoon leaders. What we thought was headlights was only signals the lead column was flashing to guide us . . .

No one is even whispering now. Yesterday's grumblers are too tired to react to anything. The only sound is the flickflack of wet shoes, the jar of a metal gun butt against a stone, or the splash of some clumsy fall into the water.

At dawn we finally find the trucks, right near where they had left us. The drivers say they watched our zigzag progress all night. But radio contact could not be established on account of the bad weather, and they had orders to show no lights, so there was nothing they could do.

As for the fellaghas, they've vanished. The men who relieve us next morning at Makouda don't even find their dead.

---

[5] Mountain stream.

# 3

Next day, return to Abbo, and rest. We make bedding out of whatever we can tear off the ground or the roofs of the houses: grass, leaves, branches. Then we lie down, too tired to think.

Many sleep as they've probably never slept before in their soft lives. Others take off their shoes and stare at their burning feet. I had never worn anything but low shoes before, and the heavy, water-soaked army boots have mangled my toes. Am I ever going to be able to get them on again? My red, swollen feet fill me with horror and shame.

A few, forgetting their fatigue, go exploring about the camp. They come back from the gardens with their pockets full of enormous oranges. The 8th Battalion of Colonial Paratroops is discovering the orange of Algeria. We shall discover also the figs of Kabylia, the dates and apricots of the Aurès, and dysentery.

We're going to be here a week, they say. The ninety men of the company, Bretons, Landais, Parisians, have become comrades. Twenty-four hours in the field has produced mutual sympathy and understanding. We have suffered together. Packs of cards come out of pockets, cups pass from mouth to mouth. A whole week! Sleep and laughter, shouts and songs, from morning till night. Life is not so bad!

Along comes a sergeant. "Attention!" shouts a professional soldier in the midst of the story of his campaigns in Indochina. The sergeant is a Corsican, a man of few words: "Guard duty, So-and-so, So-and-so, So-and-so. Reveille at two o'clock. Departure, three o'clock. In your packs, two days' rations, tent cloth, complete supply of ammunition, plus two grenades... At ease!" He goes away amid heavy silence. "Bordel de bordel de bordel!" shouts the veteran. I think of

9

my feet and wonder how on earth I'm going to be able to set off again in the morning. And sadly I remember that very young man of good family who, not long ago, dreamed happily of the outdoor life and its hardships from the depths of a warm apartment. My smile must be pitiful.

# 4

Five o'clock. Empty silence. Wandering thoughts. Our drowsy bodies bump together shoulder to shoulder with the roll of the truck, particularly as we approach the summits.

We are miserably cold. In Boufarik, the quartermaster did seem to have noticed that Algeria is not always a hot country. He issued each of us a sweater. Unfortunately, we all got No. 1, the smallest size, and apparently meant for pocket-size infantry since the sleeves barely reach our elbows.

The purpose of this second operation is to intercept and annihilate the rebel band that we barely disturbed the day before yesterday. We absolutely must re-establish our prestige, which has suffered throughout the whole region because of our first failure. Yet, whereas the first time we heard the rebels though we never saw them, this time we do not even hear them.

To make up for that, though, we march all day and most of the night. This time it doesn't rain; but, worse, from the moment the sun rises to the time it sets, it is frightfully hot. The operation is therefore not wholly useless: it teaches us to know the Algerian sun.

This Tizi-Ouzou region, which we reach at daybreak, is an endless chaos of valleys, ravines, and eroded cliffs, over-grown with thorny brush. We march till evening without encountering a single living creature, except from time to time an enraged chameleon. As we struggle through patches of brambles, footsore and half dead with sleep, we learn what a soldier's sufferings are. The rebels reported the day before must still be here. But this heath is their domain. They melt into the landscape.

The strap of my F.M. saws away, now at my right shoulder, now at my left. My five cartridge clips bite into my side like a vulture. Worst of all, I am horribly thirsty. Our rations consist of completely dehydrated foods and require a great deal of water. There is none anywhere. And besides, there is the sun. We march on. There can be no limit to our fatigue, because the rebels never set any limit to theirs.

I feel so empty and worn out when we get back that I drop onto the straw without even taking off my boots. Their weight wakes me at three in the morning. I am so sore all over that I cannot go back to sleep. Every ten minutes I hear the sentry's slow steps go by my head. In the dark, there is continual stirring. My comrades, who cannot sleep either, groan and toss in the straw.

Next day, back to Boufarik—for rest, theoretically; in fact, for a feverish bustling about in the dust. A fruit juice factory burned by the rebels offers us the hospitality of its ruined old roofs. We sleep on the cement floor. It is even harder than the ground, and colder. My shoulders and hips hurt so that I often wake up. There is one consolation: the quantities of oranges and grapefruit that we can feast on to our heart's content.

In the morning, cleaning of weapons, inspections. "How many items in your cleaning kit?" "Where is your toothbrush?" The size of my new issue of cartridges makes me wonder: twelve hundred. And there is talk of going back to France! Winter is beginning, very cold they tell us, on these mountains. We still have neither gloves, nor wool helmets, nor quilted jackets, nor pataugas.[1] Some get knitted socks and sweaters from France, thanks to generous fiancées... I prefer not to ask anybody for anything. And, since I cannot supplement my equipment out of my pay, I stay the way I am.

---

[1] Heavy canvas and rubber sandals.

# 5

November 24th. Off again at four in the morning for a two-day trip. Pure air, peaceful landscape. At nine o'clock we go through Algiers. At nine that night we reach Sétif. Stop at the city gates where, except for the men on guard, we get an hour or two of heavy sleep in the shadow of the trucks. In town, the barracks are full. Nomads forbidden. Fortunately, it doesn't rain.

The trucks roll on all next day, not stopping till they get to Khenchela, a sad town swept by a Siberian wind. The platoon enjoys the comfort of a shed and even, marvel of marvels, of a bale of straw per squad. After forty-eight hours of jolts, cramped legs and aching heads, being able to stretch is bliss. The night is sharply clear. Till five o'clock, everyone sleeps the sleep of the dead. But at dawn we leave.

The sky grows gray with heat. No more vegetation, except the six-foot cactus hedges that serve as fortifications for the increasingly infrequent villages. Between them, plains of gravelly sand. Here and there a dry hill crumbling into rock slides, or an old salt-covered lake bed. Then nothing more but sand, though never pure: the desert. And, as the trucks zigzag through this sand, it fills the air with impalpable veils. The wheels spin, showering us with gritty yellow dust. White-faced and choking, we still try to see. But there is nothing there, except on the horizon a pale line, the territories of the South.

In sight of a few gray and white earthen blocks pressed close against each other, with a half dozen wretched palm trees here and there among them, the lead vehicle hesitates, then stops. The trucks form a circle.

Nothing seems to connect this tiny desert village with anything else. Yet it is, it seems, a very important oasis.

12

Water is so scarce here that it takes us all next day to find the only well—a well with no stone rim, practically invisible, and dry, too, all summer.

The battalion pitches its tents in a square. But in shifting sand how set up a tent pole? Besides, no one has one; the army probably didn't foresee the absence of trees... The bayonets will have to do for poles. More than one later falls down on the sleepers—but they don't notice till morning.

Evening sets in. And as the sun goes down, the landscape is revealed in such immense beauty that every man, almost dazed by it, stops what he is doing. Before us the Aurès, so dazzling pink under such a blue sky that even the least impressionable are moved. Behind us, a sea of molten gold, stretching endlessly. For many, the silent blazing of the mountain walls, forever frozen between the still, burning sky and the sand, is the most beautiful thing they have ever seen. They go to sleep happy, without knowing why.

Midnight. I am on guard duty. The sand is still hot. The square formed by the sleeping battalion's tents is dotted with fires around which a few men are still drinking and endlessly telling the story of the lives they think, or want others to think, they have lived. It is a lovely holiday evening. From the millions of stars that fill the endless sky, a painful sweetness seems trying to rain down. I feel light, pure, unspotted, ready for no matter what. How far away are Paris and those I love or might have loved! Am I not totally alone, despite these three hundred fellow soldiers around me, lying like so many dead beneath the vaultless cathedral whose only guardian I am?

Next day, complete rest, and off duty. I set out with a comrade to explore the village. Not an Arab in sight. Either they are hiding, or it is too hot for them to come out. Hardly any animals, or vegetable life either. Just a glimpse, here and there, of an old gray camel, barely showing over a low earth wall. We have been told there is a miniature shop, the only one in the village, somewhere at the foot of a wall, where they sell dates. We look for it eagerly, already tasting their delicious flavor. In vain. However small this wretched oasis may be, it is so curiously laid out that we manage to lose our way in its three alleys. Soaked with sweat, we go round and round like mad dogs. The village keeps throwing us back into the desert.

One evening, about eleven o'clock, a small disturbance in the village wakes us with a start. Instinctively, I slip on my uniform, pick up my weapon, and go out of my tent. Everybody is up, gun in hand. There is burst of submachine gunfire, followed by two shots. Then, nothing more. "It's nothing," yells the sergeant as he goes by the tents on the run. "Go back to bed!"

Next day we learn more.

"Attention! Hear this report: Corporal N. is sentenced to two weeks' prison, one of them in solitary, for unlawful entry at night into the dwelling of an Arab. At ease!"

I know Corporal N. well. A little fellow of Spanish origin, with coal-black hair and eyes. He speaks little, but violently, and always seems burdened with a secret.

On our return from a very strenuous operation in the Aurès, he later told me about this little nocturnal adventure.

"You know, I can't live two weeks without seeing a woman. Or else I go crazy. Can you understand that?"

I can, if I want.

"I had charge of the watch and I was making my rounds. I began to feel very bored. I told the sentry I was going to do a little patrolling by myself. As I was going by along the wall of a garden, I heard little bursts of women's laughter. That gave me a shock. I stopped: I felt myself vibrating like a cat. I almost had to hold myself in not to start mewing. You understand?"

I understand.

"The laughter keeps on. Nobody'd heard me. So I hurried back and told the sentry not to worry about me and I climbed up on the wall... What did I see? Two little half-naked fatmas,[1] about fifteen and twenty years old, washing their faces in a pail of water. They were laughing and splashing and didn't see me—luckily, because up there on the wall I couldn't have looked my best... As the wall was starting to collapse under my weight, I slid my submachine gun onto my back so as not to scare them and, without any noise, I jumped into the garden. I didn't know how this would work, but I said to myself: It's worth trying... 'Hello,' said I. Quick as a wink, they turned round, and then ran shrieking off into their mechta.[2] You see the picture?"

---

[1] Arab women.
[2] Arab house and garden.

"I see."

"No, you don't see, but no matter... There was nobody left. I couldn't chase them into their shack. I'm not a satyr, after all. So I started to retreat. It's no go, said I to myself, and all at once I didn't want anything more, not a thing. I was quite astonished, for I rarely fail in this sort of undertaking. Without meaning to boast, I think I can say that women like me... Well, I quickly climbed up on the wall again and was about to straddle it when I heard someone shouting in Arab behind me. It was an old man, probably the father, and as he yelled he took a shot at me with a boukala,[3] produced from I don't know where. Luckily, he missed me. I let him have a burst around the ears, to scare him, and I took off. You know the rest. Enough to spoil your taste for romance..."

"But why on earth did you enlist? Obviously, your love life is being interfered with. You can't be free when you're in uniform."

"You think a civilian is free because he has no uniform? You make me laugh! In the first place, they do have a uniform, and a lot worse-looking than ours, too. You haven't seen workers coming out of a factory, or clerks out of their offices? All alike. Ugly, hypocritical faces. I couldn't stand the sight of them any more. And being one of them. That's why I enlisted. I like the faces here better."

Fourth beer. He is started on his autobiography.

"All right. So I'm a corporal, just a soldier like you. In other words, nobody. But what was I as a civilian? Not even a man. And it wasn't an army I belonged to, it was a herd... A slight difference, my boy, a slight difference!"

He's enjoying himself.

"I was a clerk. An office clerk. I was bored to death. Listen. In the morning, there was the start for the subway in the rain. I've always hated rain. Then I dive into the subway. No air. The people smell, and in Paris in the morning, they're always ugly, all of them. At eight-thirty I arrive at the office—or I'm about to arrive, for I'm more often late than early. As a matter of principle. The day starts, and it won't end till six-thirty in the evening. I sit on a chair, with a pencil in my fingers. You know what I do? I line up figures—I, who hate them even more than rain. I don't count them, no, I line

---

[3] Gun.

them up in columns. The first week, I felt as if I were doing a cross-word puzzle that would never end. The second week, I wondered if I wasn't going crazy. From the third week on, I really was idiotic. Every day I would start over again. You understand?"

"I understand."

"Well, you're lucky, because after a while I didn't understand. At first, I thought this wouldn't last. But it seems that was all they wanted of me. That was my job! I felt at the bottom of a well. No way out, no hope of a way out. And I had to wear a necktie, a sort of uniform.

"The worst was that I wasn't alone. A woman sat behind me, at a small table. An old fool, about sixty, who typed all day. I can hear her still, right behind my ears. In front of me, a fat man in a comfortable armchair shuffled papers from morning till night. You didn't get an armchair till you'd worked at least ten years. That man's face! I saw in it the picture of what I would be some day. He seemed to imagine no greater happiness than being there in his armchair. For fifteen years, this had been enough to make him think himself a man. I needn't tell you he wasn't fond of me. And he was my superior. I never knew in what. His secretary and he smoked so much that the place always smelled. No question of opening the window, though, even for five minutes. They'd have caught cold! Wanted to bury themselves!

"That lasted a year. Finally, when I came in, there were always looks and whisperings. I was an outsider. People told me this was a good job. Some of my friends who worked in factories even envied me, poor devils!

"One day in summer, the sun was too bright, even through the dirty windows. I felt something move in me! I was full of disgust, boredom, rage, and sick of being sorry for myself. I had to leave! I suddenly got up. 'I don't feel well,' I think I said. And out I went. Next day, I signed my enlistment papers in the rue Saint-Dominique.

"That day, I swore to myself never in all the rest of my life to spend more than twenty-four hours sitting down. I've served six years and I've kept my word. Of course, I'm not quite free yet—but I know, too, that no one ever is, really. Isn't that true? At least I now spend my life on my feet. I think that in itself is something. And I sleep under the stars... To sleep under the stars! My first dream. The only one I have realized.

"Now, I am sometimes happy. In all the big towns, I have my 'petite amie.' In Bayonne, in Paris, in Constantine, in Algiers, everywhere. And it was the same in Indo. I can go on leave anywhere, I always find someone waiting to be nice to me. The companionship of women—not their tenderness, for which I have no use—has become the only thing I like, along with war. I may be old-fashioned, anything you want to call it, but that's the way it is... Before, I never could have had so many easy friendships with women, but, now that I am just another uniform, why should I have any scruples? And everybody's happy, the girls and I."

"Your two fatmas, though..."

"Nothing to do with it. Those were savages."

After two days spent recalling things recent but already far away, we are ordered to be ready to leave at three-thirty in the morning. Fine, we were beginning to be bored.

With all headlights out, the convoy sets off quietly into the dark. We are no more interested in the fate of Algeria than we are in that of France. Except, probably, for the colonel, we are in the state of mind of city people setting off on a Sunday for the woods, in quest of air and sun. The trucks travel over nothing but sand, gently rocking us till morning.

Then a wild sandstorm blows up, filling the air with whiplashes. We have to unwind our long chèches[4] and wrap ourselves in them. At fifty miles an hour, hardly able to breathe, we plunge into the yellow dust. Day breaks. We are at the foot of an immense wall. The Aurès rises before us in the early morning sunlight, the whole range a magnificent, blazing red.

Through an invisible cleft we make our way into the hills, as into a forbidden domain. No more wind. Absolute silence. No birds, not the least plant. Millions of stones. Even the sun is sad, and will now ceaselessly betray us. Every night we shall be cold in these mountains, and thirsty every day. While in France people are forgetting that a little revolt has broken out in Algeria, we shall be learning what war is.

---

[4] Long Arab veil used as a turban.

# 6

The mission assigned us is neither more nor less than to annihilate the whole of the rebel army; in other words the little band which is growing from week to week and, always everywhere and nowhere, is not to be caught. Is it reported in the North? Dropping everything, we have to rush there by forced marches. Too late: the Arab telephone—those fires that at night suddenly blaze up from hill to hill—is faster than we. We no sooner arrive than we have to set off again to the South. All winter, the Aurès will be the theater of our games of prisoner's base.

Starting from the camp near the village of Tadjemout, the "mopping up" operation begins the very day of our arrival, in El Alaman, Tadjine, Biar Asckoufess. Imperturbably, the Arabs watch us burst into their villages. They remain silently in front of their mechtas. Impossible to know what they think of all this. They are waiting. The whole fate of Algeria may be at stake through these days.

Every Arab is suspect and must be interrogated, if only to verify his identity. Unfortunately we have the village magistrate, the caïd, do the questioning. He is a cross between an Arab officer and a local policeman, and the Aurasians hate him more than all the French put together.

I watch one of these interrogations. This fat, pompous caïd, an Arab like the rest, but dressed like a European, owes his position solely to his zeal. Secure because he feels our battalion behind him, he has had his village assemble in the square. One after another, the men are filing by in front of him.

An old man appears. Perhaps because he is deaf, or, like many in this country, blind, when questioned he just gazes ahead without replying and goes on his way. Has he not

heard, not understood? Such an old man. The caïd, red with
anger, slaps him hard in the face. The captain is embarrassed
and looks the other way. This caïd is a fool, but we have orders
to be tough and above all to work fast. Meanwhile, two young
men have rushed up. His sons? Shuddering, they take him
by the arm and lead him away. The procession continues. But
something has changed. A moment ago the eyes of these
Arabs revealed nothing, except a timid curiosity. Now, hate
blazes in them, like a fire.

Tadjemout becomes our rear base. At night we leave for
long marches through the douars,[1] returning at dawn, worn
out. We get so tired that, even asleep, we feel the weight of
the pack on our shoulders.

The village is off bounds, but one evening I steal into its
labyrinth of little streets that fall from the hillside in cascades
of dry stones.

Like all Aurès villages, Tadjemout is a miracle of surviv-
al. There are about fifty mechtas, from which emanates a
powerful smell of goats and sweat. I ask the Arab sitting in
front of the moorish café where the people find water here.
"In the thalweg,"[2] he replies. "But there never is any till
spring."

I am astonished at his speaking French so well. He
opens his jellabah[3] and shows me the médaille militaire
pinned to his shirt. "I am the mayor of Tadjemout . . . the real
one, not the caïd." And he adds: "The water problem is the
biggest. It often has to be brought more than forty miles, and
on muleback, in skins. It is exchanged for food, of which we
do not have enough to start with. Everybody is poor here on
account of the water. That's why the rebels come so often.
They know the young men will go off with them at a
moment's notice, because there are too many mouths to
feed."

What on earth do they live on? Around the village there
are none of those little fields that elsewhere give at least the
impression of prosperity. He looks at me and for reply makes
a vague gesture.

---

[1] Villages.
[2] Valley.
[3] Long Arab tunic.

MEDITERRANEAN

COLLO PENINSULA

Djidjelli
El Milia

Bougie

Soummam R.

KABYLIA

Maillot

Constantine

Sétif

Rummel R.

A      L      G      E

Pasteur

Batna
El Madher

N'Gaous
Timgad
Lambèse
Foum-To

Barika
Mac-Mahon
AURES
Medina
M

El Kantara
Arris
Tchenanina

Djemorah
T'Kout
Tifelfel

Tadjemout

Biskra
Khang

Sidi-Okba
Aïn-Naga

Oued Melah

NORTHEAST
ALGERIA
Scale of Miles
0  5 10    20    30    40    50

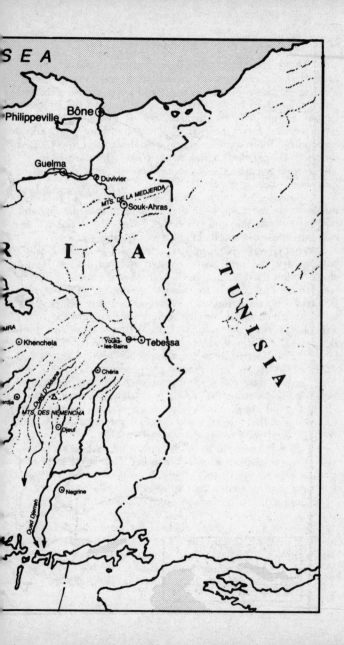

"Thirty kilometers from here is a forest. But it is occupied, and the government forbids us to take wood. People used to go there all the time. Wood is so scarce. Yes, the young men used to go there at night. We sold the precious logs at a high price to other villages. It was about our only resource. But today, how travel at night without being taken for a rebel? Too risky. The young men don't want to get killed for that. People don't know what to do. They are waiting." These men squatting in front of their mechtas do seem to have been waiting for centuries.

He invites me to come and drink "kawa."[4] He probably means to do me honor—unless he plans to call his sons and take my submachine gun. We'll see. I enter the dark hovel he calls his house. It smells horribly of dirt and goats.

What poverty. No furniture, a few piles of clothing heavy with grease and soot, some painted wooden chests. Round stones, a few earthen jars. In the middle of the room, a hole in which a handful of coals are burning. A woman, no doubt once beautiful, still young, but worn by endless drudgery, brings water.

The coffee ritual begins. The cups are tiny, but typically French, of the sort sold at fairs, white china with blue flowers. The water is dirty, but even so, the coffee is delicious. From time to time, a head appears in the doorway and vanishes. What are they planning? Never mind! Even if this is to be my last coffee, I intend to have the pleasure of believing these strangers are my best friends. I smile at them all, at the old men, at the children, even at the women, who lose some of their shyness and appear here and there in dark corners. And they respond with smiles.

I do not leave till dark, after shaking everybody's hand and then, as custom requires, placing it on my heart; after patting all the babies too—there were three—and smiling a last time at the women that were being hidden from me.

The next day, the whole camp has fleas.

The mechtas here are made of flat stones placed one on another without mortar. Their weight holds them in position. No windows. The only light comes in through the door. Whenever there is a marriage, a new house has to be built. They cannot last more than a generation. The walls are left to

---

[4] Coffee.

collapse of their own accord. But the door, and the two or
three beams that support the roof stones, are carefully saved
and bequeathed by father to son.

The thick low walls make these dark tomblike dwellings
astonishingly cool in summer, but the people shiver in them
all winter, and the children perish under their miserable
blankets. It is clear why the rebels, bred under such hard
conditions, are able to endure any and all privations. We
should be trained in their school.

On the outskirts of the villages, the Aurès goats endlessly
graze their stony pastures. Centuries of undernourishment
have reduced them to the size of small dogs. What do they
eat? You have to stoop down to see that between the red and
white pebbles they are continually moving with their tongues
there are microscopic little plants scattered here and there
like so many spiders. It is on these starved little wisps of
vegetation that the life of the village depends. The goatherds
are scarcely better fed than the goats. As they are suspected
of being liaison agents, we often have to search them. Every
time, we find the same pitiful ration in their woolen bag: a
chunk of hard biscuit, a bit of water, and a handful of dry
dates. Nothing more for the whole day. I begin to leave my
biscuits with the children in every village we come to—not
that I deserve any credit, for the biscuits are inedible. These
people are in want of everything. They live on nothing but
stones and air. Their faces reflect the pathetic nobility of the
very poor. A few of my comrades are moved, and, like me,
carry biscuits and even other foods to give away.

The 8th B.P.C.,[5] our battalion, officially named "blizzard," is plunging into the depths of the Aurès, into those
gorges where even the Roman legions never completely
penetrated. More isolated than conquistadors forgotten in a
new world, we shall be spending a whole winter in a vast and
confused comradeship with the sky and the earth.

I still don't like to kill, nor to risk being killed. But I do
like the pitiless hardship of our elemental life. Beyond a
certain threshold of fatigue, there comes a sort of happiness,
as from asceticism.

---

[5] B.P.C. Batallion Parachutiste Colonial: Colonial Paratroop Battalion.

* * *

Every two or three days, we leave Tadjemout and return after forty-eight or seventy-two hours of strenuous marching. We search every inch of the mountains. If we go through a village in the daytime, the rebels come there that night. If we camp in one for the night, they are back in it next morning, a few hours after we have left. All they want is to make fools of us and to prove to the Arabs that they can't be caught, and that even an army will never be able to force an engagement on them unless they want it.

The staff gets impatient, and we bombard several villages much frequented by the rebels—who, of course, aren't there. A few women and children unintentionally massacred make us more hated in a few weeks than a century of colonialism.

Finally a directive comes from France forbidding all preliminary or retaliatory bombardment. Henceforth, we are to work only with guns.

The rainy season begins. Within a few hours all maneuvers, even the simplest, are out of the question. The steep trails are obliterated: the mountains will have none of us.

From the 10th to the 13th of December we are on the Tadjemout plateau, waiting for the deluge to end. Huddled together in the little four-man tents, we listen to the floods of water whipping the canvas. We dare not budge: the least movement makes water drip on our heads. The tents leak everywhere, soaking packs and weapons. We spend the nights curled up, heads against our knees, waiting our turn to stand guard. Violent rages build up in the tents and from time to time explode. Strange singing, louder than the noise of the rain, breaks out now and then, and some soldier, crazy from squatting so long, goes roaring half naked out of his tent. Each time a few comrades go out, cursing, grab the man at the edge of the ravine, and bring him back.

Our situation has become absolutely impossible. The plateau is an unspeakable yellow mire. Everything, even the weapons, is soaked. Dirty, cold water oozes from the ground, and rain streams from the top of the rotting tent.

The worst is that, behind us, there are mechtas, and they must be full of straw. But these mechtas are occupied by the officers. Being too "new" to dare to complain openly, the battalion at first endures the ordeal without a word. Then, on the morning of the 13th, angry shouting, anonymous and somewhat vague, breaks out here and there under the half-collapsed tents. "I didn't enlist to rot to death," one of the old soldiers said last week. Today, he shouts louder than all the others. His tent is flat on the ground. "Les rosses! Les salauds! Les vaches!" These insults are not directed at the Aurès rebels, but at the army in general and at its leaders in particular. Nor are they entirely wasted. The very next night the order is suddenly given to break camp. We pack up joyfully, with hands that tremble from cold. The wolves left to howl in the rain will now set off again, lean and black. We have been made vicious and are ready for new hunting.

## 7

Still on foot, we start back toward the north. After marching and climbing for several hours, we come to a region as wooded as the Vosges. The varied landscape of these strange mountains continues to astonish us.

We reach Tichtat, an old stone village strategically laid out along the crest of a ridge, the crossroads of three valleys. It will be our new rear base.

We immediate establish our camp. It is almost luxurious, a mechta to a squad. What grandeur. No straw, but what of that! Inside these sumptuous dwellings, the smell of goat is strong, but that is a detail: the door will stay open. It's the only opening, and it would hardly be wise to block our view of the outside.

We are quickly disenchanted. The guard has to be doubled around the village, for the region is not safe. No one will sleep a single night here without having to mount two, or four, hours of guard.

From time to time, one of us is seized with "le bour-don," otherwise known as the blues. He quietly goes and isolates himself in a corner, like a sick animal.

There are others who get the "mal d'amour." It suddenly impels them to want to write to their absent ones.

"I've got to write a love letter," shouts one of these men.

"Write to whom?"

"To anybody!"

No one is surprised.

"Ask the Italian."

The Italian has five or six sisters, all young and pretty. He agrees, in return for the address of some girl vaguely related to the applicant, to give the first name and the address of his youngest sister.

My loader has thus decided to write to Mirella. But he never finished the eighth grade, and though he talks well, he has never learned to express himself correctly in writing. He insists on having me dictate to him. I finally consent. Then begins what could be very ticklish: writing a girl one has never seen, nor even has the hope of ever seeing, a burning love letter dictated by another.

"I love you, comma, mademoiselle, comma, I love you, period."

"It is all right to laugh?" asks someone.

The Italian looks thoughtful: it is his sister that is being written to.

This forest we have to comb today seems never to have had any air. It is stagnant with moist heat that hangs on the heavy branches of the old trees. Among the thickly growing pines and cedars, heaps of boulders mixed with rotting, broken trunks make walking harder and slower than in the hot sun. Absolute silence. One has the feeling that for centuries, perhaps since the beginning of time, no human being has strayed into these woods. Quantities of dead wood cover the uneven ground. There are no birds. Not even an insect. Only the rustling of the fierce heat on the dry needles.

All our canteens are empty by noon. No hope of water, unless we reach some mechta before night. The streams are rivers of dry stones. The battalion moves on in single file. Heads loll under the helmets. Not a word. Only from time to time the sound of a gun striking a stone.

Everyone thinks it's crazy to look for fellaghas in such woods at this hour. It would take a miracle to find them.

But suddenly it happens! At one o'clock, with no warning, violent shooting breaks out, followed by bursts of automatic rifle fire. The Bérets bleus of the 18th R.C.P.[1] have made contact with a group of outlaws in front of us.

# 8

We are suddenly like children allowed to play in the yard after a long and irksome study hour. We straighten up, check our weapons, and joyfully—yes, joyfully—we think: Here we go at last!

Ahead of us, a rebel hidden in a tree opens fire. No one can see him. In less than a minute, he has mortally wounded two of our lead riflemen. He is singlehandedly holding up the whole company, which has stopped dumfounded, deployed in line.

Meanwhile the other rebels, though already encircled, have been taking position behind boulders. Shooting begins over the bodies of our two comrades, whom we cannot yet reach. Beneath each of them, a dark stain slowly spreads.

Impossible to locate anyone. The sound of the shots, our only clue, gets confused in the branches. We don't know quite what to do. The captain is furious: "What kind of a performance is this?"

I have set up my F.M. and, though still unable to see anyone, I fire little bursts of two or three shots at the objective a lieutenant has just pointed out to me. From the other side, someone who perhaps does not see me either, but who hears me, is just as conscientiously firing at me. I reflect that he may well get me in the end, if only by luck. Perhaps that is really all war is: trying to kill someone without knowing whom, or why—and being killed the same way. Who would ever be willing to die if he knew why?

We have now been lying ten yards apart behind our

---

[1] Régiment de Chasseurs Parachutistes: Airborne Infantry Regiment.

rocks for an hour, firing at the waiting enemy similarly hidden behind their rocks. We are beginning to be bored. We would like to attack, or else go away. Some show signs of restlessness. "You're crazy!" roars the captain. "Don't move, goddammit!"

A fellagha, perhaps as tired of waiting as we are, suddenly emerges head and shoulders above a rock. He takes aim. Nervously, I fire a whole magazine at him: twenty-five cartridges in half a minute! The noise, amplified by the firing of comrades who had seen the man too, is appalling. The rebel falls on his back. His rifle slides and bounces from rock to rock, almost as far as us. There is again calm, a heavy, tense calm.

For fully three hours we have been holding our weapons and have not budged, and we have changed more in these three hours than in ten years. A heavy rain slowly starts to fall. We do not feel it. From time to time a shot rings out, a password is whispered. Despite the growing boredom, despite the stiffness, the tension gives each minute an exceptional gravity. Who knows if we shall reach the next? Sharp stones are digging into my stomach. My head aches. Is this going to keep on much longer? The fellaghas are completely surrounded—they can't move. But neither can we. We aren't going to starve them to death, are we?

Evening comes. War or no war, you have to eat. I furtively open a can and, still keeping a finger on the trigger of my F.M., I take a sharp twig and spear a morsel. I discover how hard it is to eat head down. As for drinking, that is out of the question—even if I had any water.

It is raining harder. Lovely evening in prospect. A messenger is worming his way about. "Stay where you are. The rebels are sure to try to get away as soon as it's completely dark. Keep your eyes open and let no one get by."

The dead fellagha is still there, in front of me. No one has been able to get to him. His long body spread over the rocks becomes indistinct in the gathering darkness. But I am more and more aware of its vaguely horrible, fascinating presence. It makes the idea of death, so far only a vague concept, an oppressive reality. I think how this abandoned corpse might well be mine, and that few would long remember an event of so slight importance.

I dream that I am dead, free at last and at peace. A helicopter is carrying away my body wrapped in a muddy, dirty tent cloth. I arrive in Algiers, a corpse. Seemly burial in the blue, white and red. On the flag that covers me, shines a pretty medal, pinned there that all may know I died a hero. An old man in uniform honors with a formal little speech what, though dead, I hear him call my "remains." All that is perfect, splendid, think I sleepily. The actual burial is performed quickly. They lower me into the hole. The earth covers everything. Finished. Erased from the rolls. No wife, no children. What am I leaving behind me? Nothing at all, except weeping parents. I have died without having had time ever to be really happy.

This absurd dream almost made me fall really asleep. I come to my senses. I pinch myself to make sure I am not still dreaming. No, the dead fellagha is still lying there in front of me. How did he die, furious, or happy? Was he taken by surprise? Or was death what he wanted? How many children did he have? How many wives? This idea of several widows, all equally in tears, jolts me. I drive it off like a fly... Is he young? I lean forward. But in the dark I cannot distinguish his features, and, besides, they are covered with blood. Did he die without caring? Was he only playing at patriotic fervor, like so many of us? Or was he aware of the risk he took fighting us, and simply trying to live? It is still raining.

At last! The shooting begins again. There is firing from the caves. Orders are passed from man to man, close to the ground, while between the trees flares go wavering up toward the sky, hindered by the weight of the rain. They come slowly down again, revealing a few ghostlike running figures in light-colored jellabahs. The rebels are trying to get away.

**M 1949 (MAT) Submachine Gun**

But loud music accompanies them: P.M.'s,[1] mortars, F.M.'s, rifles of all calibers, firing in all directions. To little purpose: next morning, the count will show six dead and fifteen wounded on our side, twenty-nine dead on theirs. No prisoners. Mediocre results. They will tell us we could have done better.

A work squad is commandeered from the nearest village to bury the dead. Peasants arrive trembling with fear and cold. They have never seen so many soldiers in their woods. The interpreter explains to them by gestures that they have to carry off these rebel corpses and bury them in their village cemetery. An argument follows. The head of the village, though terrified, tries to escape the gruesome task. Impossible, he says. They do not know these dead. These are not natives of the village. They have no right to the cemetery. What is he afraid of? A punitive expedition by the Army of Liberation? Or does he fear that the ghosts of these nameless strangers will disturb the peace of the village? The strange dispute grows heated, in the presence of the waiting dead.

But these corpses absolutely must be buried. It is already very hot. "If these Arabs won't have them in their cemetery," decides the exasperated colonel, "they can bury them right here!" This settles it. Long trenches two feet deep are quickly, though not easily, dug in the pebbly clay. And the rebels, most of them unidentified, disappear, without a coffin, without even a sheet, their eyes still open.

Later, their comrades will exhume them. In a ceremony to which all the mountain people are invited, they will rebury them in a secret holy place on one of those hilltops where we sometimes find Roman mausoleums. Standing upright and facing Mecca, the dead of Islam will await eternity, beneath six feet of earth.

Covered with mud—mud is becoming a sort of uniform for us—and speechless, as though embarrassed at having encountered death, the battalion moves off in single file through the forest. We do not reach Tichtat till noon. A three-hour pause. Rapid cleaning of wet, muddy weapons. And off again.

---

[1] Pistolet mitrailleur: submachine gun.

Again we take the trails of the week before. Despite the rain and the order not to throw away paper or cans, these trails are still recognizable by the trash strewn along them. Our feet slip on the crumbling rock of the steep slopes. We are tired and thirsty. But that is nothing; men died yesterday. Short of death, what would we not endure now?

We keep on, scarcely conscious. Our only concern is to avoid as many loose stones as possible, like the mules walking ahead of us.

A man can sleep standing, with eyes wide open. I have sometimes found sentinels doing that. But a man can also sleep marching. The mountains today are full of men, rebels and regulars, marching this way, haggard with fatigue. Soon they will be all over Algeria. For, more than it is a massacre, this strange and interminable war is an endurance race. Neither the tanks nor even the helicopters will change that.

In the evening we get to Tadjemout, our old camp. Everything is covered with mud. The holes where the tents were are full of water. New holes have to be dug. A few clever ones find the tent pegs they buried there just in case. But the rest sleep rolled up in their tent cloth, for there is no wood anywhere. Nobody says a word. Our weariness is gloomy. A few bottles of beer would loosen our tongues. But there's been no beer for a long time.

Midnight. All are asleep on the plateau, stretched out on the fine soft mud. The company is at rest. Somewhere higher up, or lower down, the rebel company, or what is left of it, is likewise sleeping, dead tired, in the same mud.

A full night of sleep is a night of bliss. When at dawn the last sentinel wakes the NCO of the day who goes from tent to tent and wakes the whole company, everybody's first thought is: Just a minute! Just one more minute! But half an hour later, the tents have been struck, the coffee drunk, the packs made up, and, gun in hand, everybody is ready.

Off again, once more. In trucks this time, for the north. By way of Biskra, a half-dead town that we go through without even stopping. We reach the Aurès and the El Kantara gorges. Once more, we traverse the whole length of them and get to Batna in the evening.

# 9

A barracks opens its doors to us. What luxury, we get beds! mattresses! sheets! a hot meal! wine! letters, and even parcels, forerunners of Christmas! What happiness to be able to saunter, light as a feather, between two rows of real houses, and go into the sparkling cafés.

In dress uniforms and clean shirts, freshly shaved and with money in our pockets, we scatter over the town. Batna is ours tonight!

But what a town. Only one real street. All the rest is blind alleys, dead ends, sewers opening on stony fields and bare desert. Utter dreariness. Here and there, sickly little trees grow painfully out of the sidewalks. From time to time, swift clouds of white dust suddenly sweep your face—or showers that are just as violent. A few barracks, as ugly as in any French town, a few saloons, a few Arab cafés, a little mosque, a little church, and a little town hall. Yes, it's all very little—except for the prison, which is monumental.

These will be our surroundings on our returns from operations.

# 10

The captain calls the company together in the courtyard: "At ease! The rebels have attacked the post at T'Kout. We know they are in the Chélia forest... We leave tonight: one forty-five."

We are driving once more toward the Aurès in the cold, windy Algerian night. Between Arris and Batna the road, once you pass Lambèse, is just a winding track, one hairpin turn after another, on the edge of precipices. The drivers have orders to keep moving and make time. They do. R., the transport sergeant, is leading them. A madman: we remember him coming out of the Mont-de-Marsan barracks standing on his motorcycle with his arms folded. The drivers follow him, trying desperately to keep the regulation thirty meters' interval between trucks. At 2 A.M. we whirl through Arris in the moonlight like a demented circus caravan. The legionnaire guarding the road has just time to part the barbed wire before getting out of our way.

Up there on the peaks, the rebels keep watch. Undoubtedly, they are observing our convoy as it winds through the mountains with dimmed headlights, like a long luminous caterpillar. We have to outdistance them, and reach the forest before they can send warnings. So, faster. The trucks jolt, balk, tear ahead, stop, suddenly start off again, lean to the right, to the left, shake themselves and bound over the rocks, like animals. You have to cling, but to whom, to what? We fall in heaps on top of each other. When the truck dances, everybody dances. When the truck leaps, everybody leaps. All this to the accompaniment of a furious wind. The canvas top snaps and flogs the sideboards, weapons bang together, crates break open, packs fall, grenades slip off belts and roll on the floor. We grope for them in the dark under each other's feet. We shiver, we try to work our sleeves down. They slip back to our elbows. We close the collars of our jackets. The wind rushes in anyway. We shall begin this operation as usual: limp, numb, worn out, before taking a single step.

At full speed, we go through T'Kout, the real center of the Aurès, at present occupied by the Bérets bleus. We are now in completely wild country. The trucks strain, snort, rattle and shudder. They were not built for going like this. Our convoy leader hardly ever uses his brakes. We keep on over roads which certainly no vehicle has ever traveled before, holding our breath, with only inches to spare.

It gets colder and colder. The Chélia forest is in sight. Here, Krim Belkacem will hold out against us for months, ceaselessly maneuvering, indefatigable, elusive, but never ineffective. We go in at dawn on foot.

We spend all that day, as we shall spend many future days and nights, endlessly marching one behind the other, silently lugging our bodies and weapons that grow heavier hour by hour.

At about eleven o'clock, we are told that the fellaghas are only a few kilometers ahead. Up in front, they can be seen through field glasses. But we have to move fast. Once it is dark, it will be too late, and we may lose contact with them for weeks.

We break into a half run, three hundred and fifty men limping, sweating, panting, up the trail at the colonel's infernal pace. He is a fiend! At the head of the column, in front of him or behind, the lead man charges ahead, hurdling rocks, breaking branches...

How long can we keep this up and not collapse? Sweat pours, and immediately evaporates, leaving a powdery salt which makes our lips all white. The combination of salt and sun makes our skin crack.

At noon we have a twenty-minute halt, just time to eat. But what we need is to drink. We mumble our food with parched lips. Our bodies ache. Our one desire is to lie down in some cool place and not move.

We sometimes come across the little donkeys of this country, overloaded like us and suffering without ever stopping, and we know how they feel.

We finally halt in the middle of the night, on a narrow ridge whose mica-studded rocks gleam in the moonlight, and lie down to sleep a few hours till dawn. We don't have time to dig the usual holes that shelter us from wind if not from bullets. Each man stretches out wherever he happened to stop. Is there any point in undoing one's belt? Don't we sleep with our helmets on when it rains?

A short meal: a few biscuits and some lumps of sugar. No water. I lay my head on my pack, which is hard as a rock. It has nothing in it but reserve ammunition and tomorrow's can of rations. I try to improve matters by adding my cartridge cases and the equipment I carry on my belt. The mica grates under my head. I roll up in a ball, with the strap of my submachine gun around my forearm.

I shut my eyes, but cannot sleep. A silent, dry, cold wind is sweeping the ridge. Moon. Thousands, millions of stars. Silence. At last I doze, dog-tired. I am about to drop off to real sleep when I am suddenly pulled by the arm . . . I do not even start. I know.

My watch is from one to four. I have had about one hour's sleep. I crouch among the rocks, straining to keep my eyes open and listening to the night with the utmost intentness. But there is nothing. My companions are lying here and there, pitifully cramped and huddled. It is very cold in the white moonlight.

A friend once said to me: "Three hours is too much. The third hour, the rocks move." The third hour begins. Unconsciously, I lean forward . . . I straighten up at the last moment, like a staggering drunken man. Could I, in this state, make use of the weapon I am clutching? Would I realize in time that a man slowly approaching, with his eyes fixed on me, meant death?

The sky is still very dark. I can hardly read my wristwatch. "Four o'clock. At last!" I step stealthily over my sleeping comrades.

Not without pleasure, I go over to the sergeant, who is sleeping near the captain. I grab him and shake him. "Huh?" says he. He sits up and looks at me with his big pale Alsatian eyes. "What's up? What's up?" he keeps repeating, instinctively clutching his club. He finally comes to, and says with authority: "Wake everybody. Departure in twenty minutes!"

Bitterly, everyone gets to his feet, and seems in the dawn to be rising out of the earth. We fasten our belts. We munch a biscuit. A few efficient ones manage to pour a little bag of powdered coffee into their last cup of water, and even have just time to wipe the dew off their weapons.

In exactly twenty minutes, the company is on the march. There is still dead silence. All that breaks it is the occasional rolling of a stone under the unsteady feet of men marching like sleepwalkers.

We meet the trucks at T'Kout. The drivers had thought us lost. Tomorrow is Christmas. We must get to Batna by this evening.

Everyone climbs heavily aboard, but hastily, for the motors are already roaring. What a relief to throw down your pack and at last relax your aching shoulders, your arms, your body. Generously, and in defiance of regulations, the drivers divide among us their cans of water that are provided for the motors. What a joy to have something to drink, even if it does taste of gasoline.

And tonight, Batna. Get going, driver!

# 11

We are in town. A tremendous party is in the making. The mail clerk is mobbed. Stacks of letters have accumulated, and parcels, and money orders. I count mine: what a haul! Seventeen. People I have not thought of for years are writing me, overflowing with affection. The memory of my parents wells up in my heart, which I had thought dead. Paris, and its gentle rain in the light of the streetlamps... This is the time you miss all your friends, and even your enemies. Three years... Memories pass over my heart, like a hand.

Some sit down, within reach of a case of beer, and start to answer their mail right away. All those dreadful days we spent dragging ourselves through the mud like miserable dogs become a marvelous epic.

"Dear Parents: I am writing you, squatting cross-legged under a flowering palm, by the light of tracer bullets, just back from a patrol in the perfumed, starry night. We have visited the Aurès. They are very pretty mountains. I hope to go back there sometime for a vacation. I am so brown you wouldn't recognize me. We travel all the time. Sometimes this all seems a dream, a strange, marvelous dream... etc...." That is the kind of thing the beer makes us say. The fact is that three weeks of wading through cold mud has made us all realize with rage in our hearts that in this infernal country our dreams can never translate themselves into anything but an endless nightmare. But we do not admit that, nor that we have made a mistake. If a younger friend wants to volunteer, we write enthusiastically: "It's a great life! I am writing you with a submachine gun across my knees. A beautiful fatma is making me delicious coffee. By the window, a palm tree (those haunting palm trees!) is swaying softly in

the breeze..." etc. Not a word about the stupidity of the
NCO's, or the fatigue, or the rains. Just the golden sun, the
blue sky, and the endless leisure.

When the letters have been read, and the parcels that
were so lovingly done up have been torn open, the sound of
orgy begins.

There's plenty to drink. The canteen sells only beer, but
Algerian vin rosé (14, 15 percent) gets into the barracks from
everywhere. Drink, sing, drink. They call this quietly preparing for Christmas.

There's also a slight improvement in the food, by way of
prelude to tomorrow's banquet. But this only momentarily
appeases our rage at being confined to barracks on such a day,
when the town is so near. The commandant, fearing the
rebels would take advantage of the soldiers' being drunk and
irresponsible to commit a few easy murders, is adamant: no
personnel, except the patrol, will leave barracks before noon
tomorrow. "Who cares about murders?" shout the men. "We
want to get out, whether we get back or not!" They are
sincere, though a bit naïve to think this is tender solicitude:
the point is that a good soldier dead isn't a good soldier any
more, because unusable.

In the evening, not even a mass. Just a double ration of
food and wine.

I encounter army drunkenness for the first time.

During the jump training at Pau, I had seen eighteen-
year-old volunteers collapse on their beds in a state of nerves,
simply because they had been cut off for two weeks from the
outside world and had nothing more to smoke. They would
prowl like sick dogs around the huts, looking for butts in the
dirt, even in the garbage... But still sadder is the twenty-
year-old alcoholic.

By ten o'clock, half the battalion is completely drunk. By
eleven, the courtyards, the stairways, and the dormitories are
spattered with purplish vomit. The songs and the laughter
are becoming more and more raucous.

For no apparent reason, a young Breton volunteer, weeping and trembling, suddenly starts to smash everything around
him. This is a comical sight at first, but it soon becomes
intolerable. It takes four of us to hold him on his bed, where
he struggles like an animal. The sergeant is beside himself
and hands out prison sentences right and left. There is

fighting everywhere, over nothing, and not for fun: blood flows. All the weapons have been chained to the gun rack, but some are already laying hold of the bayonets. The bayonet of the Mas 36 is no toy, and it has to be pulled out of the hands of more than one maniac who clings to it till his fingers are covered with blood.

I remember that rookie who was killed by one, at Mont-de-Marsan.

This fellow, a born thief, had been in the army about two weeks. One day, when detailed as dormitory guard, he decided to help himself to something really worth while, and set to work forcing the trunk of the dormitory corporal.

Unfortunately, the latter was excused from drill that day. He was just back from Indochina, malaria-ridden, feverish, and universally known for his extremely difficult and suspicious nature. Either because he vaguely suspected something, or by pure chance, he went back to the dormitory during the drill hour. He opened the door without a sound, came on into the room, stealthy as an old wolf, and, from behind, saw the guard bending over his trunk. He drew near, holding his breath, and discovered that the man was reading his letters, after taking out the money enclosed in them.

His letters! Still controlling his rage—which, however, being stifled, instantly started his daily fit of fever—and still without making a sound—the boy was too absorbed anyway to hear him—the corporal went to the arms rack, took a rifle, attached the bayonet, drew near again . . . and without hesitating, without even trembling, though in the paroxysm of his attack, with one spring, with one blow, he planted the bayonet in the bent back, wham! as if into a tree.

Thus, in mid-twentieth century, like an owl crucified on a barn door, was a young thief of eighteen nailed in a French barracks to a corporal's trunk. The unlucky boy was killed outright, and probably died in complete bewilderment. The first man to see his corpse, when drill was over, was so astounded that he dropped his gun, which rolled down the stairs. The bayonet, planted straight in the back and to the hilt, had not shed a drop of blood.

In the dormitory, there is now no question of sleeping, or even of writing the briefest letter. I slip on my jacket and go for a walk in the moonlight. In the courtyards the night is

cold, but beautifully clear, a true French Christmas night.
Gun carriages, 30's, 75's, are gleaming here and there.
Where to go? At each gate a sentry challenges me, cheerily,
in a resounding voice. I retreat into the dark. Alone.

The sickly trees of the main courtyard are almost beautiful under the moon's rays. Suddenly, I stop, amazed:

> *Mon enfant, ma soeur,*
> *Songe à la douceur*
> *D'aller là-bas vivre ensemble . . .*

> My child, my sister,
> Think of the sweetness
> To go yonder and live together . . .

Someone reciting poetry in this yard? I also hear the
bellowing of an off-color song from the dormitory windows.
But in the Batna night where I thought myself alone, the
voice proceeds, imperturbable and serene:

> *Aimer à loisir*
> *Aimer et mourir*
> *Au pays qui te ressemble . . .*

> To love at leisure
> To love and die
> In the country that resembles you . . .

Something lets go in my heart.

> *Les soleils mouillés*
> *De ces ciels brouillés*
> *Pour mon esprit ont les charmes . . .*

> The wet suns
> Of these murky skies
> To my spirit have the charms . . .

If sadness, self-displaying despair, is the most mortal sin,
this cleanses me of it.

I go forward. The yard is deserted. The voice continues,
calm, full, and sure. It seems to rise from another world.

Each syllable forms and falls like a drop of rain in the black
air of the night. The voice stops.

"Oh!"

Seated at the foot of a tree and half hidden in the shadow
of the trunk, Private Marc R. looks at me. On his lips is a
faint smile, like the expression of an unhappy cat:

"What are you doing here?"

"And you?"

"Nothing."

"I?... I am singing!"

"Why?"

"I don't know... I've got to forget that I'm a soldier, at
least for an hour!"

I move away. And the song continues. But with such
intensity that I go and sit down a little farther on and listen in
the dark.

> *Là, tout n'est qu'ordre et beauté,*
> *Luxe, calme et volupté.*
>
> There, all is order and beauty
> Luxury, calm and volupty...

Sitting on the dirty pavement of the yard, insensible to
the outer world, the trash cans, the dirty papers, and the
cannons, R. sang on for an hour: Rimbaud, Baudelaire,
Valéry.

He came to see me next morning. Not a word about his
poetical spree. I realized, though, that I had made a friend of
him. The best I ever had.

This somewhat odd boy later revealed himself to all as a
model of courage. Throughout three years, he was the one
man I never caught in an act of baseness, or even of petti-
ness. The one man!

I never saw him show fear. Not even fear of reciting
gravely—as though to himself alone—in a cattle car, sitting in
the straw, among thirty exasperated young men, verses written to be read in the quiet depths of a wood:

*Les sanglots longs*
*Des violons*
*De l'automne . . .*

The long sobs
Of the violins
Of Autumn . . .

We were traveling from Algiers to Batna in frightful heat.
There were thirty of us soldiers in that car, like animals,
furious, though sleepy, quarreling, shouting. I remember the
hush that came over the whole car at the word "automne." All
immediately listened, breathless:

*Blessent mon coeur*
*D'une langueur*
*Monotone.*

Wound my heart
With a monotonous
Languor.

In the midst of an engagement, this same Marc R. would
give his water to those who had none, with perfect grace and
naturalness. Once, in a parade exercise, he seized the detachment leader by the collar. The latter, Sergeant G., famous for
his ferocity, was maltreating a young recruit who couldn't
keep step. Result: thirty days' prison, fifteen of them in
solitary, which he served serenely and proudly.

Next day, big celebration! The entire company is assembled around the long tables. Liqueurs, cigars, cigarettes,
wines, coffee, till late in the afternoon.

The day before, there had been a spectacular arrival of
turkeys, airborne and parachuted onto the Batna airfield, to
let everybody know that "our little paratroopers" were not
forgotten.

That very night, with the sumptuous fowl barely digested,
we are off again for the Aurès. It's Christmas, but the war
continues.

# 12

During one particularly harassing operation, some of the draftees staged a small revolt, which amounted to a refusal to march. This immediately roused the fury of the rest of the regiment. *We* were volunteers and, in a spirit of contrariety, we suddenly discovered ourselves proud that our dream was combat.

"Combat!" said the draftees, who had been promised they would be back in France in three months, "you can have it!"

Two factions were forming: the draftees, potential malcontents and complainers, who, to be sure, finally marched like everybody else, though always unwillingly; and the volunteers, a muddled and vocal conglomeration of hotheads, all of them malcontents too, but who, even though their hearts were no longer in it, never admitted this even to themselves.

Divided between these two parties, a few, who neither wanted to kill nor feared to die, formed a clan apart. They had nothing to unite them but a certain independence of mind. They were equally scorned by both sides, because they would not join either the draftees who grumbled out of mere rebelliousness, or the volunteers who would have accepted anything from the army.

Marc R. was the very soul of this party of free spirits. He did not know it, but his superiors did, and at once took a dislike to him. He was picked for all fatigues and details. Nevertheless, when he stood at attention, waiting for the sergeant's "At ease!" as the latter read him the reason for his punishment and blew cigarette smoke in his face, it was always the sergeant who seemed punished.

He was already classified as a nut, as a subversive, even, when, as a result of a very characteristic incident, he finally came to be considered a defender of the fellaghas—and that condemned him permanently in everybody's eyes.

Second Lieutenant C. had just taken what he proudly called "prisoners." A few men having remained behind in one of the villages, he had had them herded together with rifle butts. Their hands and feet were firmly tied and then secured to their necks by a very short rope. In that constrained position, they were left to spend the night. For six hours they groaned with pain and humiliation on the ground, where they had been thrown like animals.

At daybreak, Marc was the first to see them. "That's outrageous!" he shouted, red with rage. But the lieutenant was already giving orders: "Untie them fast, we're leaving!" One of the men cut the ropes with his knife, not very skillfully either. But the Arabs couldn't move. "Get up!" "They don't register," observed someone. The prisoners feebly moved their feet in the dust. We waited.

Thereupon the lieutenant, who perhaps hadn't slept either, came up to the prostrate prisoners, and, to show that he thought them no better than dogs, began to kick them in the ribs, then in the face. At that point, Private Marc R., speechless and wide-eyed with rage, went up to the lieutenant, still busy kicking a suspect's face. He grasped him by the arm and forced him to turn around. He didn't even give him time to be surprised, but took him by the lapel of his jacket and with one heave sent him hurtling back about ten yards into some bushes. The oldest among us, the famous veterans of Indochina, declared to me later they had never seen anything like this.

The lieutenant got up, wild-eyed and paler than his prisoners. The affront was intolerable. He ought to have settled matters on the spot, man to man, uniform or no. But, being cowardly like all fake toughs, he didn't dare. Becoming suddenly respectful of the regulations, he just mumbled pathetically: "You're crazy, but you'll hear from me, R."

"I can see people killed, even unjustly," Marc said to me later, "but those kicks in their faces, I felt them on mine."

He got three months' prison for this. Purely symbolic prison, of course, because he was campaigning with us in the Aurès: what cell could they have put him in? These three months, though, he had to serve without pay, liable to unlimited extra duty, with his head practically sand-papered, and a target for all the humiliations the lieutenant, who now hated him with black ferocity, could think of to inflict on him. Most of his former friends dropped him, for fear of compromising themselves.

"In those three months," he told me later, "I don't remember spending a single night without at least two hours' guard duty. That was the worst. The rest just made me smile. But two hours' loss of sleep every night is really hard. It's contrary to all regulations too. But the regulations are like the Geneva Conventions: people do as they like about them."

# 13

We return in the night to Batna, but only to leave again. A list of eighty names, one of them mine, is read in the courtyard by the lights of the trucks. "Get up at three o'clock. Leave at three-thirty." It's now one.

Curiosity makes us forget our fatigue. Wouldn't this be the reward the colonel talked about at the Christmas banquet: the jump training, secret dread and secret desire of every one of us? That glamorous training, interrupted after its preliminaries by our hurried departure from France, November 2nd... After all, we aren't paratroops yet, except for the beret.

That's just what it is! As we drive toward the coast, the heavy air of the Aurès gives way to the sea breeze. Late in the afternoon we reach Philippeville, city of fountains, greenery and light.

We throw our weapons and packs on our beds. The sea is so near we almost think we are free, and we are just setting out, hands in pockets, to have a look around when a shrill whistle stops us short. Three fox-faced instructors are coming toward us on the double. Assembly.

"One: here, we go everywhere on the double. Two: you have all more or less completed your ground training at Pau.

So, you know everything. Consequently, tomorrow morning, get up at four: first jump session."

Deep impression. Anguished looks, which the instructors seem not to notice.

"Meanwhile, a general review: single file behind me!"

Our pathetic column goes skipping off, under the eucalyptus trees. "Always limber and relaxed!" Easy to say. We already feel sick.

First, the practice tower, otherwise known as the "chicken coop," a flimsy, surrealistic metal construction that sways in the slightest wind, almost like a Calder mobile. You climb up a wispy, shaky ladder and arrive exhausted on the railless platform where the wind is always blowing. You'd like to pause, but you're allowed just time to fasten the strap that stops your fall a foot from the ground. Then you have to jump. And right away. No hesitating.

This string on your back is so light you don't feel it. You feel exactly as you would if you jumped from the tenth floor with a closed umbrella in your hand. You jump all the same, and find yourself back on the ground, dazed, with ears buzzing, not knowing how you got there. Then an instructor shouts at you: "Start over again, that won't do." And you start over again.

The point is to experience the sensation of a free fall, that terrible fall into space so contrary to human instinct.

The top of this tower is the stumbling block to the faint-hearted, or weak-willed. Many would rather jump from a plane. More than one, at Pau, rather than leap into the void, had preferred the shame of being made to crawl on all fours in the grass in front of us, till transferred, forever "deflated," to the colonial infantry.

But today everyone jumps without hesitating, in one rush, twice, three times. We have to be held back. The instructors declare they never saw the like. Have a few weeks of merciless hardship been enough to permanently strengthen our wills?

At night, nerves are taut, and none can go right off to sleep: deep in our brains, a little lamp has gone on, and it burns all night, making us groan in our sleep till morning. An instructor had warned me: "Never hope to get rid of that, never hope you can go out the hatch of a plane the way you go out your front door. Make up your mind to that. Yesterday was my 307th jump; well, I was afraid, like the first time. Not as much, but it was the same thing. I've always been afraid. I know this won't stop till the day I become a civilian again, after my last jump! But you get used to everything, even fear."

At four o'clock, the sentinel's brutal pummeling ends our nightmares. Up! Hasty washing. Coffee. Lots of coffee. Ah, the perfume of the "kawa" in the slightly rusty cup! We take deep drafts: we are pulling ourselves together. Refreshment before effort.

We go down the hill in silence. What a marvelous morning and what a pretty town! The painted flagstones of the square glisten above the glassy sea. How pleasant it would be to idle away the morning on some terrace...

The trucks take us to the D.Z., the *drop zone*, which is reserved for us—a great empty field between the vineyards, the sky and the sea. The "sticks," our paratroop squads, are assembled, and arms are stacked. We check the string that ties the helmet to the parachute to prevent its being torn off when the 'chute opens. That done, despite dread that grows with the growing light, we have but one desire: to jump, yes, to jump at once. And get a good breath of air, at last.

But you don't jump, just like that. You first have to endure a good long wait.

To start with, we miserable beginners have to wait for a favorable wind. "Up there, I'm telling you, there's always wind," an instructor informs us. "We try to keep down the number of broken legs. Get it?"

So we wait in the frightful heat, already worn out by our emotions.

At last, in our innocence, we think our turn has come. But it's just the business of checking and trying on. They throw us two parachutes: ventral and dorsal. We immediately find that they are horribly complicated. Paralyzed with anxiety, everyone thinks: How can I ever get all this on straight?

The instructors soon see that we've forgotten all we learned at Mont-de-Marsan. None of us can tell, when he takes hold of his parachute, which is the top and which the bottom. "Your umbrella's upside down, young man. That way, you'd go up, not down. Here, give it to me!" They buzz around us like flies, kindly and cross at the same time, with occasional roars of laughter. "Look at the way this one's tied up! These peasants! What innocence!" They poke and nudge us. "Look here! See that strap? To the right, it opens the parachute. The other way: it's death. Yes, sir, death." We are in a cold sweat.

At last we and our parachutes are somehow or other tied together, and all we still have to wait for is the inspection by the last instructor. The parachutes are all the same, but not the men; and, though adjustable, some of the "umbrellas" seem to overwhelm those they are meant to support. More dead than alive, we wait in line for the inspector: checking of instruments, checking of the ventral parachute's ripcord ring, checking of the ventral and dorsal ripcords, above all checking of the S.O.A.,[1] the automatic opening strap. "Turn this way. Now all the way round!"...A smart slap on the back pronounces you fit to jump. "Next!" Like fish being hauled from the water, we emerge one by one from the sea of creeping things.

Six o'clock...I shall not jump till eleven. Cruel hours, severe ordeal. You ought to have something you could do. Anything: play cards, drink, move about, take a walk...But there's nothing to do, just wait, and sweat.

Every ten minutes, ten men, staggering under the double weight of their parachutes and their fear, climb weakly up into the plane that has come for them. One by one, they disappear into the shuddering fuselage. Horrified though we are, we envy them: they are on their way.

The plane is a black Junker, narrow, with no airworthiness at all, but making up for that by vibrating like a violin. It roars off the runway, rises heavily, at last turns, climbs into the sky, and disappears. Less than a quarter of an hour later, it has cut its motors and glides back at two thousand feet to disperse its load of paratroopers like a scattered handful of salt. Until their green corollas open, the little toy men are microscopic black specks, pitiful particles of living dust, tumbled about by the wind.

Down below, we amuse ourselves giving names to these specks: "The fourth one, that's the sergeant! That one's got nerve: he's gliding!...And that other one doing a high dive.

---

[1] Sangle d'ouverture automatique.

He's crazy!...And that one there. He's forgotten his parachute...Ah! he notices...He's trying to open the other one...They both open, they tangle...He's in a mess, hasn't a chance! Why, no...And this one trying to open his ventral and pulling the wrong string, I certainly know him, it's N., the little know-it-all. Say, he's not having such a good time now!" From below, it's easy to be funny.

The scattered squad drops like rain, then disappears as though swallowed by the ground.

"Next!"...Our turn!

I read my own fear on the face of every one of my comrades. A moment ago, their eyes were swimming; now they're sinking, going under: shipwreck...

"Hurry up!"

The air churned by the propellers flows back along the fuselage and pushes us away. "On the double!" We climb the short metal ladder. Someone trips and falls. No one laughs.

In the cockpit, the heavy smell of gasoline half chokes you. And what boiler-room heat. Not even a bench. Barely room to stand. "Close up, close up!" If only my S.O.A. doesn't tangle with someone else's...

The overloaded plane takes off like a drunken June bug. We are stifling and crushed against each other. I used to dream of travel by air. Another lost illusion. To the smell of gasoline is now added that of fifteen bodies sweating sourly with fear. We don't dare look out the portholes. Some have turned white, others purple. "The jump itself lasts only one minute," I tell myself. "In a quarter of an hour, you'll be on the ground. It's your body that's afraid. No disgrace in that..." Useless rhetoric. It's dark in this plane's belly! Just one little red lamp, up near the pilot, glowing like an altar light. The air roars and whips our legs.

"And now, a song!" yells the instructor. The little shot of rum before the charge. Oughtn't one rather collect one's wits, meditate? On the contrary, we oughtn't to think at all: if one of us with frayed nerves starts to yell "Aaah!" we'll all go mad...

Last inspection. The instructor hangs with all his weight on the cable that carries the S.O.A.'s to make sure it's solid. It that cable snaps, not one but four or five of us will be owing our death to it a moment from now. "But sing, for heaven's sake, sing!" Our voices are pathetic, strangled, croaking.

The final minutes. Carelessly and as if fooling, the instructor picks up the "umbrella" behind him and throws it over his shoulders, as a man in a hurry slips on his jacket. He's a great comedian.

"The first man ... In position!"

With knees on the floor and hands flat on the edges of the open hatch, Sergeant R., the squad leader, is nearing his crucial moment. He feels bound to feign nonchalance, with his face up, according to regulations. But why does he close his eyes? Behind me, someone is panting softly, like a person dying. I don't dare turn around.

Three more minutes. Silence of the abyss awaiting us. We have to go through with it: jump, or die of shame.

One more minute. I am furious at not being able to find the irrefutable argument to free me of my dread. I am still doggedly searching for that argument, still continuing a quite useless soliloquy. I keep repeating to myself: "Whether, beyond this door, which is but a door, there are two thousand feet of vertical emptiness, or three steps down into a quiet garden, it is only this fateful threshold I am dreading, nothing else." But my fear is still there.

"In position!"

Nothing more for thought to cling to. The jump is there, imminent. Think no more.

"Go!"

A man has vanished. The sound of the wind he cuts tells us distinctly he is falling like an arrow.

"Go! ... Go! ... Go!"

The S.O.A.'s snap, lashing the cockpit like whips. And each time a man drops with a whistling sound, body thrust forward.

"Go! ... Go!"

No more fear. All the last men are afraid of is of not jumping. I feel that I am being pushed, and that I am pushing. Quick, quick, get it over. Go! Go! Still one man in front of me, the last obstacle. He dives. My turn.

"Go!"

Brutally, the four winds slap me, shake me. But they do not hold me at all. I can't breathe. Nothing holds me to anything. My body is all cramp, an immense contraction. I want to clutch myself. I am falling, falling, and that is now my whole life. I have become a sheaf of air and light.

The instructors had warned us: "The hardest part is before the opening. That will at first seem very long, but at the most it is only about ten seconds." Can these be called seconds? Just as others take forever to die, so I take forever to finish falling. I think: Is my parachute in working order? Then other thoughts come and torment me at dizzy speed. Formulas, physics courses of long ago, dance in my head. If mass increases with velocity, what is my mass now? How about my kinetic energy? The enveloping air burns me. I feel myself blazing like a meteor. I am suffocating. Weightless, how can I go on living?

I've not yet opened my eyes. My lids seem fastened forever. Is it the dread, the horror, or the speed? I am spiraling like a dead leaf. I am but a blind weight, inertly mad, plummeting to earth. I do not know where my head starts, or my legs and arms end. An inhuman time, seconds I can never describe, nor compare with anything else!

The terror finally clears just enough to warn me that this parachute on my back absolutely must open, now! Immediately! I had almost forgotten it. Vision of being crushed on the ground, dislocated bones, flowing blood.

Ah! A tremendous jolt. I am yanked back into life. With a sound of giant wings, an immense bundle of silk is spurting around me. One parachute has at last opened. Saved!

Caressed by the infinity of light and wind, I yield myself to the sky, with wide-opened eyes. Joy. Laughter. Am I bird or fish? I swim and glide and float and fly. I am the center of this world of blue light, drunk with joy and air. How strangely gentle is the silky wind that lulls me, and this sky where for the first time in my life I am free. Never more than in that moment shall I have the sense of liberty.

The pure air is filled with joyous shouts. Beneath their ample sails, my comrades are slowly gliding here and there, now drawing near each other, now drifting apart, as the wind blows them. I had forgotten all about them, so synonymous are liberty and solitude.

I hear other shouts. From the earth. Instructors are scurrying about, very small. What are they shouting?... "Keep to the right! to the left!" To whom? Why? The speed of the descent becomes perceptible. The wind is gusty.

I remember that I must check everything. Is it too late? Test the ropes, trim the cupola, etc., etc. Someone overtakes me. His parachute brushes mine, he gets entangled, and shouts something. How pale he is. The wind veers, and I draw away from him.

The earth rises. I am coming to it. It is coming to me. Lovely hills roll like waves below my heavy boots. Oh, gracious Earth, bordered by the blue of the Mediterranean!... Three hundred feet. A hundred and fifty feet. Thirty feet. Fear, for a moment forgotten, seizes me again. Instinctively, I draw up my legs.

Like the rest, I reach the ground at the speed of a bicycle coasting downhill. I roll as best I can, like a bundle. And the earth, so soft from up there, now offers me only a jumbled mass of sun-baked clods that thoroughly rasp my sides. What an embrace. I bounce, amid a multitude of resounding stars. My parachute tows me along the ground, and I run and seize its vent to master it like an animal. The wind comes up again, and again I flounder among the ropes, overwhelmed by the enormous silky mass.

I finally succeed in unbuckling myself and getting my body free. With difficulty I get my legs out: they are painful but undamaged. Not even a sprain. My whole body is suddenly seized with a great weariness, right to my hands, which tremble.

In spite of its being expressly forbidden—for, when beginners are jumping, the sky is always full of falling helmets torn off by the shock of the opening parachute—I take off my sweaty helmet: we make it a point of honor to reach the assembly point bare-headed. I pick up my parachutes and, staggering a bit, I head for the trucks.

Meanwhile, other planes are gently gliding, and other men are already diving and spinning, sublime clowns in a pale blue sky.

A man from another company, to whom I don't remember ever having spoken before, comes up to me: "Hi!" He hails me joyfully, affectionately, almost tenderly. "You know, what scared me most," he says, "was..." I look at him in bewilderment, then understand: he is just pursuing a mono-

logue begun a few hours ago. I respond in a confidential
tone: "As for me, imagine..."

Cool drinks. Cheerful voices. Each of us is recounting
his vicissitudes, convinced that his jump was quite out of the
ordinary. A little to one side, a few old soldiers, stern and
silent, are smiling pityingly. They consider such effusions
ridiculous.

Assembly. "Column of two's, to the trucks. Forward,
march! One... Two... One... Two..."

End of the interlude. For ten minutes we have enjoyed
the greatest of freedoms, that of the birds. Now, we are back
on earth with folded wings, regimented as before: "One...
Two..."

What, after all, is the first jump? Just a leap into the
unknown. Beware of the next ones: they will be leaps into the
known, which is worse.

We have to complete eight jumps before we can adorn
our chests with the famous "license plate" so envied by
rookies, a metal badge in the form of a big winged parachute,
on the back of which a number irrefutably attests it your
personal certificate.

There are a thousand ways of wearing this prestigious
symbol. The elegant chrome it and make it shine like silver,
even at night. The careful mount it on red leather to show it
to advantage. Still others, obeying a profounder ethic, twist
it, abuse it, tarnish it.

As we return, our joy wears out and we meditate on the
seven jumps to come, of which one, if you believe the
veterans, will inevitably be the "Jump of Fear."

The jump of fear is to the paratrooper what Death Valley
must have been to the California pioneers, the decisive
passage. Once past this test which spreads terror among the
novices and of which the veterans themselves speak only with
respect, a man can break all the rules. He can almost jump
without a parachute! But first you must experience that
inevitable jump. Will it be the second, or the third? Will it
be tomorrow, or later?

The fragrant dawn beguiles our awakening. We jump
again this morning. We must be quick. Far off in the Aurès,
others are waiting their turn to taste these horrible delights.

"Keep step!" shouts the instructor. "Elbows in! Don't be so sloppy!"

Still on the run, we come back to the base at noon. We've all jumped without hesitating.

Lunch: second helping all round, more if you want. Build yourself up!

"This afternoon, on account of the continuing good weather, double jump," the instructor informs us. Some faces fall.

"Dogtrot behind me!" Good, let's get away from this table, before our courage melts. No time for digestion now. Later on, perhaps: as civilians?

We jump twice more, but not all of us. There are three spectacular refusals, failures of nerve that show what can happen the minute you relax. The wind becomes violent after the second jump, and for most of us the third is the jump of fear.

Ever since the take-off, the instructor has had his eye on M. M. is in front of me. The rest of us are not exactly at ease, but it is only too obvious that M. is really afraid. He has lost control of his hands, which keep making sudden, meaningless gestures. And why is he red one minute, and white the next? Fear can be read in our faces as in an open book. But M. has gone beyond fear. In utter horror, he is breathing in and out at the same time. I catch a glimpse of his eyes and look away, not to offend him. But does he see me? His eyes are like a dead man's—the eyes of a dead man still in pain. He keeps opening his mouth as if to speak. He makes feeble motions. He is obviously at the end of his rope.

I would be the one behind him! What luck. If only he jumps... Watching him disintegrate with terror, I feel it taking hold of me too. One jump this morning, another a moment ago, and now this third jump, without even drawing breath. They are overdoing it.

"In position!"

M. is fourth.

"Go!"

The first man, an air force sergeant, jumps with his arms and legs spread and his face up: the swan dive. A pretty start, but wasted beauty. Nobody is seeing anything now except himself.

The second man's turn, the third's: "Go! Go!"

In desperation, M. throws his S.O.A. on the cable. He

even makes a perfect turn toward the hatch. His toes are already out of the cockpit, past the edge of the void. He leans forward. But too slowly, much too slowly. Already it's too late. This has to be practically automatic. M. is thinking, and he's done for. He knows he won't jump. The instructor knows it too. So do we all know it. But we all shout, almost forgetting our own fear: "Go! Go! Go!" The instructor even tries pushing him gently with his finger, in violation of the regulations. In vain. M.'s convulsed hands continue to grip the hot metal edges of the hatch. His eyes are shut tight against the light that is killing him. He is utterly horrified by his failure, and yet all refusal. His body, powerless but unshakable, has betrayed him: he cannot move. A cocked pistol at his temple would not budge him. With arms spread, like an ineffectual Christ, he is slowly perishing of shame and horror.

Three minutes. Without a word, the instructor moves the great suffering body out of the way into the back of the cockpit.

"Next!... No! Hold on! Too late!"

I was about to jump. The instructor is holding me by my jacket. The D.Z. is too short. We have to circle and come back.

"Stay in position!"

Stay in position. Just what I most feared. I have to stay on my knees, bent over the horrifying void and forced to contemplate it, knowing that in just a moment I am going to have to drop into it like a bomb.

No! I must not close my eyes: the others are looking at me.

The plane is slowly making its turn.

And then, on my hand comes and lights—a fly! Now, where did that creature come from? How drive it away? Move my hand? That might seem a little nervous gesture of fear. No, don't move. The fly is now rubbing its hands, looking at me, and winking. Is it making fun of me?

The plane has cut its motor and is flying straight. This is it. Careful. I am squad leader now.

"In position..." I do not wait for "Go!" I dive. I must break out of this hell. I want to pierce the sky, to give myself wholly to that blue abyss which alone can free me... Free, now I am free, all shackles broken. What could I fear in this world now?

We jump twice the next day, and twice more the day after, in great haste. The morning of our eighth and final jump, just as we finish and are thinking we can loaf a little, or even have a celebration in the town, which looks so lovely from the hill, we are ordered to assemble.

We are leaving! The graduation ceremony is rushed through in a few minutes. The metal badges are awarded. A three-minute speech... "At ease!" And reassemble in one hour.

That evening, we are back in Batna. Our replacements have already left. We never again see M. and the others who have "chickened."

We do not even have time to wear those badges we naïvely consider so impressive. "Everybody in combat uniform! And take off those insignia! We're leaving tonight for the Aurès. No jewelry!" Hard times. Not even a night in which to baptize the badges with a bottle of wine.

---

# 14

A new year is beginning: 1955. A year so painful and confused that, though I remember our first operations perfectly, from then on my mind retains only fragmentary recollections, so rapidly do combing operations, and even engagements, succeed each other. Without respite, day or night, we are dispatched to the four corners of Algeria, a big place when you have to cross it on foot, with a pack on your back. The life of hardship makes us as tireless as wolves, and as pitiless. It does the same to the rebels. A fierce, relentless struggle begins, and is finally called by its right name: the Algerian war.

We adopt the customs of the country: commandos of ten paratroopers, in jellabahs and with close-cut hair, are dispersed through the central Aurès.

We forget the landscapes of France. Our villages are

Foum-Toub, Arris, Tifelfel, T'Kout, Lambèse, Louestia. Yesterday citizens of Paris, today hill-men of the Aurès. Nothing can any longer surprise us. Whatever happens, the reaction is always: c'est normal!

On January 4th, on the Foum-Toub–Arris road, four men in a jeep are surprised by the rebels and burned alive. No cries of horror. Their epitaph: "C'est normal!"

As soon as we finish combing the mountains, back we go into the valley, which is burning and seething all over again. We spend days going from one to another. Of course, we always arrive too late.

Meantime the rebels are winning the savage hearts of the people. They are cleverer than we, and do not hesitate to use persecution and cruelty. They know the mentality of the country, whereas even our distribution of wheat works against us, only causing smiles of contempt. As they go through the villages ahead of us, they always announce our arrival. "Look out, the French are coming. They will kill you all and destroy everything. Run away, or follow us!" And the frightened Aurasians run off, scatter, and hide in the rocks and caves so abundant in their mountains. If found there they are likely to be mistaken for the fellaghas, while the latter are getting away. We usually find only women and children in the villages.

These unfortunate people are as much suspected by the rebels as by the French, and their only course is to take one side or the other, no matter which, in this tremendous quarrel which they never do quite understand. Guerrillas, counter-guerrillas, pacification, army of liberation, army for the maintenance of order: some peasants in their innocence even confuse the uniforms.

Their scanty grain supplies give out, and their wretched cattle are massacred in ever greater numbers. We find whole villages practically deserted. Couscous, their daily food, is lacking everywhere. In the dark mechtas, children, undersized and pale, huddle around the little heaps of embers that smolder day and night, crying with hunger; and, almost instinctively, we throw them packages of biscuits and cans of food.

# 15

We had been marching for several days through infernal country. Even the pack mules couldn't follow. We'd left them the other side of a high ridge. One was lying maimed at the bottom of a ravine, so deep no one has gone down to finish him. No water since morning. At nightfall, camp among the rocks. We sleep if we can. I think of the mule, who's sure to be eaten alive by the jackals. But who'd be affected here by the death of an animal?

At daybreak, we set out again. Morning thirst is a terrible thing. We again march all day in country where perhaps no human being has ever set foot before. A strange band we are, climbing on all fours over the enormous rocks that reflect the sun right into our faces while thirst throbs in our veins.

Our eyes are swollen by the glare, as well as by fever and lack of sleep. Our seven days' beards are full of salt and dust. Fierce faces! But no one complains, or even speaks. What's the use? We've not eaten since morning. Beyond a certain limit of thirst, all appetite ceases. Life is but the hope for water . . .

We leave the trail. Marching on a path was much too luxurious. We again have to climb an enormous peak, a perfectly gigantic one, all one great rock. Cascades of rolling stones make a hollow, sinister sound. A falcon is slowly wheeling around the summit. No talk, just the hard breathing of aching chests.

We are on top, fanning out, grenades ready. You never know . . . But today, no ambush.

The descent is hard on the feet, even harder than the climb. One by one, we bestride the crest, a rocky spine, sharp as the peaks in children's drawings . . . Look! There,

58       THE WAR IN ALGERIA

practically at our feet, lies a tremendous valley, lush, luminous and green, and the water is shining. The water!

"Water...!" shout the men of the 1st company at the
top of their lungs to those still on their way up in a welter of
sweat, rage and dirt.

"Water... Elma," softly murmurs the Arab guide near
me. Elma! His voice is that of lovers murmuring "Darling!"

We are still at least ten kilometers from it. But what of
that? The water is there. It can be seen. What fatigue could
keep us from it now? The way down grows dizzily steep. At
evening, we are on the banks.

We all reach the water in one final rush. Orgy! We duck
our heads in it; we fill our dirty helmets with it. And in
enormous swallows, we drink and drink, till we are almost
sick.

I take out my old tin cup. Slowly, I raise it, dreaming of
joy. Still more slowly, to intensify the delight, I very gently
plunge it deep down. The water streams over my parched
fingers, which are thirsty too. And, slowly, in long drafts, I
drink as I would drink life.

We pitch our tents on the terraces of rich soil bordering
the stream. The abandoned beanstalks make us luxurious
bedding. In spite of weariness, we are all happy as children,
just to be here on the edge of this clear water, under these
pomegranates heavy with red, cool fruit.

In the deserted mechtas scattered here and there under
the trees, we find plenty of onions, dried dates and figs: all
we need for a fine civilian meal, with no canned rations, and
no biscuits. We sit down in groups of two, or three, or four,
around the fires rising vertically toward the sky. Some take
care of their blistered feet, others go and soak themselves in
the water, which is icy in the shade, warm in the sun.

"Aren't you hungry for fish," Marc asks me, "big, fresh
fish?" We load our belts with grenades and move off along the
shore, jumping from stone to stone. Quick, before others get
the same idea! We spot a wide, deep pool. I pull the safety
and throw. The grenade disappears sputtering beneath the
calm surface. We wait expectantly: one, two... three. Suddenly there is an enormous rumbling. The water boils, and
amid strange glaucous vegetation, up come dozens and dozens of huge silver-bellied fish. We dive in among them.
There are so many that we scorn the little ones. The whole

camp feasts on fish, covered with salt and onions and baked in the coals.

Night falls. The air is still warm under these thick palms. Everyone goes to sleep on the fine, soft earth—like pure flour, and almost as white. Tomorrow, we don't get up till eight!

The two planes from Telergma circle a long time before spotting us. The terrain jumbles our radios. And the white canvas T we spread for them is not very visible on the white sand. But they finally drop us mail, messages, and even huge cans of wine. Wine! After the water, wine: more and more remarkable!

"You needn't climb the palm trees with joy, boys," declares an old soldier. "If they've sent us all that, it's because this operation's going to last another two weeks, at least. And it's not likely to be two weeks fooling around on this river, either." We leave that very same day at noon.

The march is resumed. From time to time, at a bend in the road, we meet a long line of trucks that have been waiting for several days. We think: This time it's over, we're going back. We joyfully empty the water cans as we drive along. The trucks take us a little further. Then: "Everybody off!" And we start marching again.

**G.M.C. Truck**

# 16

Even the matériel is worn out. The powerful G.M.C. trucks are stalling, going to pieces, falling apart. One day, to get us going again, helicopters have to bring spare parts.

Sometimes a whole platoon gets lost in the rocks or woods, and we have to make an extra day's march to find it.

Not even the old career officers back from Indochina are fit for this disheartening guerrilla warfare. We expend immense quantities of energy; we go without sleep, rest, food and water, not to mention fun, all to no avail. The fellaghas are still there, in all the valleys, on all the mountaintops, though invisible. Except for an ambush now and then, cunningly set for some isolated detachment, we can hardly ever make contact with them. They always slip away. More than anything else, this sense of futility saps our morale.

We are riddled with dysentery, for, in village after village, the dried dates and figs left behind in the deserted mechtas are spoiled. Likewise, certain springs, apparently pure, are not wholesome. There is talk of poison, but when we're dying of thirst we don't care. We drink anything, water that is stagnant, green, without even diluting those bitter-tasting pills in it. That takes too long.

Finally, we get back to Batna. Our socks are stiff, muddy, torn, our eyes red and inflamed, and we are wretched and furious.

These days of rest in Batna! We spend them running about like lunatics. You have to get an F.M. part, replace some worn-out piece of equipment, or your torn combat jacket... This leaves, at most, two hours of leisure. Two hours to answer two weeks' letters, go to town, buy what you need, see people who are expecting you, and have some fun. It's not very much. Many stagger as they go out of the barracks. They are so unused to a two-hour leave that they are drunk in advance.

This very evening we are leaving by the six o'clock train.

The cars are still hot from the cattle as we climb aboard with our weapons and our packs: these take up more than half the room, and we have to sleep with our knees drawn up. All those long months of marching just to end in this foul car. Seeing me sad, Marc says amicably: "Wouldn't we be less miserable if we weren't always thinking of ourselves?"

# 17

Here we are in Biskra. A change, anyway. On the shore of a blue—yes, blue—river, we quickly pitch our tents in the sand.

Off duty till midnight! The palm groves, the façades of the deserted palaces, the gardens, call to us. By noon, the camp is empty, except for the sentries sweltering in the sun.

I set out, alone, toward the Arab quarter. In the little streets white with sunlight, the people, astonished at seeing me go by with a P.M. slung from my shoulder, turn aside as though I were a leper. In the low doorways, old men squatting on their sand-colored burnouses cast distant glances at me through half-closed eyes, now like a venom, now like a benediction. How forget these old men who, never moving, concentrate their soul in their gaze: eyes that fasten on you, fierce and impenetrable, unresigned to the misery of their dying life that never, even in dreams, was anything but hunger, poverty, and suffering. The Arab town is full of eyes: under all the porches, in all the shaded corners.

Little children in multicolored rags leap about and rush from stairway to stairway. I make the mistake of offering one of them a bit of money. The crowd around me at once becomes a swarm. I have to run, and run a long time, to get rid of them.

The women are phantoms, sometimes black, sometimes

white, always furtive as ghosts. They seem to disappear from one wall to another. The most one can see of them is one eye. Though they are draped from head to foot, a quite superfluous veil is added to hide one of their eyes. Both eyes would be concealed if that were possible. It's not ugly, though: a single eye couldn't be ugly. Why not suppose that all these women passing so close to you are marvelously beautiful?

As for the men, they avoid me, and it's just as well. Some are probably rebels. At the most, they gaze at me askance, like men with the sun in their eyes.

Before I know it, I am in the marketplace. Under the white clay arches, a great variety of things is being sold, in grass baskets, in jars. Stones—blue, black, white, red, green— that cure this or that, depending on their color, even the mal d'amour! Locusts, by the measure, or the bushel. They don't look unappetizing. Out of curiosity, I buy a small measure. I shut my eyes and crunch one of these enormous insects between my teeth, not without a sort of horror. Like potato chips. Not bad; not much flavor, though. I try another, a smaller one: perhaps it will be different, being less old. Equally tasteless.

Children are beginning to collect around me again like flies. I start to move away, almost knock someone over, turn round sharply and apologize: it's one of those miniature donkeys so numerous in North Africa. He pricks his enormous ears, and eyes me angrily through his long palpitating lashes. We stare at each other a moment. Then I roar with laughter, and he instantly responds by laughing heartily himself, right in my face.

I come to the abandoned palaces and casinos, and slide over the cool marble flagstones. What a splendid sight, these pink and white buildings under their palm trees, after the squalor of the Arab hovels. But the war shows here too. Luxury has vanished from the courtyards and the deserted rooms. From time to time travelers sleep on the magnificent stone floors once trodden by the richest idlers in the world. Today, André Gide would be arrested here by the sentries, as doubly suspect.

But the gardens are still so beautiful that, without being tired, I sit on a bench to breathe the light breeze, so warm and yet so fresh. Under the heavy-scented trees, little blue streams are singing as they run.

I notice a little school, half hidden in a clump of mimosa. How can a child study under such trees, in such a climate? What sweet mildness comes down from these palms! I am enchanted, overwhelmed. Give me twenty-four hours in this languorous city, and I know I will desert.

I run across Bernard.

"I am going to show you something out of the ordinary. You've heard of the Ouled Naïls? Women of poverty-stricken tribes who train their young daughters for a certain profession: you'll see.

"What makes it interesting is that it's all done innocently, with the bishop's blessing, if they have a bishop! The good papas bring their daughters to Biskra to make little courtesans of them, the way in France well brought-up little girls are sent to school in a convent.

"The best street in town is reserved for these young ladies and their activities. It's all very primitive, and very refined. When their necklace of gold coins weighs enough to make a good dowry, they go home and marry! Come along. We're going to have a look."

A labyrinth of winding streets. Then a spacious thoroughfare, between rows of little houses prettily decorated with red flowers whose petals rain down on the sidewalk. Groups of women in rich dresses of many colors await you on the green wooden balconies, all invitation and smiles. On their arms, legs and feet, all of which are bare, bracelets, necklaces, pendants, tinkle at their slightest motion.

We enter the first house, through winding sky blue corridors.

"Remember, now," Bernard feels obliged to warn me, "this is not, properly speaking, a house of prostitution. Think of it rather as a harem, or something like that."

There is a faint smell of bodies and of smoke. Bernard explains: "Now they're going to offer us mint tea, or coffee, or something. I warn you, it's awful. But you've got to drink it. It would be boorish not to." In unbelievable little cups, hardly the size of a thimble, we are served a few drops of some bitter liquid, black, syrupy, but not recognizable. It certainly is horrible.

Meanwhile, a fringed silk curtain has been let down in front of us. We are left alone. The only light is from big

copper lamps on the carpet where we sit like buddhas. No
window. A quarter hour goes by. Still nothing happens.

"Like the movies, isn't it?"

"More like a puppet show. This curtain..."

"Just wait, you've not seen anything yet."

Curtains slowly rise. Women are dancing slowly, way in
the back of the room, which the lighting makes seem
tremendously long. This greenish half-light prevents our
seeing their shapes except vaguely. You might think they
were fish.

A weird, enervating music suddenly begins all around
us. Young women come and sit near us. Some are beating
tambourines, others are rattling some sort of castanets. The
light goes up. Those long green dolphins draw near, slowly,
dancing on tiptoe. They are very young women with tall,
supple brown bodies. And all they have on is their silver
medals and their bracelets, which they wear around their
necks! They are smiling vaguely, a sad little smile, and
swaying their bodies in a curious negligent manner, as though
unconsciously, absentmindedly.

A sort of shame seizes me. An entire hour goes by.
Dance, dance, and fever.

"Enervating, these shows," finally observes Bernard.

"Yes, enervating and grotesque. Let's get out of here!"

"Can't. You have to wait till the dances are over."

Some of our comrades arrive, noisily. They settle themselves. "We're delighted, absolutely delighted," they declare
to the directress. Serious customers. They receive delicate
attention.

The curtain falls on a final entrechat.

"Some of the little young men like to sleep in little
bedroom with little artiste?" murmurs the directress. "This is
the way!"

Stampede. Five or six of the "little young men" rush
forward. We slip out. "I smell sin," says Bernard, half seriously, half jokingly.

At the last big European café still open, we sit in the
shade of the palm trees to watch the people go by, as in Paris
on the Champs Elysées. But almost no one goes by. The few
that do are following the narrow paths of shade, close to the
walls. Europeans or Arabs, they all have a guilty look.

Our waiter seems nervous. He never stops wiping our table. Finally he can keep quiet no longer. Without our asking him, he informs us that there are almost as few people left in the houses here as in the streets. "They are afraid. Many have left. The city's unhealthy. At first it was just now and then a body, in the morning, against a palm, with a knife in the back, one of those 'douk-douk' knives they sell in the bazaars. Then, more and more bodies, panic, murders every-where. They even found children strangled in the park, and Arabs too, not all murdered by other Arabs," he confides in a low voice. "You understand me?"

We are astonished. It's true this is only the beginning of 1955. We shall soon be used to it, and learn that people can get away with anything in war, especially if not in uniform.

The waiter continues: "All the big hotels closed when the first body was found. But, here, we're not leaving. Not yet. We're waiting to see. A few months from now, all these horrors will be over, won't they—with you here?"

Bernard looks at me. We say nothing.

In camp next morning, we learn that one of the young Ouled Naïls we saw dance has just been found with two 9-mm. bullets in her chest, her necklace of gold coins gone. An investigation is begun in the battalion and in all the other units occupying the city. They never find out who killed her. We leave the next day.

## 18

This time, we are going into the Aurès from the south. We enter the African night: mild air and fragrance under the trees. We drive on through the dark, thinking of nothing in particular. I am vaguely remembering the poor sad little smile of one of the young dancers of yesterday. Was she the one murdered? Tonight more than ever death disgusts me.

Headquarters is dissatisfied. Results so far are ridiculously small compared to the means employed. We are going to strike a big blow, Operation Veronica. For this, all available Algerian battalions are rounded up, five or six "operational" ones. And, forward march! Each to its own mountain. While the rebel bands are on the march in the night, convoys are converging, with all lights out, on the heart of the range. We don't get off the trucks till dawn.

Sidi Okba, Aïn-Naga, Houlach: miles and miles of trails. In the afternoon, brief contact, but violent: two lieutenants and a sergeant killed at Khanga-Hourdeau. A few enemy dead remain on the field. But it is not isolated detachments that we are after. There are cynics who maintain these weren't even real rebels.

Next day, we "comb" the village of El-Amoun. Not even a cat in it, but we make much noise, confusion and dust. The day after, still at full speed, we mop up the Amar Khadou mountains: much in need of attention.

Finally, twenty-four hours' halt at Biskra; on its outskirts, rather, for we're forbidden the town since the last outrage there. Generals Cherrières and de Linarès insist on coming in person to congratulate the battalion, we never found out what for. Anyway, all they do is march past us, without saying a word. On the whole, it's just as well. We had to wait for them three hours in the sun, standing still and looking at the sand like idiots. Tardiness is the impoliteness of generals.

We leave next morning at four. The party's not over. But now it's Operation Violet. We're becoming modest.

We start right in with a mopping up: the village of Djemorah. Actually, the inhabitants have done the mopping up themselves: when we get there, there's nothing left. After much searching, we finally find an interesting item: a magnificent wooden gunstock. Too bad it was only the stock. In the evening we find a superb pistol at least seventy centimeters long, a flintlock. It's a museum piece, and I still have it at home.

**M 1 Rifle**

The following days, from morning till night, fellagha-hunting—still without success. On January 26th, having achieved nothing, they decide to call it off. Especially as a cold wave of unheard-of severity has suddenly hit the mountains. We are half frozen, our feet are swollen with chilblains, and we make hardly any progress in the sticky, ice-cold mud.

The trucks should have been here yesterday. But the road has been blocked by landslides due to the rain, as well as cut by the rebels' auxiliaries, the people of the villages. We just have to wait. Luckily, it's not raining now.

Next day, when the trucks finally arrive, we find that the battalion's interpreter-guide has modestly retired to the heart of the mountains, taking with him as mementoes a subma-chine gun and an American M-1 rifle, that, trusting in the médaille militaire pinned to his jellabah, we had thought safe to entrust to him.

It begins to rain very violently. The streams overflow, and the convoy has to stop. We wait three days camped along the road.

We start off again. But a jeep and its occupants are carried away by the torrent: a lieutenant is killed. The drivers are terrified and proceed with redoubled caution. Wheels spin, we make little progress. Next day, another jeep falls into a ravine: a corporal killed, two sergeants injured.

Another stop: still rain. We pitch our tents at Abramur, and they are soon soaked through. The showers seem likely to go on forever. We head for Batna. Ragged and covered with mud, we again go through Biskra, El Kantara, MacMahon. We reach Batna at noon. We have to reorganize the platoons and get new matériel and ammunition.

## 19

These days of rest are depressing. They give you a taste of civilian freedom, but it is spoiled by the prospect of having to start off again almost immediately. Will it be tomorrow, day after tomorrow, or in three days? We are never told, for the enemy has to be deceived. Unfortunately, the Arabs often know of these secret departures two or three days before we do.

It is a pleasure, though, when all the chores are done, to be able to escape for a few hours from barracks and uniforms with the few thousand francs that constitute our monthly pay. All that counts is this money I have in my pocket, and whatever pleasure I can derive from it. No worry about wife and children to feed. No concern about the immediate present. We drift at random. Past and future are erased. Neither hope nor despair. If it is time to suffer and march, we suffer and march, without knowing why. If it is time to enjoy ourselves, we enjoy ourselves, also without knowing why. We sleep on the stream of days and nights, which bears us off, as if dead.

We are going by train again, without yet knowing where. Nobody worries about that. "They're probably taking us to China . . ."

After forty-eight hours of drowsing, we are completely bewildered as we jump down onto the platform of the little station at Boufarik. We had left it only a few months ago, foolish as puppies and full of illusions. Now we're back, minus the illusions.

Boufarik is the city of orange planters. It is also for these people that we're fighting. Wealthy colonials, Italians, Spaniards, Levantines, even Frenchmen, most of them appear to be but shortsighted exploiters of this region's excellent soil and native population.

The day after our arrival, I succeed in getting a few hours' leave and in thumbing a ride to Algiers. The good old lady sitting next to me, probably the mother of the man at the wheel, suddenly breaks the silence and says in a gentle little voice: "They've all got to be killed."

"I beg your pardon?" I think I must have misunderstood, because of her accent.

"Yes! All killed! These, and those," continues the old woman pleasantly, pointing first to the laborers breaking stone along the sun-baked highway and then to other Arabs going by on donkeys.

"Killed? Why?"

"Why, because they're a pest. Lazy, sneaky trash. Look at their faces! You're still young!"

"Did you kill a lot of them in the Aurès?" chimes in the driver, suddenly attentive. His fat face is both good-natured and cruel.

The old lady continues sweetly: "We can never kill enough of them!"

A glance at her little green eyes convinces me that she is perfectly serious and that, if she could, she would joyfully massacre every single one of those roadworkers with her own wrinkled, shaky old hand.

After a week in Boufarik, everyone feels the agonizing physical need for diversion. This idleness is eating away at us like a cancer. Some, confined to barracks or not, leave camp in the middle of the night and rush to Algiers. There is always a woman involved in these little excursions—certain women of the Maison Carrée *lupanar* undertake to copulate gratis, in consideration of a certain quantity of cartridges, which they afterwards resell to the rebels. The expeditions always end the same way: between two military policemen. We see our comrades returning in the early morning, in the most incredible costumes, half civilian, half military, heads bloody but unbowed. Whatever the number of days of "clink" they are going to get, they consider themselves fully compensated in advance by their "nuit d'amour" and the prestige their exploits earn them. Those, however, are the extreme cases. A bit of flirting with young girls as bored by their little town as we are is enough for most of us.

Rest is doing us no good. Many of us, who can't distinguish between an Arab village, where anything is permitted, and a European city, cause scandals every night in the cafés and even in private homes. Enthusiastic when we arrived, the population is now thoroughly sick of us. "Messieurs les Bérets rouges, we have seen enough of you! Go get killed somewhere else!" Like the ancient poets, we are first strewn with roses, then driven from the towns.

We therefore soon break camp, and head for Batna— departure so sudden that many who have run up bills in every café, shop, and restaurant have to leave without paying.

To their great regret, they say. But their regret will be more sincere a few days later when the colonel is deluged with letters from creditors, and they find their pay proportionately reduced.

## 20

Batna, the most sordid, depressing, icy cold and suffocatingly hot little city in North Africa! The shopkeepers are delighted: whatever finally happens, in the meantime our presence means excellent business. The other Europeans give us a cool welcome. They are beginning to know us.

Nor is there much room for us in Batna now. Our old barracks are full of recruits just arrived from France. But what do we need a roof for, accustomed to the open as we are? We are assigned a vast empty area at the gates of the town. There we pitch our marabouts, heavy group tents in which we shiver at night and swelter when the sun is up.

Our only visitors are a few thin stray dogs and fever-ridden beggars who hang around the edges of the camp, hoping for something to eat. At six o'clock, the cook tosses them scraps over the barbed wire. Everybody else avoids us.

Yet we are not absolutely alone. Besides ours, there is another camp peopling the sadness of the plain. A camp embellished by high gateways of painted wood. A camp whose impeccable alignment and spotless cleanliness are surprising in this ever swirling dust: the Legion.

Wherever weather conditions are so bad that no commanding officer would risk having his men camp more than three days, we encounter the Foreign Legion. In the now icy, now blazing deserts between the Aurès and the Némencha; in the heart of the most impregnable rebel bastions: Soummam, Némencha, Tunisian frontier, Collo peninsula; on the peaks and ridges most exposed to fire, in the great days of those famous skirmishes of Djeurf and of Négrine, we have the

Legion with us. And, more particularly, the R.E.P.'s,[1] foreign paratroop regiments, also called the Bérets verts, because in place of the white képi of the old Legion, they sometimes wear the green beret of the Legion paratroops.

Many of us later become friends with these men. They are the only ones in the whole army not afraid to see themselves as just what they are, mercenaries pure and simple, neither ashamed nor proud of it.

"Honor and Fidelity," in letters a yard wide, made of stones painted and arranged with care, is the motto at the entrance to their camp. All about, the ground is carefully sanded. The whole area is perfectly kept up... Our base is still neglected, uneven, strewn with foul-smelling refuse. Shall we ever succeed, we supposedly ingenious, but in fact inefficient, Frenchmen, in turning our camp into such a simple, dignified garden as this?

Between the tents, which are raised and ventilated by foundations of hewn stone, the legionnaires come and go. They are at work, bareheaded in the blazing sun, silent and grave. The muscles of their backs and chests gleam like the breastplates of their Roman predecessors. The average age of these men is about thirty, and, compared to them, we twenty-year-olds feel like ridiculous boy soldiers.

I try to imagine what can be going on in the head, behind the narrowed eyes, of the legionnaire standing at the main gate. In full uniform under the noon sun—white képi, red and green wool epaulette, white shirt and green tie, the German color, he has been mounting guard for two hours at imperturbable attention. Is there someone, somewhere, waiting for him to come back?

Legionnaires as a rule are taciturn, and loath to mingle with the other troops they encounter. Nevertheless, the day after our arrival, while choosing a book in the Batna bookstore, I made the acquaintance of a legionnaire who happened to be looking for the same book, Gunther W.

He was a German, and well born, as he carefully made clear. He spoke French fluently enough to be understood by a soldier, and he was good enough to tell me over a drink what had caused him to choose his curious profession. It was, in the first place, his knowledge of French, result of the

---

[1] Régiments Etrangers Parachutistes.

Occupation; then, the fact that, having enrolled in the Hitlerjugend at fifteen, he had never learned any trade but soldiering; and, lastly, because he came back from the Russian campaign, penniless, to find he had no family left and no way of making a living.

When French troops occupied his village after the armistice, he took the opportunity to enlist: "I ought to have been made prisoner, but they always take you if the job is getting killed.

"I started by fighting against France, but without hatred. I can just as well fight for her. Anyway, what good are convictions for making war? What I like is war for its own sake. Any war! War leaves me free, free from care, and nothing else does. Our minimum enlistment is for five years. I took ten. I'm going to take five more."

"And what do you think of Algeria, and of the fellaghas?"

"I'd like them well enough, except for one very bad fault they have, for me the worst: they're dirty! I know there's not much water. Even so, they go too far. They smell bad, even dead."

The Legion's tradition of cleanliness! We French paratroopers are always a bit untidy, if not ragged, sometimes not even shaved—trying to look "tough." But the legionnaires, even dead drunk, are always impeccably dressed: ties in place, whatever the temperature, trousers sharply creased, three V-shaped pleats in the back of their shirts, boots polished till they sparkle, even if three minutes later they are going to be covered with mud.

Gunther is very proud of having never killed or stolen, as a civilian. The stories of young men enlisting in the Legion to atone for some scrape are true only in movies and dime novels. "You can sign up under a false name and keep it all the time you are in the Legion. But your officers know the real one. You can, of course, enlist after some misdeed, but only if they're willing to have you. And it's better to tell them about it, because, sooner or later, they're sure to find out. Hotheads, expatriates, cynics, outcasts, we have all sorts of men. But not pimps, or pickpockets, or dandies!"

I accompany Gunther W. back to his camp. Even strolling, you'd think him on parade. He walks with the Legion stride, very long, seemingly very slow, but in fact very swift.

As we reach the entrance to the camp, he points out

something to one side of the tents. All I see is a sentinel standing with fixed bayonet in front of a hole.

"You see the hole, in the sand?... There's a man lying in it. His head, body and legs are bare. It's le tombeau, the tomb. He's not allowed to sit or stand. He's been there twelve hours."

"It's crazy! He could die in this sun. And what about the night?"

"Same thing. He has to endure the cold, too, and wind and rain, all without a shirt."

"How could they! Who started this?"

"It's old as they world! Discipline! You people don't ever have le tombeau?"

Horrified, I lean against the barbed wire to get a better look. The sentinel is watching us with a vague but unfriendly look. He obviously does not enjoy having to stand there two hours in full uniform under the blazing sun.

The poor man in the hole has his head shaved to within a centimeter: "la boule à zéro." He is literally streaming sweat from head to foot. His eyes look as if they were being consumed by fire, and his lips are so white with salt one would think him dead.

I am speechless.

"He's there of his own free will, you know. He dug the hole himself. Everybody here thinks this normal."

"Normal!"

"For several years, le tombeau has been forbidden all through the army, even among us. But it still exists, as you see. Only, now, you volunteer."

"Volunteer!"

"Yes. During our last operation, this man raped a little fatma, in the Tighanimine gorges. The captain himself caught him in the act. The fatma's family, moreover, knew enough French to complain to the magistrate in Batna. So, the captain wasn't able to hush things up in the usual way.

"When we got back from the operation, the day before yesterday, the captain at once sent for Konrad D., that's the man in the hole, and said to him: 'You're in serious trouble. And, what's worse, you've made even more serious trouble for us! I ought to punish you severely. But, as this is your first major offense, I'll give you your choice: either I send you to the military tribunal in Constantine, or you volunteer for le

tombeau, thirty-six hours, without eating or drinking. I grant
you this favor only because you've nothing on your record
and because you're in line for corporal. If you go to Constantine,
take my word for it, even if you stay in the army fifteen,
twenty-five years, you'll never be more than a private. So,
make up your mind: Constantine, or le tombeau?' Of course
he chose le tombeau. 'Good,' said the captain, 'take a spade
and get out of here. I don't want to hear any more about you!'
You see how simple it is!"

This was the same legion regiment that distinguished
itself a year later in the Némencha.

For three days, two of its companies had been blockad-
ing a cliff. They couldn't get the better of a strong rebel band
solidly ensconced in the caves. They had tried everything,
including flamethrowers (which are forbidden by the "laws" of
Geneva, but issued to most of the regiments). It's no use.
The caves are impregnable. They think of using smoke, but
there's no wood, and it would take hundreds of smoke
grenades, with caves of this size. Then an idea occurs to them
that only a legionnaire would think of. They get helicopters to
bring them mortar and building stone, and, one after another,
covered by machine guns, they calmly seal up every last cave
in the cliff. That done, they leave.

Several months later, they come back to see. They
cautiously dismantle the walls, which are still as they left
them. Out comes an overpowering smell of death. The stiffened
corpses massed on the other side fall into their arms. Smothered
or starved, probably both.

"The rebels would do the same, if they could."

We spend two days of so-called rest, under the fierce
sun, stripped to the waist and barefoot, pitching our heavy
tents, unloading matériel and food, stringing miles of barbed
wire. Out of this filthy area, we have to make the spacious
camp that is to be our rear base. The strict and perfect order
of our neighbors' post obliges us to produce something at
least halfway decent. But we are tired. There are snakes and
scorpions under the stones we have to move, and a few of us
get bitten. An anti-scorpion shot has been provided, but it
hurts as much as the bite itself.

Before we have finished this work, we have to leave once more for the Aurès.

## 21

The 8th B.P.C. did have one holiday, though, in April 1955. That was the day we went as tourists to Timgad, the largest of the old Roman cities in North Africa. ("As tourists" may be exaggerating a little, because we took along our submachine guns, and, out of habit, slipped a few hand grenades into the pockets of our dress uniforms.)

Timgad! At first glance, the mere presence of this great stone city in the midst of all this desolation is a complete enigma. How, you say to yourself, after driving from Batna over miles of desert, without seeing a bush or even a blade of grass, could people have lived in this dead region of sand and dust? Here were a spacious marketplace, a magnificent temple, three of whose columns are still standing and impressively beautiful, even a spacious amphitheater. All this was built for the use and the luxury of an intelligent and numerous population.

Must not this desert have been once, if not green like Normandy, at least planted with olive trees and cultivated with love? Is it possible that, in a few centuries, a few invasions, by the Arabs and others, have been enough to reduce to this pass a country where life must have been beautiful and happy?

We leap from stone to stone, so plunged in thoughts of Rome that we half expect a detachment of legionaries to appear around the corner of some marble-paved street, led by a broad-shouldered centurion, close-shaven and in full dress uniform. The whole battalion is deeply impressed. "Ah, these Romans! They were strong. You don't see men built like them today." We have the temerity to compare ourselves with those men of bronze!

* * *

Next day, we are back at work. Escort for the linemen on the Batna–Arris road. Over some dozens of miles, there are hundreds of poles down, cut through at the base. The rebels, just to show they are still there, get the peasants to do this work, five or six poles a night, and keep a watchful eye on their more or less willing auxiliaries from positions above the road.

Poor Aurasians! All night, they cut down poles and dig wide ditches in the stony roads. They no sooner finish this exhausting labor than in the morning they are resetting the poles and filling in the ditches, still under the threat of guns, this time ours.

In Batna, and even in its outskirts, there are Europeans who still refuse to admit that they are in an insecure area. Their capital and their "life work"—nine times out of ten it's really the work of others—are committed, and they would rather be massacred like sheep than get out in time. Not out of patriotism! The real homeland of these people is wherever they make money. In town, they go right on putting up expensive buildings.

On the night of the 17th, while on guard duty at camp, I suddenly notice an immense glow rising into the sky. The emergency platoon and the fire detachment find that gasoline had been poured all over these new buildings: they get there just in time to see it all burst into flames. The rebels who set the fire are already far off. It's still early in the night, the perfect time for quick operations in town. They have till dawn to get back to the mountains.

In Batna itself, in spite of all our troops there, little skirmishes are becoming commonplace. The Aurès are near.

We hunt the rebels like wolves, and they, growing more and more savage, are beginning to burn everything modern, hotels, schools, model farms, forestry centers, power plants, often massacring everybody in them, without regard to sex or age. Ex-convicts and common highwaymen take advantage of the disorder to form little independent bands. Unafraid either of the real rebels or of the French, they loot, kill, rape, on their own account, in the villages and towns. This leads to more reprisals and new hatreds.

The staff has finally seen that all our shuttling back and

forth between Batna and the Aurès does not prevent the rebels' getting away safely after every coup, and therefore decides to post us high up in the mountains. One fine April evening, we set out for T'Kout to relieve a Legion regiment that had been there since the beginning of winter.

T'Kout is in a hollow enclosed by red mountains, "like Dien-Bien-Phu," as the legionnaires point out. "But you're lucky. You'll be able to do your night patrolling in peace. We've killed every last dog in the villages here, within forty kilometers."

These big, shaggy, yellow and white Aurès dogs are very fierce, and they have extraordinarily keen ears. At more than a kilometer, they can detect the approach of a six-man patrol in espadrilles. If you crack a single twig, they sound the alarm at the top of their lungs.

"There's no water yet," continue the legionnaires. "This isn't the season. The stream's dry. You'll have to wait for the tank truck. Ours used to bring water from Batna. But watch out! By the time it gets here it's boiling. Don't drink right away. Aber das ist Krieg, n'est-ce pas?"*

The legionnaires have very small packs, just ammunition, rations, change of clothes, but rare is the man without some mascot, a big green chameleon perched on his shoulder, a desert fox, a puppy, a cat, a young jackal, or even a snake wound languorously about him. It's somewhat irregular, but here they don't separate a man from his pet animal.

They leave the camp spotless, and we, feeling very relaxed, begin getting ready our suppers in front of the tents, with the prospect of a long peaceful night of rest ahead of us.

Suddenly, we are being shot at from every direction! We throw down our plates, kick out the fires, and rush into the tents for our weapons. The rebels must have been watching us all day from the mountaintops.

We are taken completely by surprise. Not having dug our foxholes yet, we are fine targets down on our plain. Next morning, we learn from the size of the holes in the tents that the rebels were using 12-gauge slugs, which are deadly.

They keep right on firing after dark. Our green, red and white flares spurt up toward the sky, and come slowly down, as pretty to watch as 14th of July fireworks on the Pont-Neuf.

---

*But that is war, is it not?

For two or three minutes, as their parachutes brake their fall, they light up the mountains and a few shadowy running figures. But they make us visible too and enable rebels hidden in the dark to take better aim.

We finally spot a group of rebels crouching in some brush. The mortars are now brought into play and the summits get a shower of little 60- and 81-mm. shells. There are a few yells, then silence punctured here and there by a final shot.

A company goes up and patrols the summits all night, returning empty-handed in the morning except for one wounded man the rebels had left behind.

The insolence of these outlaws' daring to pot us like rabbits the moment we arrived gives us food for thought. From now on, one squad goes up every evening about a

**81 mm Mortar**

kilometer from the camp to serve as a buffer and give the alarm, in case of more enemy attacks.

A few days later, I have to go to the gendarmerie—the only European building in T'Kout—and there I chance to see the wounded rebel who had been captured during the night.

Two gendarmes specially sent from Batna to interrogate him had not been able to get a thing out of him. So they had left him to slowly rot in a close little room, till "ripe" for further questioning. I say "rot," and I mean it. I both see and smell the putrefying of the untended wounds in his hand and chest. Unbearable smell.

The medic explains: "I disinfected and bandaged him the first day. The doctor is in Batna. He probably doesn't care, and he hasn't even been told. I have orders not to do any more, because the man's going to be shot anyway. The bandages came off, that's why he twists and scratches all the time. The flies have gotten into his wounds. I expect it will start gangrene or something."

I watch the man through the peephole in the cell door. All that's left alive of him is his eyes. He is writhing slowly on the filthy stone floor.

"I wouldn't like to be in his place," says the guard, joining us. When the prisoner failed to respond to the usual slaps and kicks, the gendarmes had used a "394" battery, in army slang a "gégenne." They had connected the electrodes to the most sensitive parts of the man's body and then varied the intensity to make him "come," that is, shriek, and talk. This method of investigation soon became common practice in a number of units, because it is the only way that immediately useful information can be obtained from prisoners in the field, before they are disposed of.

For another whole week, the wounded rebel stubbornly refused to talk. His screams were often heard through the walls. Then he yielded. On the basis of the information he gave, a vast operation was set up. It accomplished nothing. As for him, he disappeared.

One evening, worn out after a day of "rest" spent digging trenches, we are waiting for the flies to go to sleep so that we can perhaps sleep a little ourselves (it's true the mosquitoes take over from the flies) when a gun goes off in our marabout. We hurriedly put out the hurricane lamps and seize our weapons, convinced there's a rebel in the tent opening about to let fly with his automatic rifle. But loud laughter ends the excitement. "It's Grand-père!" shouts somebody. "Grand-père!" we all say with relief and pride. "What a man, what a man!"

Grand-père is a professional soldier who's been in the army about twelve years and already has a few gray hairs to prove it. He's been a corporal more than once, but busted every time for drunkenness and scandalous behavior in public and private, and is now just a tough old wreck. He drinks—as only Breton soldiers drink, to drive away the "blues": at night, during the day, the whole time; and anything at all. The whole of his miserable pay is spent on drink. Alcohol is his one refuge from the savagery of life, the one thing that keeps him from going under. An excellent comrade, too, full of kindliness, even drunk, which is uncommon.

But tonight Grand-père is beside himself. The heat, the dark—he hardly ever sleeps—the inactivity, are too much. He's at the end of his rope. Sitting on his bed, gun in hand, he has started shooting, and the bullets go whistling through the canvas right over our heads. If only he doesn't decide to grab the grenades. We'd have just five seconds to get out. We pretend nonchalance but stay ready, with one leg already out of bed.

"I've been in Indo, I have!" yells Grand-père. "I've been wounded four times" (actually only once). "And it wasn't to fool around in this stinking bush. I'd blow myself up for a nickel. But first, to hell with them all! Merde alors! The fellaghas and all the rest! You laugh? You won't laugh so much when you're sweating where I've sweated, you rascals! I've sweated on the Chinese border, I have!"

"Grand-père's laying it on tonight," observes Bernard, greatly interested.

"The hell with T'Kout! I'm getting out of here!" And, suiting the action to the word, Grand-père starts out of the tent, gun in hand. Still holding his barrel up, he goes on firing at the stars. We like this better.

By this time, the whole camp is up, armed to the teeth, and running in every direction, with the colonel out in front. Grand-père pays no attention. He goes right on shooting and nobody dares go near him.

A lieutenant finally takes the bull by the horns.

"Stop that, stop it," says the little officer, not afraid, but wary.

No response. The shooting continues.

Going up to Grand-père, he insists: "Stop that!"

"But I'm fed up, mon lieutenant, I'm fed up, do you understand?"

"Yes, I do understand. I'm fed up too. We're all fed up here. But, all the same, put down your gun and go to bed, old man."

Old man! This works. Grand-père goes back into his tent without a word. He throws down his gun and stretches out, moaning, on his bed. It's all over.

That day, for once, he hadn't had a drop to drink.

## 22

The governor of this region, probably reassured by our presence, decides to go and visit the surrounding douars.

We have to escort and guard him on his tour. In his Mexican field marshal's uniform, with oak leaves on his képi, riding breeches, dark brown boots, and a submachine gun at his side, he wears an air of fatuous good-nature, and is a perfectly ridiculous sight.

At each village, we begin by holding an assembly of the important citizens, if any remain, to whom the governor makes a benign little speech, which the peasants absorb in dead silence, with half-closed eyes, being as sly here as anywhere else. After that, it's checking of identification cards, goodbye, and thank you. All very peaceful.

Our worthy governor is obviously as much a stranger in his villages as a Bantu in the Place Pigalle. No doubt this is the first time he has set his elegantly booted foot in them. He intones: "France, whose mission it is..." Talk, talk. It's late to save face with words. And the governor knows it.

\* \* \*

Life continues, death too. Escorts, ambushes, combings and mop-ups follow each other endlessly. Despite our efforts, despite the truckloads of suspects we send to Batna, despite the rebels we manage to put out of action here and there, there are still just as many of them, even more. For every outlaw fallen, a dozen young Arabs rise. There's no end to it.

Knowing they are still not strong enough to attack us openly, the rebels make known their presence in a thousand ways, for example those apparently meaningless murders becoming more and more frequent in the villages. Any Arab suspected of collaboration or sympathy with France is marked down. Sooner or later, right in his own village, specialized rebel killers come and attend to him.

Through a mixture of promises, praise, terror, falsehood and truth, there has been set up in all the villages and even in the outskirts of cities a very real though shadowy extra-legal government that manifests itself by strikingly bloody examples. Regularly now, as we approach a village, we find the body of one of the local representatives of France, caïd, policeman, or mayor, lying in the bottom of a ravine and half eaten by jackals.

These victims have not been shot. Powder and bullets are still scarce in the Army of Liberation. But, more important, the offender must be made to suffer a long time before he dies. People have to be impressed. We discover bodies without hands, without feet, necks half severed with a razor, or trunks cut in two. On examination, it is apparent that the executioner has at first confined himself to mutilation that does not quickly cause death. He has begun, for example, by putting out the eyes. And always horribly evident is the unspeakable mutilation of the lower abdomen, the height of pain.

The Arabs won't talk. They refuse to say who killed that old man we've just found, though he's their father. Even if the killers were caught and shot down in front of them, they would still keep silence. Their tongues are paralyzed with fear.

Even in Batna, we encounter Arabs without noses and ears, furtively trying to conceal their shame. They are first-degree mutilees, perhaps with death sentences merely postponed, and meantime serving as walking examples.

One morning three weeks after our arrival in T'Kout, we

find the village policeman with his throat cut and his eyes put out, in his own cottage, where he had asked me to coffee a few days before. A piece of paper signed F.L.N., Front de Libération Nationale, had been pinned on his chest, right to the skin. Thus, despite our sentries on duty day and night, a rebel can come within a hundred yards of the camp and kill without risk. The colonel is furious. From now on, we're forbidden to go even two hundred yards from camp, unless there are at least two of us, and armed.

The insecurity keeps spreading. A convoy is sure to be stopped within ten kilometers of the camp by a trench dug across the road during the night. It takes endless time in the hot sun to fill up the hole, for there's not always a village at hand, where labor can be commandeered. We're lucky, too, if a few hundred yards farther on we don't come on another "gap" treacherously opened in some dangerous curve. We sometimes strike five or six of these ditches in one day and spend the whole afternoon getting to a point we should have reached in half an hour. Life is becoming impossible.

The rebels have intensified their attacks, now that the hot weather has set in. They are better able than we to find water, and better able to do without, too.

The T'Kout–Batna road is our only link with European civilization, and we have to maintain and guard it ceaselessly. We often spend the whole day on the ridges to protect a returning convoy. A day among the rocks is long, with only one canteen per man. At night we double the sentinels. They are posted everywhere. The camp itself is threatened. Even off duty, there is no more real sleep for anyone.

The peasants, manipulated by the F.L.N., seem to be provoking trouble with us. In the general state of nerves, repression is becoming more and more brutal. Fear engenders cruelty; cruelty, fear.

At the start, the villages seldom give us a hostile reception. Quite the contrary, there are endless greetings and salaams. Our lead detachment hardly ever encounters anything but a highly dignified reception committee of honorable old men, abundantly decorated ('14–'18 and '39–'45). A few Indochina veterans, with the T.O.E.[1] on their chests, are

---

[1] Théâtre d'Opérations Extérieures: colonial decoration equivalent to the Croix de Guerre.

with them. "Asma! Asma! Brave soldiers! Brave France! Come eat the méchoui of friendship!" Congratulations. We're all soldiers, aren't we? As long as the company is on its way through the village, at a slow and cautious pace, doing no more investigating than is required, the whole village loves France, even the France that we represent.

But, as soon as the last soldier has his back turned to the last mechta: "bang . . . rat tat . . . rat tat tat . . . !" The honorable old men seize the old boukala hidden in the woodpile and open fire, solidly supported by a few authentic outlaws among them.

It is hard to imagine more puerile treachery. Tactically, it is, of course, idiotic. From that moment on, the village's fate is sealed. Less than a week later, the air force will come by, and leave nothing at all. Let the survivors shift for themselves. Isn't that just what the fellaghas want, though? As much hate as possible? To have the war endless, atrocious and pitiless, and the whole population of these mountains so desperate and so destitute that it willingly joins their side?

A stiffened corpse leaves hardly a trace in a soldier's memory. But one remembers certain wounded men a long time.

It was April, and we were returning from a patrol, bringing back two suspects. They were walking in front of us, with their hands bound—but this did not prevent our talking, and even joking, with them, for nobody thought they were in serious trouble.

Evening comes, very fast. We close up a bit. The suspects put out the cigarettes we had given them. We look rather like a troop of boy scouts. Seven o'clock: in five minutes, it will be dark. We are all silent now, and walking along the crest of a narrow ridge. On either side, there is a perpendicular drop into the night.

All of a sudden: "Aaaah . . . Aaaaah! Aaaaah . . ." An appalling yell, a caveman yell—wild, demented, more animal than human—rends our drowsy ears!

We stop, chilled by terror. At this instant, in spite of their bound hands, the two rebels dive madly off either side of the ridge, leaping from rock to rock at a rate to dislocate their legs, hurtling like a pair of jumping jacks down into the pitch-dark.

"Shoot, for God's sake, shoot!" yells the sergeant, who has nothing but a revolver himself. It is already too late to hope to hit the fugitives with a rifle.

We do succeed, however, in wounding one with our P.M. We rush down to him. He is lying among the rocks, in agony, with his eyes wide open. He can't speak. No papers. We never find out his name. He is beginning to die in the darkness.

"Come back up, we're going on!" they shout to us from above.

"What about the wounded man?"

"Leave him!"

A shot of morphine, and we go away.

Next morning, the patrol sent to look for his body has trouble finding it. He is thirty yards below where we left him. The man had slid on his back during the night. And he is not entirely dead. He is still gasping spasmodically. He can't speak. But he casts a glance at me that turns me pale. The sun is rising. Hundreds of flies cover his body, buzzing on it in black swarms, eagerly sucking the exposed blood.

The patrol leader is perplexed. He has orders to find a corpse. And to bury it. What's to be done? How move a man in this condition to the post, five or six kilometers away? "Why couldn't the fellow hurry up and die?" says someone. This recalcitrant corpse is a nuisance to everybody. Thirteen .30-caliber bullets in the chest, a few more in the head, quarts of lost blood, and still those black eyes move. Blood everywhere, nightmare of blood. Blood all round the body, on the stones, blood already black, and red blood oozing from the long yellow face.

We give him another shot of morphine. Was it really morphine? He dies instantly. A last glance, in which all the world's hatred is accumulated, and the head falls on the panting chest, in a nod.

In the very midst of horror one can still be bored. After one month at T'Kout, whenever there is any rest everybody becomes bored to tears, almost to screams. The thirst, the anger, even death are not sufficient.

Charles R., whom we called Charlot, had the look of someone repeatedly taking an examination he never passes. One day he simply began to "take off." In every sense of the term. We said: "Charlot's cut his motor." He certainly had, and his wings were in poor shape too.

"What's the matter, old man?" a smiling comrade would ask now and then, sitting down on his camp bed. "Here, have a drink."

Charlot would drink, but be no happier.

"When I see a man sad, I think he is falling in love," someone has written. Charles R., French paratrooper, twenty-one, tall and strong, and no more stupid than the rest of us, was in love. He loved a star, or rather her picture. Some say that where there is no hope, love dies. But what do they know of either?

We often saw Charlot absorbed in a book whose pages he never turned. He used it as a screen for uninterrupted contemplation of his idol's publicity shot. I saw the picture one day. At the bottom, standing out like the brand name of a chocolate, I read, Marina... Marina Vlady, if I remember correctly. Above was a woman's smile, nothing but a smile under some hair. La Bruyère said that a human face is the most beautiful of sights. Well, Charlot certainly had this face on the brain.

Did Charlot ever try to write this woman, this young actress further removed from his soldier's life in Algeria than a toad from a lost planet? However that may be, his sad romance ended on a stretcher. For he had completely stopped eating. From the Batna hospital, where I would go see him every chance I got, he was sent on to the hospital in Constantine. After that I never saw him again.

The ridiculous little idol he had chosen for himself had accomplished her mission.

# 23

April 30th is the ninety-second anniversary of Camerone.[1]
Preparations are being made for a tremendous celebration at
Arris, where such Legion affairs take place. A detachment
from our battalion, including me, is invited. A great honor:
the Legion is the most exclusive of clubs.

When we arrive at their spotless camp in the morning,
all the legionnaires are drawn up in dress uniform on the
great sanded space in front of their tents. They are awaiting
*us*. These people couldn't think of living without a parade
ground, even here.

Wearing képi and white leather shoulder straps, heavy
red and green wool epaulettes, white leggings and triple
fourragère, most of them covered with decorations won in
combat, our hosts are like picture soldiers, except that they
are very much alive. Compared to them, we in our dusty
uniforms seem like peasants.

Trumpet blast. Followed by evocation of the proud dead
of Camerone. Submachine guns and bayonets sparkle in the
sun. The music goes to the heart.

Long silence. The colonel moves slowly along, like a
ramrod, and here and there pins a medal on an outthrust
chest. The rich ceremony, full of pomp and dignity, unfolds
itself in the religious silence of the entire regiment.

Sounding of taps, poignant with unavailing sadness. And,
once more, a strident trumpet blast. Eight hundred men at
impeccable attention, chests out, eyes front, await the colonel's word as briskly now, he passes in front of them, face
severe, stick in hand. "Honneur et Fidélité, voici la Légion!"
*Legio patria nostra!* The ceremony closes with wild acclama-

---

[1]Battle fought in Mexico, April 30, 1863.

tions. And the legionnaires' dogs, silent till now, burst into tumultuous barking.

After ceremonies like this, some men re-enlist in wild enthusiasm. Perhaps the main strength of armies is the mise en scène.

The men disperse into the tents. There, vast tables await them, loaded with food, and even delicacies. Under the tables are dozens and dozens of bottles of beer and wine. The revels begin.

Roast chicken: each man his own bird. Wine: each man his bottle. We paratroopers participate actively. "Et vive la Coloniale!" they shout to us.

By about five o'clock, everybody, Legion and paratroops alike, is "cané," at the zenith of intoxication. One after another, legionnaires strike up some fearful Polish, Spanish or German song. The discordant airs mingle and clash, but remain poignant with melancholy. They are always about departing for death, and loss of sweetheart and country. What with the songs and the drink and the heat, some of the oldest legionnaires have tears pouring down their cheeks.

Others tell the stories of their lives: strange tales of confused and bloody wars, hair-raising adventures, endless successions of misfortunes interspersed with a few joyless pleasures.

Toward evening, we have to tear ourselves away from this magnificent party. Quite a few have slid under the tables, their superb white uniforms stained with wine. The shouting is such that no one can understand anybody.

After many handshakes and pats on the back, we reel out of the camp, with our pockets full of cigars, our hands full of bottles. Even the dogs are drunk.

Our little convoy starts zigzagging down the road, which is not very straight itself. Guttural voices follow us with good wishes. "Ach So! Donnerwetter!"

The driver of our lead truck is that acrobat of a transport sergeant, and he is loaded to the gunwales. He proclaims that he is going to drive like a circus rider today. Like a danseuse. "Go to it!" we shout at him. "Hit sixty." We want sensations.

We really do take curve after curve at sixty miles an hour until, about ten kilometers from camp, the truck leaves the road, rolls over five or six times, and stops thirty feet further on, upside down with the wheels still spinning.

Everybody is suddenly sober, and sore all over. We shake ourselves. But a few yards off two of our number are lying still and very pale. "They're dead?" It's the sergeant's turn to grow pale. This affair could cost him dear. We crowd around the two bodies. "Ho! Ho!" We shake them. No reaction. Someone suggests slapping them. They thereupon receive a rain of blows, and one of them finally opens an eye. "Oh! Come back to us!—Ah! There we are!" Drunken tenderness. They were only unconscious.

Next day, the fellaghas, probably informed of these revels, attack the tabors'[2] post at Tiffelfel, halfway between the Legion and us. A rash undertaking, for the post is in a solidly built stone schoolhouse, and you don't storm a building like that in daylight, with nothing but rifles, unless you have friends in the garrison. Perhaps they did. Algerian soldiers have been known to surrender their posts to the rebels, after massacring their officers.

At any rate, this coup failed, and the rebels lost one dead and two captured, one of the latter wounded.

But it proves that, even in broad daylight and in a region bursting with troops, the rebels may appear in arms at any moment, out of a village or a fold in the mountains.

We are beginning to say to one another that all these good people we see cultivating their stony little fields or driving their mules along the quiet roads are probably rebels out of uniform. "They're all rebels, all! We're silly! We should talk to these people with submachine guns! And flamethrowers!" We are getting excited, just when the newspapers are starting to talk about mediation and possible negotiators.

---

[2] Moroccan infantry.

# 24

The rebels are at it again. The commandant has been reprimanded. The result for us is a series of spectacular operations.

The first is in the mountains near Medina, in collaboration with the Legion, who have two men killed the very first day, and others on the way back. Being less French than the rest, the legionnaires are always chosen for the hardest operations. They are the ones most often asked to die for France.

One evening, eighty rebels in uniform set fire to the Balcon de Rhouffi, a luxurious hotel for millionaires, built on a cliff in one of the deepest gorges in the Aurès. They also burn the school and whatever other buildings are "European," massacring and overpowering all in their path. All this in less than a quarter of an hour. Then they disappear. It's 1955, the evening of the 5th of May.

The news reached the camp at nine o'clock, just as we were starting to rest after a forty-eight hour forced march from which we had returned that afternoon.

At ten o'clock, in moonlight hot as the sun, the battalion is again on the march. Ahead of us is a gigantic mountain, like a wall.

In the moonlight, we advance slowly, tiny specks lost on a vast plain that sparkles like a snowfield. The heat pours down on us. The silence is broken only by the sound of the gypsum breaking under our feet. Not a blade of grass. Not an insect. Nothing but the bare sky, the bare earth, the flat and burning white perspective.

The mountains, which a moment ago seemed near enough to touch, are endlessly receding. We have been marching only four hours, but already our faces are streaming. Our eyelids are soaked with burning moisture. The sun-baked crust conceals a fine, suffocating dust that blows out when we break through. Each step is a jolt, like missing a step on the stairs.

We are getting farther and farther behind the rebels. We try running, with the captains in the lead. But the more we run, the further we fall through, and the more time it takes to lift our dusty, bloody feet out of the broken ground. We might as well be running through water. We trip, weapons roll on the ground. We get up, and fall down again.

One after another, the men in the lead disappear in front of us, as though swallowed by the earth. I reach this fateful threshold and stop dead. At my feet is a chasm, more than three hundred feet deep.

Unable to see a thing, I slowly grope my way into the Rhouffi gorge, with my F.M. banging against my sides and upsetting my balance. We inch down step by step, feeling our way with our feet. If rebels are posted in caves on the opposite cliff, they can shoot us like rabbits, with our noses to the wall, and we won't even be able to turn around. But, intent as we are on just getting to the bottom, nobody is thinking of any other danger for the moment.

After an hour of this, halfway down we are blocked. The rest of the wall seems to be completely smooth. The sound of swiftly running water has grown much louder, and we are suffering acutely from thirst. But we have to climb back to the top, try another way down, then another, and another. We finally get to the bottom at three in the morning.

The company now divides in two in order to comb both shores of the river at once. We go happily down into the deep water. It is running tumultuously in some places, silently in others. Drink, we're going to drink!

The water's undrinkable. This is a river of liquid mud, and hot—not warm, actually hot. It is waist-deep, and we struggle through, raising our arms to keep our weapons dry.

We reach the other bank dripping like dogs and, bending forward, force our way into a treacherous forest. At the foot of every tree, date, apricot, fig, or pomegranate, a little clump of cacti faces us with its assorted venoms. Six-foot hedges of barbary figs block our way, and in the dark we sometimes run right into them nose first with cries of rage and pain. Often we have to go back into the water to get around them. We slosh and slip and tear our cheeks on the thorns. But we have to keep up and stay in touch with each other. Thirst tortures us more and more, while the water ripples about our legs.

In some places the moonlight comes right through to the river, and wading waist deep in the dense water we seem to be moving through warm liquid silver. As we become more skillful at avoiding the cacti, we begin to look further than our feet. The strange beauty of this valley rises to our hearts like a song of love. We lift up our eyes to the stars.

Three hundred feet above us, on the surface of the earth, the world goes on. But here we are, deep in this shadowy and luminous canyon, hidden in the very heart of the loneliest of African lands. The giant perpendicular cliffs seem ready to close upon us like the waters on Pharaoh's host. And the moon moves ever higher! Its light streams down on helmeted ghosts with pale blue faces.

We went through Rhouffi. The handful of terrified survivors were waiting for us, and also the corpses of their families, neatly laid out along the road, with their chests riddled and their eyes put out.

We climb back up the cliff, and at about nine o'clock we finally surface, like divers, our uniforms torn and a number of weapons broken from having crashed into rocks.

"Halt." We laugh, congratulate each other, slap each other on the back. "Well, we'll remember this..." Several have already stretched out ecstatically, full length, on the ground.

"Everybody up!" shouts the captain. "We're leaving!"

"They're crazy... Must be kidding?... It's impossible!"

"On the double, forward!" And off we go.

The mountain is six thousand feet, straight up. We climb on all fours. On its flat summit live some of the cruelest and most repulsive animals in the world: falcons, jackals, snakes, inhabit this sun-scorched hell.

About ten o'clock, at the start of the climb, a man falls in a faint. We add his pack and weapons to our own loads, and set off at once, faster than before, to catch up.

The colonel is displeased. "These aren't men," he said on learning the man fainted.

At ten-thirty, another fainting. A strong man this time, no little Paris boy, a real peasant from the Landes. He falls in a heap, without a word. His helmet rolls on the stones, making an eerie sound. We pick him up, limp, deadly pale, with his face bruised and his mouth half open. "He's dead," says someone. But our Landais finally starts to make feeble motions.

Three minutes later, it's an old F.M. man's turn to collapse. His weapon strikes the stones with a resounding crash that makes everyone turn around. These mountains are sonorous as a gong.

Three faintings in less than an hour. We continue the march and the steep climb...

## 25

May 8th. Triple anniversary: Joan of Arc, the Liberation, Dien Bien Phu. We're not so sure how our victories and defeats balance now. Dien Bien Phu's the hope of the rebels: let's not emphasize that. Joan of Arc's better, but a pretty old story. As for the Liberation, who achieved it?

On this triple occasion, there's a slight improvement in our food.

The heat's becoming frightful. We're going to try a new system: operate only at night, as the rebels have been doing for some time.

We get in the habit of leaving camp every evening about seven o'clock, and of not returning till four or five in the morning. The wild animal schedule.

We form commandos of ten or a dozen men who work well together. We wear espadrilles to walk without a sound, wrap our gun butts in dark wool socks to prevent any reflection, black our faces with burnt cork—nothing is more luminous at night than a face, and we scour the mountains like wolves, in search of a choice encounter. At our own risk, of course: if we chanced to intercept a company, we'd have plenty of time to get ourselves massacred, before the arrival of reinforcements.

Fortunately, the rebels don't seem to be seeking combat.

They are there, though, and let us know it the very first night we apply our new system, and think ourselves unnoticed. While we are gone, seven telegraph poles are cut along the very road we took. Night and day, the surrounding mountains are full of watchful eyes.

After marching all night, we ought to sleep during the day. But how can we, in the frightful heat of these big tents? Thousands of flies, those angry, noisy flies attracted by the refuse around the camp, never stop harassing us.

Not infrequently, too, when we've come in at five in the morning and had a few hours of nominal rest, we have to leave for the mountains again at two in the afternoon, in the heat of the day, to intercept some suspicious caravan.

Out of frustration, rage and despair, to show we've accomplished something, we begin to arrest all Arabs, whoever they are. Only to let them go, two or three hours, two or three days, or two or three months later, often a hundred kilometers from where they were arrested, and without a penny, without water, without food, sometimes in the desert. Let them fend for themselves. You give the Arab a good slap on the back, and off he goes. (At first, slowly: he's suspicious, with good reason. To get rid of a bothersome prisoner, there's the old trick: "Get going, fool!" When he runs, you blast him in the back: attempted escape, no complications. Our regiment's not using this method yet.) Like as not, he's rearrested ten kilometers farther on by another post with nothing better to do.

Thus, especially in the mountains, there are unfortunate Arabs who spend months being sent from one camp to another, often without knowing why—any more than we do. As a result, we see peasants begin to cry, cry like children, at the slightest questioning. It's not pretense, nor dread of eventual execution, but simply nerves, confusion! They get mixed up in their answers, and then all they can do is stammer. That is the way to arouse suspicion. More than one has got into bad trouble by going to pieces this way when sharply questioned by an armed man appearing suddenly round the corner of the road.

Lucky are the Arabs who, after their mule has been confiscated at the first post and their papers scattered among a succession of five or six soldiers, and after enduring every indignity, finally do get back to their village, which they sometimes left a month or two before—for an afternoon trip after wood. These could have fared worse. Some don't get back.

Why be surprised if in their poverty and rage they take the first opportunity after getting back to their much-raided village to go over to the rebels, and murder even the children of the landowners they manage to catch in their beds?

One fine morning, millions of locusts alight on the camp, from exhaustion probably, for there is nothing to eat here. They fall to the ground in clouds. The air is dark with them for miles. It's amusing at first. We walk about in them as though in straw. Then it gets disgusting. We close up the tents. But they get through everywhere. And from time to time a grasshopper as big as your finger drops from the roof onto your neck, your head, or your plate.

The heat is horrible, and it not only favors grasshoppers, it is also the great season for rebels. They capture four soldiers in broad daylight within three kilometers of the camp. But, on our side, we make fourteen prisoners of fourteen rebels unsuspectingly strolling about in a village at midday. They confess they supposed that in heat like this we were all lying half dead in our tents.

In order to question them "carefully," we bring them back in trucks to T'Kout. The orders are to "execute prisoners immediately in the event of attack made for the purpose of freeing them." Two men in each truck are designated for this responsibility. But who wouldn't volunteer? To kill without risk of being killed, what a refinement of pleasure!

It is now the turn of our friends down the road, the tabors (all these Moroccans will very shortly go home), to be attacked. In broad daylight the rebels capture them all, along with two automatic rifles and forty-one carbines.

Everything suggests that the tabors put up but a feeble defense. No doubt they are anxious not to get themselves killed without knowing what for. Only the three Europeans who were with them were found dead, killed by whom?

During the night of the 19th to the 20th of May, we leave on foot to set an ambush a few kilometers from the camp, in difficult terrain. The night is very dark, with no moon. The trail is soon lost. We have to go by compass. We lose several hours taking our bearings every few hundred yards.

At last we reach the appointed spot and settle ourselves as best we can among the rocks. The wait begins. At first it's rest. We're sweaty and glad to relax. Then the icy wind comes and lashes us, and we spend the rest of the time shivering and shaking, for we have no shirts on under our jackets.

Our leaden eyelids struggle furiously against sleep. To sleep would be a crime. A man who sleeps during an ambush is not only derelict in that he has left his post in the face of the enemy, but also a traitor, for in the dim light his motionless form inspires false confidence. He can be shot for this. We know it. However, we do now and then go to sleep.

The ambush is a failure. We are coming back toward the camp, still seeking contact. Several of our most recent prisoners have definitely informed us that rebels will be passing this way tonight, and we can't return empty-handed.

At about one in the morning, we set a new ambush on the road just outside the village of Djemorah. The ground is covered with thousands of stones, over which we trip as we take our positions, dead tired.

An hour, two hours, go by. Nothing happens. Absolute silence in the pitch-dark. If only we could sleep! What a bore this is.

Suddenly, there is an explosion of shots and shouts right in among us, like a succession of thunderclaps.

Everybody jumps up, vibrating from head to foot, wide awake, weapon in hand. "What? What's this? Who's there to shoot at? What can we do?" We can't see a thing. To my right, I hear a violent melee, with the crackling of automatic rifles and submachine guns. Then off goes a grenade. Everywhere, men are firing wildly, by guess, at everything that moves. How be of any use? Too many kill their best friends, or are killed by them.

This goes on at least ten or fifteen minutes; then there is silence again, broken only by the groans of the wounded. We find out what happened.

A group of rebels had walked into our position without knowing it and without our knowing it either. The night was exceptionally dark. Their lead man mistook us for rocks.

Wearing espadrilles, he glided along without a sound. Suddenly he found himself within two feet of a long shape, made still longer by a weapon. A man stretched out, perfectly still.

It was Private B., sound asleep. And every ten yards were other men posted like him among the rocks and supposed to be watching, sitting on stones with their heads in their hands and their guns between their knees. They may not have all been sound asleep, but they were all at least in a doze.

The rebel scout realizes his luck. No one has seen him. If he wants, he can go quietly back and tell the men following him. Then they can all bypass us completely unnoticed, simply by changing their course a little. That would be the wisest thing to do.

But this rebel is young. He chooses the bolder course. The new automatic rifle, so near, shining a little in the dark, tempts him. What a triumph to go back to his leader with that weapon under his arm! He bends over B., takes hold of the end of the barrel, and gives a very gentle tug.

To prevent such a thing from happening, the quartermaster had distributed short chains by which to attach your weapon to your wrist at night. But who would ever use one? They scrape your skin and keep you awake. B., of course, has his chain in his pocket like everybody else. When he sat down, though, he had slipped the strap of his F.M. around his leg, the way every automatic rifleman does when he's resting. The rebel doesn't know this. He keeps pulling the weapon toward him. B. wakes with a start. Still confused, he mutters: "Why, lieutenant..." (so his loader told us next morning). But that doesn't make the rebel let go. He just pulls a little harder. B. then looks up sleepily, and suddenly understands. "Oh!" he says, in a loud voice this time.

He says no more. The rebel has a long curved dagger in his other hand, and with one blow he plunges it to the hilt into B.'s bare head.

B.'s horrible dying shriek rends the air. Everyone leaps to his feet as the bold scout runs off with the F.M. in his hand.

The first to see him is B.'s loader, who is now responsible for the F.M. and determined to get it back. He rushes after the outlaw and catches up with him just as he's reaching his comrades. At that point, he finds his rifle is on safety. No time to cock it. He leaps on the rebel bare-handed and tries to tear the F.M. out of his hands.

Encumbered by the F.M., the fellagha couldn't use his rifle either. They grapple furiously and roll to the ground. Neither side dares shoot into the wild confusion of their bodies for fear of hitting the wrong man.

There is plenty of shooting all around them, however. And finally our platoon leader, Officer Cadet C., who has been in the thick of it from the start, kills the rebel scout with a burst in the back.

The rebel commander, a tall man who seems truly gigantic in the darkness, saw this happen. Fearless of our second F.M., which never stops firing, he stands up and at ten feet kills the officer cadet with a burst square in the chest.

The fight rages around B.'s F.M. as around a treasure. Everyone is frantic. There is now a short but very violent scuffle, so confused in the darkness that for several minutes no one knows what's happening. Except our platoon sergeant, who seems as much at ease in all this as the rebel leader. When he sees our officer down, he yells: "Riflemen, follow me!" and plunges into the middle of the rebels, as if unconscious of the danger. He is almost immediately killed by a bullet in the face, fired by a man he did not see.

Day breaks and the rebels withdraw, without carrying off the much fought over F.M. The engagement is over.

The long dagger in his head gives B. a horrible grand guignol look. It is the medic's job to pull it out. We look the other way.

Two more of our men and three of the rebels are lying dead. All six have the same disillusioned, faintly contemptuous expression, and their wide open eyes seem to be staring into space. We roll these poor fellows in their tent cloths, which are too short to cover their dusty shoes.

From the rebel dead, and also from their wounded, we take magnificent Italian Static rifles, practically new.

Having no stretchers, we carry the dead and the wounded by the arms and legs. A rebel wounded in the chest dies on our way back, worn out by the strain of breathing.

We reach camp at noon, not much pleased with ourselves. On learning that one of his lieutenants has been killed, our commanding officer is in a fury. He takes it personally, and imagines the villagers in their mechtas commenting on the news. "The Bérets rouges were caught napping last night. We killed three of them. They are not so good . . ."

The artillery comes out from Batna and mounts three 105's opposite the village. It is a threat to our camp. The rebels' being there last night proves the villagers on their side. We are going to strike a big blow.

The cannon are lined beside each other. The heavy shells are taken out of the caissons. Orders are given to fire all three cannon together as a warning. The villagers are given one hour to leave, and if they fire a single shot, they will be bombarded.

For the next hour, we watch through field glasses as up

**105 mm Howitzer**

on the ridge the inhabitants of Djemorah come out of their
village and run down the slope with packages in their arms.

At the end of the hour the evacuation is complete, and
not a shot has been fired. That changes our plans. Yet, come
to think of it, we oughtn't to have brought the artillery all the
way from Batna for nothing.

And at exactly five o'clock, the first three shells go
whistling over our heads. Every two minutes for the next
hour, three more shots are fired. The gun crews work me-
thodically, stripped to the waist. Heavy roars echo and re-echo.

Their work finished, the artillery goes calmly back to
Batna, without condescending to check the results. We can
see nothing more of the village, even through field glasses. It
seems to have melted into the horizon.

Comments: "That's what we should have done long ago,
everywhere, to all the villages. When they've no one left to
help them, the rebels will have to disband, or come down
onto the plains and get caught. We're too soft on these
people." Up there, people may be dying under the stones of
their houses. We're too soft!

In the evening, the belote players get out their cards and
resume their game. Men always have the strength to endure
the misfortunes of others.

# 26

The next day, as we return in trucks from a trip to Batna, we
suddenly hear the whistle of bullets. Some rebels up on a
ridge above the road are taking shots at us as we go by.

An attack in full daylight. Up to now, neither the Legion
nor the paratroops have been assailed so openly.

The convoy stops. We are ordered up onto the ridge, a
fairly dangerous undertaking, for the slope is almost bare.
But we all break into a run. It's good to stretch your legs after
six hours on the bench of a G.M.C.

As soon as the fellaghas see us coming at them like lunatics, they disappear, and all we find is a few cartridges, some empty shells, and a little blood. We go back to the trucks, somewhat annoyed.

A Colonial Army chaplain comes and says a mass for the battalion's dead. The rite is performed in complete silence; not even an address. I was expecting him to turn to us and say: "My children, let us pray also for those whom you have killed!" But no, not a word about that. It would be against regulations.

The same day, at three in the afternoon, just when we are so stupefied by the heat that we can hardly move, we are routed out by a new emergency. Only three kilometers from camp, the fellaghas are attacking the convoy of tabors that just went by.

By the time we arrive, there's nobody there except dead and wounded to pick up. One of the trucks is still burning.

At seven o'clock another of our convoys, this one from Arris, is attacked in the gorges, perhaps by the same band. We go out again to counterattack, but by the time we get up the cliffs, the rebels have gone.

The convoys have two techniques for getting through gorges. They either roar through full speed, not stopping even when fired on; or else they go through very slowly with field glasses and machine guns trained on the ridge tops at an 80° angle. Both ways are frustrating and humiliating.

The Aurès have become a vast fortified camp. The rebels are creating more and more impregnable areas among their rocks.

Just as we do later on in the Soummam valley, here we already find the green and white banner of the Insurrection flying from the largest mechta, in every village that we enter unexpectedly. Four hundred thousand men are powerless against that banner.

The staff in Algiers is beginning to take serious notice of us. Last week, we were expecting M. Soustelle. But so much happened and there was so much shooting that nobody came. Even so, we spent long hours waiting for our minister in the hot sun. We don't forget that. Some are malicious enough to say that M. Soustelle is a jerk, and that the reason he didn't come is just that he was scared. It's true enough that the Batna-T'Kout road is not exactly safe.

This week, we're expecting a general. I've forgotten his name. Same comedy all over again. All the posts—Legion, tabors, paras—distribute groups of armed men along the crests of the ridges, to safeguard the journey of our adventurous commanders. We're not asked to clap as they go by. But pretty nearly.

From seven-thirty in the morning to five in the afternoon, we await these gentlemen's arrival, which was officially scheduled for 8 A.M. Not a drop of water. Not a bite to eat. We sit on stones in an angry stupor with our guns between our knees and our helmets on our heads. Sweat oozes from every pore. Nobody says a word. Why talk? What's there to say? The saliva sticks to the roof of your mouth like glue. There are seven of us here, like old forgotten statues. Somewhere else, nine. Over there, twelve, invisible, melting into the stones.

We get back in the evening and learn that the general isn't coming. Today counts as a day of rest.

That night two good friends go for each other in grim silence with commando knives, on the childish pretext that a stone loosened by the foot of one had hit the other in the back. They bristle and gasp like fighting dogs. We have to separate and disarm them. The human machine is breaking up.

This same week the fellaghas kill a governor, a second lieutenant, a corporal, and a private, and capture twenty-four more tabors—all in our zone.

His Excellency the Governor General of Algeria decides, for the second time, to set out, escorted by Generals Cherrière and Allard, to take a look at this theater of operations. But—was it good luck, or bad?—their helicopter gets caught in a little sandstorm and can't land at T'Kout. They prudently return to Batna. From now on, they won't venture out of the cities.

# 27

In the night of June 3rd, we leave T'Kout for Louestia, a village on the edge of the immense Beni-Imloul forest, the domain of the rebel high command's very mobile headquarters. For ten days, we are billeted here in cool, shaded wood and stone buildings, never going out except to patrol the approaches, or to soak ourselves for hours in the deliciously cold water that runs from a big waterfall right through the middle of the village.

A rebel messenger intercepted by a patrol informs us, after "interrogation," that two large bands of outlaws are headed our way. They plan to rendezvous in the forest and attack us this very night.

This news fills us with jubilation. Two bands for one company, how complimentary. In our huts, where a moment ago we were drowsing, limp with the heat, we now clear for action. Everyone rushes for his slightly dusty weapon, and cleans and oils it.

In the afternoon, helicopters land a detachment of Legion Bérets verts to reinforce us.

By sunset, everybody is in position. The advance sentinels are tripled. The F.M.'s are mounted on the roofs. The captain goes nervously from one foxhole to another, delighted, absolutely delighted.

The night goes by, warm and very quiet. Not a thing happens. "Boors, filthy savages! They'll pay for this! We could have had such a good sleep!" The informer pays next morning. He has a bad, and final, quarter of an hour.

Probably, the rebels learned form some villager about the arrival of our reinforcements. That night, they confined their activities to cutting all the roads converging on us.

The Bérets verts go back.

Our information, however, was not unfounded.

The air force spots one of the bands as it begins to retreat, and from our roofs we watch it being destroyed less than a kilometer away.

In front of us, the forest stretches away, lit by the setting sun. The planes glisten, swift as arrows. This is the parade before the show. We snatch the field glasses from each other's hands. Four Spitfires and a small bomber are circling above the trees. They open fire.

The rebels run in all directions, trying to disperse. But over and over again, like wasps that will not leave their victim alone till they have stung him to death, the planes turn and come back over their objective. What chance has an infantryman against the 20-mm. bullets of a plane's machine guns? Very bold rebels have been known to shoot down a Piper Cub, or even a helicopter, with an F.M., but you can't shoot down fighter planes with ordinary rifles. The only thing to do is to take cover if you can.

**Spitfire**

Through the field glasses, we can see the rebels scattering among the thin pines. Scant shelter against that hail of steel. There are no rocks. These men have to die.

We can see the gunners leaning from the cockpits: they are terribly calm. Their seriousness is like that of children playing. What have they to fear? The rebels are falling one by one, blasted in mid stride. A 20-mm. bullet striking the back or chest of a running man not only annihilates him, it throws him into the air before crushing him to the ground. These men are being snuffed out, like drops of water falling on a hot stove.

One last circle, and the planes start back toward their base, shining and swift like fish. As they pass in formation above us, they dip their wings.

I put down my glasses in shame and pity. And yet, I know the horrible death of these men will not keep me from sleep. My comrades are already busy with other things. We've lost emotion.

I know perfectly well that had these rebels lived, and captured me in these woods of theirs, they would not have hesitated to torment my body, to make me talk, till I was shrieking in my death throes. All the same, if at times they were cowards and wild beasts, so were they also very brave men.

The day after our return to T'Kout, a regiment of Legion infantry relieves us there, and we leave for good.

On the way back to Batna, just as our first truck is reducing speed on entering the territory of our neighbors at Arris, fantastic music bursts forth: the Legion march. The whole regiment, in full dress uniform, in two ranks along the road, with the colonel in front, is there to honor us. We are moved as well as astonished. The legionnaires look at us, and we at them. Neither they nor we could better express our feelings for each other than by that music and those looks.

# 28

There is a slum, the "Village Nègre," on the outskirts of Batna. It is so astonishingly filthy that the Europeans never venture into it. A few Negroes live there as pariahs, mixed with a few white Arabs and all sorts of prostitutes of such mixed race that one can't tell whether they are black or white, the whole lot of them in utter poverty.

Soldiers are strictly forbidden to go into the "Village." It is full of rebels in civilian clothes who are there to recruit their labor force. But it is not unusual to see one of those old barouches so common in North Africa leaving Batna in the evening, headed for the village, heavily overloaded with soldiers in it and all over it, lurching along at a breakneck pace, with the Arab coachman no longer in control.

The evening we return to Batna, the village is full of paratroops. Three young members of our regiment are drinking in a sordid little bar. Suddenly there is an uproar. Falling chairs, breaking bottles. Nothing out of the ordinary in that, and no one would have thought twice about it, but for the report of a firearm which suddenly drowned out the other noises.

Bernard and I heard the shot. It was very near where we were. Without a word to each other we run, and are the first to enter the bar, a wretched little place with mud walls. At first all we see is the usual signs of a drunken brawl, bottles flying, a stool hurtling through the air, etc. But then we catch sight of two of our comrades backed into a corner and hemmed in by a small crowd of excited Arabs. Our friends have a bottle in each hand and are pale as death. They do not see us. At least a dozen Arabs are furiously attacking them with anything they can lay hold of, bottles, benches, clubs. From all sides, others are rushing up, threatening and shouting. There is no garrison in the village.

With great difficulty, we fight our way through this mass. Both our comrades have blood all over their faces. They are worn out, and not putting up much of a fight. However, when they see us their courage returns, and they shout: "Look out! They've killed L.! One of them has a gun!"

Only then do we see L., lying flat under a bench, with his arms limp and a hole through his shirt in the middle of his chest. Bernard whispers: "Looks bad! There are too many of them." Trying to hear Bernard, I fail to dodge an enormous bottle that lands square in my face. I see a thousand stars and my head rings like a bell. I sway like a drunken man and lean against the wall. Is this my turn?

Then there is a second loud report. But this shot was badly aimed and only hit the wall. I have time to think: Must I die so stupid a death?

There are now at least twenty Arabs yelling and waving their arms. A few are only taking advantage of the confusion to steal a few bottles. Others obviously regard as providential this opportunity to kill four paratroopers. They press us hard. Bernard the Magnificent is unrecognizable. He is covered with bruises, and kicking and punching away at three adversaries, whose chèches have come off. They are trying to draw him away from me.

Suddenly, the taller of the two paratroopers, so drunk he seems likely to have been the original cause of all this, bursts into roars of laughter—not that he stops pounding away with both enormous fists at everybody within range. This is the pay-off, he's gone crazy. He's going to dance. His beret falls off, exposing his close-cropped head absolutely shredded by broken glass. Streams of blood are pouring over his beaming face, a horrible sight. I am afraid. The Arabs look like angry cats, and there are more and more of them.

All at once, I hear familiar voices outside. Over the heads of the Arabs, I see five or six red spots, the berets of comrades running up. We shout at the top of our lungs: "In here! Give us a hand, paras!"

In two seconds, the bar is empty. The Arabs vanish. Doors slam: they are barricading themselves. Three minutes later, the village is a desert. Not even a cat.

"Les salauds," Bernard keeps repeating, "les sales bougnoules, les sales boukaks!" His hand is slit right across—a knife he had tried to grab by the blade. His torn knuckles are oozing pinkish blood. He thinks his nose is broken, and feels it, moaning.

The tall "para" without a beret has stopped laughing. He is looking at L., whom we have just laid out on the bench. I open his jacket. He is dead. Quite dead. The bullet had gone in without shedding a drop of blood and drilled its dark little tunnel to the heart.

"We were drinking. Just drinking," explains the man without a beret. "All at once, I felt there were too many of them around us. L. felt the same way. 'Let's get out quick, boys,' said he, very pale. At that moment, in came a fellagha. He had on a uniform under his jellabah. He stopped in front of the door. Perhaps he'd just come to scold the other Arabs about something. How do I know? They were all watching him. Without a word, he pulled out his gun, perhaps to set them an example, and with one shot killed L., the one nearest him. L. didn't even have time to yell. Then they all fell on us. The fellagha watched without saying anything. He was one of the first to leave."

"How can we catch them now?"

"We'd better go back first!"

We load the body into a cab, in spite of protests from the terrified driver. And we go back, feeling like fools.

On the way, we decide to say that L. was killed in the street. An inquest would be fruitless. The letter to his family will say: "Killed in action," and the Cross of Military Valor will be awarded him posthumously.

As for us, we get ten days' jail. Our bloody faces gave us away. We had no business being there. Bernard still has a scar on his palm and cannot yet completely close his hand.

Marc feels worse than anyone else about this wretched little affair.

Being a prisoner, I am confined to my tent, and he comes to see me the next day. Months of pent-up sadness break forth.

"Life is too stupid, too sordid! More and more so! L. died completely drunk didn't he? That's symbolic. Won't the world end the same way? Hasn't it already begun? This Algerian war may be only the start. Others will follow . . . I can't like people any more. The world I am living in disgusts me. I see nothing in it that doesn't make me angry. And yet I can't help feeling part of it. In a way, I pity the dead less than the living. Even happiness—which perhaps isn't very much—doesn't exist; we had to invent the word to be able to live and not kill ourselves... I pity L., as I pity the dead fellaghas, as I pity all those we never speak of and sometimes even laugh at, for idiots laugh at what they don't understand. I pity the animals who suffer all their lives for nothing. I pity the young girls we see in the subway, so ugly we hardly dare look at them... Being hopelessly ugly at twenty, when you're dying to love and be loved like the rest, can any greater suffering be imagined? Having nothing but one's miserable ugliness. And not even intelligence to console you... I can't get over the ugliness of our world... You know, in the last circle of Hell, the damned stand still: some day we'll all be standing still, all of us paralyzed by cruelty, stupefied by endless wars..."

"Don't you know you mustn't talk to prisoners?"

The sergeant comes into the tent. Marc goes slowly away.

## 29

One night when a comrade and I are on guard duty in the Domaine Saint-François, near Pasteur, a plane with no lights flies over us. It seems to be trying to find its way. Before we can aim our machine gun, it disappears in the dark.

We make our report, and next morning are highly commended for our vigilance, though this was just luck.

The next night, the same thing happens with two of our comrades. They fire one burst, and then the mysterious plane disappears. While Batna is relaying the report to the Telergma air base, we are hastily routed out of our straw. Are they expecting a squadron to arrive? The old soldiers rub their hands. The guerrilla war is over! Now for the real thing, with planes, tanks and cannon. When he is not killing, the soldier is a child.

* * *

One day, by the merest luck, we discover twenty rebels half asleep in a ditch between two fields on our Domaine Saint-François. They were waiting for night, and the plane that was to take them back to Tunisia.

As they were caught lying down, with nowhere to take cover, they made practically no resistance. They couldn't have escaped to the mountains, which are much too far off. Sixteen are killed on the spot with submachine guns. Four are temporarily spared and kept as prisoners, on the chance of their being useful.

A rebel hardly ever surrenders, for he knows the outcome will be the same either way. That's why we don't immediately execute the ones who surrender. They are the most cowardly, the most likely to talk. The rest die bravely on the spot, like men, standing erect. They sometimes blow themselves up, pulling the safety of a grenade on their belt. Everyone here respects their courage.

Much grumbling in the regiment. First, because we barely get leaves any more. Next, because we're ordered out every night, even when not on operations. We're tired of it. The other troops are staying in town, and can enjoy a fair that we are dying to go to. It's no fun wasting your life in a country where there's nothing to see.

Except for the Legion, which never comes back except to bury its dead with great pomp and ceremony, all the rest, artillery, service corps, infantry, tanks, are puttering around here and there, doing nothing three days out of four. The staffs still hesitate to use the draftees in our bloody "police operations." For instance: a violent skirmish is going on at N'Gaous. An infantry regiment is camped right near there, but they send for us, in Batna, a hundred and twenty kilometers away, and dispatch helicopters to bring us. "It's an honor for you. You're the elite of the army." That doesn't even make us laugh any more.

On July 1st, we have what is called a combined operation. The infantry stands in the shade down in the valleys and waits for us to make contact. We scramble from peak to peak, hot, footsore and half dead with thirst. As we look at our comrades lounging around three thousand feet below, we almost prefer the rebels, who at least are marching, like us.

\*      \*      \*

N'Gaous has become an outfitting center for rebel convoys and caravans. We have to occupy it. We leave our old camp in Batna one fine morning to go and bury ourselves there.

This ugly little village is at first sight just a pile of dust, scarcely higher than the dreary plain on which it lies. It consists of little hovels made of sand bricks and all crowded together. But in the midst of this desolation is a huge patch of green. Trees! This is the garden of monsieur the governor. He, by the way, has disappeared—he's been attended to by his villagers. But his park remains. We pitch our tents under the spreading boughs of his mangoes.

Very high earthen walls surround this incredible domain, and in it grows grass, green, thick, silky, velvety grass! Here and there are fig trees heavy with luscious fruit, cascading vines, big oval grapes, shrubbery and foliage that cool the air like rain. And amid all this, there are dozens of murmuring little streams, and cold springs from which dozens of blue crabs retreat awkwardly at our approach.

What a man, this governor! He must have intercepted all the water for miles around. We'll not mention the thirst of the people he governed.

N'Gaous is such a small village that we might have hoped to find peace in it. No such thing. We are soon reminded to be wary, by a grenade tossed over the wall one evening onto our tents. We attract rebels like flies. How monotonous life is.

About thirty outlaws have just attacked an infantry detachment on the road that will henceforth be ours. The soldiers were stupefied by the heat to start with, and they were still further confused by the Arabs' having put on our camouflaged paratroop uniforms, before attacking them with Mas 36's in their hands.

MAS 36, 7.5 mm.                \*      \*      \*

Recent cases of sunstroke on operations seem to be having an effect. The quartermaster has been so harassed by reports that he is finally issuing a peculiar wide-brimmed hat, called a bush helmet, that makes us all look like weary old clowns. The more simple-minded among us won't be happy till they've had their picture taken in it.

The quartermaster even goes so far as to issue us real gauze mosquito nets at the same time. Very inflammable, unfortunately. Careless smokers burn up three of them the first week.

One evening, some rebels who are perhaps as bored as we are set fire to the Bou Amamam sawmill in the Beni-Imloul forest—the last one in the Aurès—and kill everyone there, even the dog.

We get there much too late, of course. There's nothing left of the sawmill but great black heaps and a few corpses. Seven wooden bridges have also been burned or demolished on the forest's only road. We came in on foot and have to go out the same way, without having fired a single shot.

I am marching under the hot pines. And suddenly I remember that I am theoretically still a prisoner, on account of the Village Nègre affair. What liberty for a prisoner! I am armed, and can even take prisoners myself. But how much better I would like a nice cool cell. Life is poorly arranged.

Suppose like any good self-respecting prisoner I were to run away? It might be fun to wander about in this great forest, if only for a few hours or a few days. How tempting. For a moment I hesitate. At times the wildest folly lures a man like a chasm. But no. Leaving the beaten path is too much trouble... This evening I shall regard myself as a great coward for having been so sensible.

Not even a shepherd in the forest. No life at all except for insects. Here and there, the charred remains of a farmhouse, or the wreckage of a bridge. A few shots, very sharp in the still air. But we are discouraged and don't stop. Looking for men in such woods would be silly. Even a Piper couldn't find anything. The cover is thick enough to hide an army.

Typical operation! We knew when we left that it was sheer waste of time. But orders are positive: go as fast as possible to wherever the rebels show themseves, there and nowhere else. The surest way to never find them! Like the flies of this forest that are prisoners of the heavy air, we are flying lower and lower.

When we get back to Batna, they decide, as a special favor, to let us rest there a few days. Unfortunately, some sordid business of broken bottles in the largest restaurant gets us confined to barracks. Twenty-four hours off in town is more than we need to make ourselves unpopular with everybody. We aren't fit any more for the soft life in warm city barracks. We behave too badly. Before long, we won't go through towns at all except at night.

We come tearing into N'Gaous, and tear right out again, this time headed north into a region unknown to us, a vast flattish semi-desert area. Over several hundred square miles are scattered something like a dozen farms dating from the time of the Conquest.

First, thirty-six hours at El Madher, which is only a farm but big as a village. The place is deserted. The day before we came, the farm laborers had been attacked by rebels detached from the mountains to punish them. They had been warned not to work for the colonists but had continued to do so. As a second warning, the rebels cut off their noses and in some cases their ears too. Next time they will be killed. They've all gone back to their village, filled with shame and fear.

There's nobody left but the colonist's family: a dozen men, women and children, and one Arab laborer who has already been condemned and knows what's in store for him if he leaves. He alone dared give the names of some of the rebels who disfigured him. Strangely enough, it was when we arrived that he began to be really afraid. Unless he gets out of this country—and without money how could he?—he knows that as soon as we leave the sector he will be found murdered in some ditch. We are leaving in thirty-six hours.

The farm consists of about a dozen buildings arranged in a hollow square. Around the outer sides, there are no windows except narrow loopholes. Insecurity must have been the rule in this country ever since 1838. A man must be obstinate to insist on planting his wheat here.

Around the buildings run ditches full of green water, a rare thing in this region, and within their walls they seem to have collected the only clump of trees on this whole immense plateau: three palms, four eucalypti and one maple.

The Europeans here are armed to the teeth. They say they never heard a thing when the rebels broke into the Arabs' dormitory in the barn. Not a thing! That sounds queer to us. They have about fifty cows, and seem more worried about them than about their employees. Closemouthed people, not at all friendly. Though they could house a regiment, they refuse to let us in, and won't give us more than a third of a bale of straw apiece in the barn with their stinking cows.

The only congenial creatures on this farm are the storks, whose monstrous nests crown all the roofs. But how nerve-racking they are, yackety-yacking away like so many idiotic old women. A sentinel shoots one, thinking it's a submachine gun! As for me, I steal a black-beaked young stork out of his nest, at the risk of having an eye put out by his mother, and I keep him three weeks before he flies off.

That same morning, when we go down to the ditches to wash, dozens of gigantic turtles retreat into the depths of their green water. They are flat, glaucous, horrible, with great flabby carcasses, more repulsive than soft-shelled crabs. The Arab with the cut-off nose tells us they're excellent eating. But nobody tries them.

In daylight, the hundreds of acres of wheat around the buildings are like a sea. Though very short and thin, it must bring in a great deal of money. The owner is a miser and a skinflint. We sleep among the cows but can't have a drop of milk. We chew our biscuits, and our throats are dry with rage as we think of the civilians in other places who almost fought each other to gorge us with wine, fruit and milk.

Bernard goes over to the long row of great white backs, and shouts, "A helmet!" He slips between the shuddering brutes, and here and there he strips a teat—never the same one twice, to distribute the losses evenly. He fills the helmet to the brim. And we all come and lap it up.

"You won't catch me getting my nose cut off for those people," says one man when we learn that the mutilated Arab gets only there thousand francs a month.

Last weekend, a skirmish. One killed and three wounded on our side. The rebels lost three dead and fourteen captured, as well as seventeen rifles and three thousand cartridges that we picked up.

To sit on a café terrace and read that such and such a number of outlaws have been "wiped out" and that "we deplore a few losses among the forces of order"—that's not much, to be sure. It's hardly an event. But to see a comrade five yards from you go down in a few minutes into the night of death, disappear entirely, with his bad character, his pack on his back and his pockets still full of letters—that's something different, very different. Because he received so many bullets in the chest, because he didn't pay attention and didn't see the rebel lying in wait for him in the brush, Paratrooper X., aged twenty, is dead.

A day will come when the newspapers don't mention the butcheries till about page four, and, even there, only the most spectacular ones. And by then no one will care how many corpses on our side three hundred rebel dead represent. Nobody's interested any more. Let those sent to die, die . . . and keep quiet!

The Algerian infantrymen in the sector fall into an ambush. The outlaws abominate them, even more than they hate us. They kill nine, including the commanding officer, and take nineteen prisoners, nineteen men well out of it, who will probably be perfect rebels themselves in a few months. All we find on the road is naked corpses. The three trucks are charred wrecks. All weapons, including two F.M.'s, have disappeared. It was a big coup, for then.

Barika is a big trading center, fifty kilometers from our base. The mountain people come down there to sell their produce. As this traffic has doubled since the rebellion began, we decide one day to surround the place, very quietly, and check up.

In order not to rouse the dogs, which, like us, never sleep at night, our trucks stop ten kilometers from the village, with all headlights off. We carry out the maneuver on foot, very slowly. When we get in sight of the village, we all lie down among the rocks. The peasants and their caravans will go to market as usual.

The day breaks. We can hear the buzz of the market. Now's the time. We get up from our rocks and go bounding ahead, pleased to be stretching our legs. General consternation! Three minutes later, the whole market is enclosed in a perfect circle. For once, we achieve complete surprise. Counters and stalls are upset. The animals protest vociferously, especially the camels, who get up on their enormous legs and rend the air with their unbearable womanish shrieks. The fatmas screech too. They whirl crazily about, tripping over parcels, amid swarms of children beside themselves with fright or joy and yelling even louder than they. Motionless before the delirious mob, we wait for orders.

The checking up begins. While one of us keeps his gun aimed at a suspect, the other examines him from head to foot. You can't be squeamish. Arabs are not very clean. Water is scarce.

The men keep their dignity. Without a word, yet with looks of boundless scorn, which we ignore, they let themselves be searched like automatons. I notice one who seems nervous. While Marc R., my teammate that day, is controlling him as courteously as possible (he is holding his submachine gun like a great fountain pen), I set to work. With an abrupt gesture, I lift up one of the tails of his jellabah. A magnificent, black, brand-new submachine gun is hanging from his belt. He reaches for it instinctively. I have just time to snatch the weapon away from him. Anyone but Marc R. would meanwhile have cut that fellagha in two, without thinking twice about it.

Several bursts of submachine gunfire are exchanged in mid-market, wounding a child and killing one of the rebels, seven of whom are finally captured, all with weapons under their burnouses. These are supply men for the A.L.N.,[1] liaison agents, half quartermaster and half political commissar, who come down from the mountains every Sunday and levy a tax in kind on the market. All the people in Barika know them, but, though periodically fleeced by them, they would let themselves be killed rather than say a word. One of the captured rebels is an old man, one of those respectable old men with white beards that are everywhere in Algeria.

A general comes to see us. "Delighted!" He says he's delighted with the outfit. He must think we're on vacation.

---

[1] Armée de Libération Nationale.

But he doesn't ask us what we think of the food. He wouldn't have to wait long for the answer: "Foul, mon général!" We've been living for several weeks on a stock of rations which left Marseilles in 1949 and then soured for a long time in the moldy warehouses at Hanoi. One day, several men couldn't even get up, they were so completely poisoned.

One fine morning, we discovered that the insignificant little green grapes hanging in front of our tents had turned into marvelous, enormous muscatels. At first, we had them guarded by a sentinel; he patrolled the vines with fixed bayonet. But we soon found he was eating them himself. We gave that up.

Every time we come back from operations now, we have a feast of grapes. Some men ravenously snatch the first bunches they come to. Others, more fastidious, take their time, and in the moonlight select by touch only the ripest and best; then they retire to their beds to savor these fruits of the Land of Canaan, and to dream in the darkness.

One night, as we came in from a fruitless four-hour march, the men in the lead stopped opposite the first tents, ready to make the usual rush for the grapes.

"What's wrong with you?" yells the sergeant. "I didn't say anything! Go on!" Doesn't he see that we're here? "Well, go on!" he roars again. "The operation's just starting! What do you think you're doing? Going to bed?"

We didn't get back till ten next morning. We were crazy with thirst. Our heads ached. That day, the last grapes disappeared.

The scorpions are furious. We had scraped the ground to get it level under our tents, and it was just when they were laying their eggs. They are counterattacking now, coming out, hatching, all over the place. This is their big season. We even find them on our mosquito nets. Or did someone put them there?

Some of us get bitten. "You won't die," say the old soldiers scornfully. Perhaps, but it makes the victims so sick that everybody becomes careful, though pretending not to be. "And suppose it did kill you?" remarks an old corporal bitterly.

\* \* \*

A patrol ferreting about near the camp finds a fresh corpse in a mechta, and the murderer a little further on, with his pistol still in his hand. We expect a big roundup and start clearing for action. There must be more of them. Too bad, the man turned out to be just an ordinary murderer.

Algeria is full of people like him now. Arabs and Europeans take advantage of circumstances to settle private quarrels in the name of the F.L.N. or of France.

During an operation in the vicinity of Barika, we discover a rebel dying in one of the mechtas. A retreating band must have left him behind. We don't worry about sacred obligations to a wounded fugitive. No moral problems for us! The mechta is soon on fire. Amid smoke and screams, the women try to get out their boxes of clothing. They barely have time. Let it all burn! The fierce heat sears the already burning sky.

We watch with fascination. Some almost clap their hands! The women have stopped screaming. I notice that one has sat down by herself under an olive tree. She is crying. I would like to be able to measure the weight of those tears.

The next few days are marked by two important events.

First, the desertion of a sergeant who coolly goes over to the rebels with a jeep and three 30-mm. machine guns, in the hope, they say, of being made a captain.

Next, the interception of a Legion convoy at Taberdja. We find thirty legionnaires dead on the road and seventeen wounded, whom the rebels didn't have time to finish this time. They had only thirteen killed. All the trucks were burned and all the weapons captured.

That same day, we see the first "official" uniforms of the F.L.N.: gray-green-yellow treillis[2] and black American-chauffeur-type cap with metal badge showing a green crescent and a red death's-head. The death's-head will disappear later, perhaps because thought in bad taste, though possibly as a concession to Islam, which forbids depiction of the human form. The following year, in Kabylia, I unpin a different badge from rebel caps: a green and white rectangle bearing simply a crescent and a red star.

---

[2] Twill. Fatigue uniforms.

# 30

They are giving leaves again. My turn comes. I find out one morning on returning from an all-night operation. Sleep is forgotten. I'm leaving!

A comrade lends me one of those little cardboard suitcases carried by young men leaving for their regiments. I pack it in five minutes.

A Legion convoy comes by. I jump aboard a truck, the only unarmed man in it, and as we thunder along, full speed, I already feel like a civilian. A rebel attack would embarrass me considerably. All I could do would be to take cover behind my little suitcase.

In Sétif, after a glance at the city, which has the dubious look of a disreputable suburb, I hurry aboard the ten o'clock train for Algiers, a shabby, smelly little local that the S.N.C.F.[1] must have been ashamed of for years before palming it off on the C.F.A.[2] It takes it a whole day to get to Algiers.

The Arab passengers are looking at me. I sense their hatred: hatred of the fatmas hidden in veils smelling strongly of musk and camphor; the hatred of their adorable dirty-faced children scrutinizing me with shining eyes; above all, the immense, irreconcilable hatred of the men, who express it by a pursing of the lips as if to spit—which I'd advise them not to do, if there were a hundred of them!

Though I bear them no ill-will at all, every one of these people has a deadly hatred for me, that's only too obvious. And it's natural, in a way. What am I to them, till proved otherwise? A bloody brute with hands as red as the scarlet beret I am nonchalantly holding. A base, evil beast they hate because they fear it, even unarmed, a "para," a Béret rouge, a murderer!

---

[1] Société Nationale des Chemins de Fer.
[2] Chemins de Fer Algériens.

Give me France, where, even if no one loves you, no one hates you like that at first glance.

I am so happy at the prospect of seeing those I love, and Paris with all its sadness and beauty, that I try to make these Algerians understand that I am just a civilian in uniform. At all the stops—and there are plenty of them!—I get off and buy oranges for the sleepy, crying babies—at some risk of being left behind, too, for these trains always start up without the least warning. I am full of deference for the old people huddled on the floor in the corridors, and humbly apologize as I step over them. I am courteous to the women—but I don't overdo this, because their husbands are terribly jealous. I even try to start conversation . . . "Salam! Salam! Alec salam! Asma! . . ." say I at random to anyone who'll listen to me. I even talk with my hands.

The first to thaw out are the babies. They begin to gather around me. I take out of my suitcase everything I have in the way of jam, chocolate, sugar, etc. This is a success! I distribute all my cigarettes to the men—no credit to me, I don't smoke. They hardly know what to make of it.

When we finally get to Algiers, I find myself saying goodbye to real friends. Shaking of hands, hand on lips and on the heart, and all the rest of it. Fraternization! I know, of course, that if we meet again on the street, they won't dare even to look at me. They have to hate me, and I them. That has been decided for us, once and for all.

After the picturesque but sad confusion of the Casbah, the sight of the Hotel Aletti, a huge pink and white building facing the bay, reminds you that Algiers is a great European city. A great city that is white and shining in front, and whose rear is wretched and dark. A city, where, as in all so-called civilized capitals, the rich are in one place and the poor in another, and where it would be very bad taste even to suggest intermingling them.

To give myself a change from the dirt and poverty of the mechtas, I make my way into the spacious rooms of the largest restaurant in Algiers, all high ceilings, gilded woodwork, intricate chandeliers, and enormous cushiony armchairs just right for the great flabby bodies slumped in them. My nostrils are filled with a very strong aroma of money.

A little dancing. Much drinking. Young women cast you glances so heavy with lascivious languor that you wonder if their irresistible eyes aren't going to drop out on the polished floor. A few creatures who think themselves men because they have on dress shirts sway clumsily about them, wearing that serious, vexed expression of fools trying to think. Their fat faces loll gravely as they talk and drink.

I notice only one dignified face, that of an old Arab beggar. He wandered in here by mistake, and is promptly put out. I go out too.

I walk up toward the Casbah. The names of the streets delight me: rue du Diable, rue de la Lyre, rue des Lotophages, rue Scipion, du Cheval, du Palmier, rue Jugurtha, Caton. Above the doors, the five fingers of Fatima, the daughter of Mahomet, are imprinted in the porcelain or in the wood itself, to keep you from the evil eye. The round spot you see on the women's foreheads makes you think at first of a beauty spot, but it is the Eye of Knowledge. For you can see the women's foreheads in Algiers. An embroidered handkerchief covers only the lower part of their faces.

I slowly make my way through the labyrinth of winding little streets, endlessly climbing and descending rickety stairways. There are three stories of cellars below. Under the dark, low houses, there prevails a coolness of the deep woods. In three minutes, I am going round in circles, completely lost. Two or three times, I notice the same faces. They express astonishment at my walking here this way, alone and unarmed. Several of my comrades have been killed in this inextricable maze. It is strictly forbidden to soldiers, though it won't be till next year that the Casbah is surrounded with a triple wall of barbed wire.

Some children, well trained by their parents, greet me with a shower of stones. What's to be done? Face about? Counterattack? The whole Casbah would fall on me and cut me to pieces. All I can do is retreat full speed with this pack of howling urchins hot on my heels. I get a bit ahead of them, turn a corner, and hide in a little doorway. They go by without seeing me. I go back the way I came, leaving the Casbah ingloriously, but still in one piece.

Once more I plunge into the European crowd. What a joy to stride through a city after being away from civilization for more than a year! The shops especially attract me. I come back to them again and again, irresistibly drawn by their displays of non-utilitarian objects. I can't keep myself from voluptuously touching all these fine things made of cloth, or metal, or wood. To think that for a year I've had nothing but my gun and my cartridges! How wrong we are to laugh at old maiden ladies in their quaint parlors who gently end their days fondling their treasures of a bygone time!

I go in everywhere, and buy anything at all. I'm not the only one. Other soldiers, equally ecstatic, rush about, hurrying the shopkeepers, shouting and laughing, filling their packs with quantities of strange objects. They look forward wild with hope to the long imagined moment when, after embracing father and mother, they will run to their fiancée and present her with this moorish silver bracelet selected from among a hundred thousand horrors.

On the ship taking us to France, there are but a handful of us soldiers among the civilians.

A group of young Swedish girls on vacation sings on the deck all night. We gaze nostalgically at them, feeling awkward in our uniforms. We've not had time to be young or free; and it's already too late. Still practically children, we were taken from school or factory or farm and thrown into war, which ages the spirit even more than it does the body, and now we all have the mentality of tired old men. We can't laugh till we're drunk, and, as for freedom, we can't even imagine it.

This uniform! Some take off their black tie and undo their collar. But, careful. Being on leave doesn't mean you're any the less a soldier, "twenty-four hours a day." At the Gare Saint-Charles, there are military policemen with not a thing to do all day but watch from behind pillars and notice boards for unfortunates who naïvely think themselves free and saunter along with their berets in their hands. How many have been caught!

I had a somewhat similar experience myself. I was seated on the terrace of a café on the Cannebière, blissful at being back in France and dreamily writing a postcard, when into my range of vision came an old dodo of a colonel, probably more or less retired. Being absorbed in my thoughts, I go on writing. He slows down. I am looking more or less in his direction, but do not really see him: I'm still dreaming. Then

I notice that the old idiot is staring hard at me. I get worried. Have I got ink on my face? He stops in front of my table. I still don't move.

A pause. And he starts barking: "Name, first name, rank, regiment?" Yap, yap, yap! He scribbles it all down in his notebook. "You'll hear from me!" He goes away . . . I never did hear from the old bird.

A sailor on the train makes a complete change from head to foot. He got on at Marseilles in uniform and is getting off in Paris a civilian. I envy him.

A twenty-day leave seems very short. Especially when you've waited a year for it. The trees, the light of Paris! The bridges, the squares, where all is poetry mixed with life . . . The soft warm rain on the old sidewalks gleaming in the night. The Place Furstenberg, where even the trees seem intelligent! The Place de la Contrescarpe, where velvety bats fly in the evenings. I've hardly begun to live, and already the twenty days are gone, and the evening comes when I have to tear myself away. For two more years!

The return is always dreadful. A great many men on leave prefer to trade thirty days' prison for another twenty-four hours of happiness. Some even desert.

Marseilles is full of depressed soldiers about to leave. We pass each other without a word. I walk twenty or thirty kilometers, like a somnambulist. I go up long avenues that always become dirty, dreary little suburban roads. I wish I could lose my way on them, and stay lost.

I get back to the Saint-Marthe camp at one in the morning, worn out. My comrades are asleep. Later, in the rue Tubanneau, the patrols will pick up the last stragglers. The great army machine is running again.

Painful awakening. A last postcard to Paris, then good-bye France. This is the hour of regret, which even wine cannot deaden.

Night falls. The sea is so rough that the old ship, reserved for Arabs and soldiers, pitches and rolls, and we are sick in body and mind.

# 31

Most of us are still horribly sick when we come into the harbor at Philippeville next morning.

Everything has changed since we were last here. The happy, flower-scented city is now an armed camp bristling with barbed wire that has been stretched among the trampled flowers and across streets.

I had of course read about the "Philippeville affair" in the Paris newspapers last week, but only a short article couched in vague terms that had made little impression on me.

As I get off the boat, there is no mistaking the atmosphere of tragedy and ruin. Death is still master of the city: its traces are everywhere, even spots of dried blood on the paving stones of the big square. The streets which had been full of young girls when I was here a few months ago are now tramped by squads of tense, anxious soldiers. The few European civilians that are visible at all scurry across the street in no more time than it takes to open and shut a door. They sometimes look like hunted animals and sometimes like animals hunting.

I come across a Béret bleu of the 18th R.C.P. whom I had known during training at Pau. He asks me to have a drink at the Grand Café de France, and we go and sit down on the terrace. This is the only restaurant still open, in spite of its broken windows and cracked mirrors. A guard detachment has taken up position here with their backs to the grenade-splattered wall and their F.M. commanding the length of the main thoroughfare. "I'm going to tell you what happened," says my friend.

He talks fast, as though to unburden himself. The sea in front of us is calm and beautiful, but I have ceased to see it.

* * *

"For weeks there was a rumor that the rebels were planning a big coup. We didn't believe it, because we'd never seen them except in the mountains. We thought they wouldn't dare. The civilians had heard that the anniversary of the Mouloud was going to be terrible this year, and, when it went by just like any other day, they became blasé.

"So all was quiet on the morning of the 20th. We were still asleep in our barracks, after a night operation, when the first group of rebels were coming down to the city! When they gave the signal, all the Arabs in Philippeville came out of their houses at the same time, armed to the teeth. They had been told this would be a general insurrection in all the towns and villages of Algeria.

"Imagine. It was early morning, with the troops confined to barracks and probably not three soldiers anywhere in the streets, when suddenly the rebels turned loose all the Arabs in the city—you understand, all—to massacre all the Europeans, men, women and children. They went to work with rifles, submachine guns, grenades, knives, stones, billhooks, clubs, and they went on killing till they were out of breath, more than an hour.

"We in our barracks, way off from the center of town, knew nothing about it. We were asleep. The mob was so well directed by the rebels that no civilian could get to us. Very soon the city was literally strewn with bodies. The Arab children were wildly excited. They ran screaming among the adults and finished the dying. In one little street, we caught three of them crushing an old woman's head with their feet. We had to kill them on the spot. It was the same everywhere, in the square there in front of you, in the streets, on the stairs in the houses, in the yards, blind butchery and yells of pain, rage, hysteria, and madness.

"At the barracks we began to notice unusual sounds coming from the city. A patrol was getting ready to go down, when a civilian arrived, yelling at the top of his lungs.

"The sentinels wouldn't let him pass. He wanted to see the colonel. We thought he was drunk. He got mad and pushed through. A sentinel fired a shot and missed him. He got to the colonel's office, and immediately there was a general call to arms.

"Three minutes later, we were on our way into the city on the double, half dressed.

"We were already much too late. There was nobody in the streets but the dead. I had never seen so many! We had to walk in it all, stepping over sprawled bodies that were still bleeding but already buzzing with flies! The first corpse I saw was that of the marketplace guard. His skull had been split, probably by an axe, the wound was so wide. Corpses of half-naked women were lying in the drive that leads to the public gardens. In the houses it was even worse. Women in their beds, completely naked, stabbed with billhooks and douk-douks. Children strangled. No wounded. Nothing but dead. There was nobody alive in the streets, except dogs licking blood and looking terrified. It made me choke. A man in my company fainted.

"A hundred yards ahead of us, there were rebels hurriedly retreating. They had seen us coming. They were taking with them civilians who had taken part in the massacre, and therefore had to get away. But these were hampered by their jellabahs and couldn't keep up. We fired indiscrimately on the whole lot of them.

"The farther we went, the more dead we found, and the company commanders finally gave orders to shoot all Arabs. You should have seen the work! Most of the rebels in uniform had time to get away. They had too much head start on us. But the ones who lived in the city were soon caught. For two hours our submachine guns never stopped firing. In addition to the dozen armed rebels we shot at the start, there were at least a hundred and fifty others. Some still had fresh blood all over their clothes. We executed them on the spot.

"While half of us continued the pursuit toward the mountains, with the air force in support, the rest of us came back to mop up the city. It was still full of Arabs who hadn't had time to get away. We found them in alleys, under piles of blankets in the mechtas, even in the cactus hedges, in spite of the thorns. 'It wasn't us!' they would scream when they saw us coming. It was awful! We'd shoot the whole lot of them. The barrel of my P.M. got so hot I couldn't touch it.

"At noon, we got orders to take prisoners. That complicated everything. As long as it was just killing, it was easy. But catching them one by one and tying them up was hard work! It went on till evening. We brought them into the barracks yard in truck loads. By seven o'clock we had several hundred. Only men, but of all ages. They were to sleep where they were. But we didn't give them anything to eat. We had only two days' rations on hand. Anyway, they had to die. If we'd kept them too long, the Europeans who escaped the massacre would never have forgiven us. They were already angry enough at our getting there too late. They would have come and killed them themselves.

"At six o'clock next morning, all the regiment's automatic rifles and machine guns were lined up in front of this mass of prisoners. They started to yell, but we opened fire. Ten minutes later, it was over! There were so many of them that they had to be buried with bulldozers.

"So you see why there are so few people. What Europeans survived are still afraid to go out, and the Arabs the same. As for me, I'd sure like a leave!"

# 32

Back to N'Gaous. Dust and sand whirl over the road in gritty yellow clouds. No rain here since winter. We can't breathe, we can't swallow, our eyes sting. Those cool mornings in Paris, with rain on the eyelids like a kiss!

From time to time, we pass slow caravans of nomads driven from the desert by the heat. They never use the road itself, but travel to one side of it, covered with dirt and dust. The camels have a look of contemptuous sadness. On their backs, under high semicircular canopies, are perched women with downcast eyes. How dreary, tired and languid they seem. The landscape is so mournful, and their guardians look so ill-natured and morose. Indescribable tedium of the desert.

The evening of my return, I go out on an operation.

Sunday, another operation. No rest, even on the Sabbath! Score: three rebels, also three weapons captured. Like taking a drop of water from the sea.

We leave N'Gaous one evening for Foum-Toub and bivouac in the quadrangle of a Legion camp. We think we're going to rest. Wrong: at three in the morning, everybody's waked up. The legionnaires set out in one direction, and we by truck in the other, for Yabous. There, just after sunrise, we are picked up by helicopters and dropped on neighboring mountaintops. "The outlaws are sure to be there, and you can't help taking them by surprise!" But, as usual, it's too late. The fellaghas have left. The only sign of them is their fires, which are still hot.

We pursue them all day from one village to another, in helicopters, in jeeps and on foot, without stopping, for they never stop. As we go along, we set fire to all the mechtas where we find traces of them, and to a few others. A simple way to let them know of our presence!

In the evening, rendezvous in front of immense caves where we must by this time have bottled up the rebels. We sleep opposite the yawning, silent entrances. At dawn, we go in one by one, a bit nervously. Too late again. Not a thing here but flour sacks and unwrapped packages of combat uniforms.

At N'Gaous, there are no more grapes, the trampled grass is brown, the figs are rotting on the ground. Everybody is cross. There are more and more quarrels. Today, R. does his best to pick a fight with me. He tries so hard he finally succeeds.

# 33

Liaison with Constantine. I seize the chance to have a look at the Médina, in spite of its being forbidden to go there alone.

This Médina of Constantine is much more dangerous than the Casbah of Algiers, if only because of the deep gorge of the Rummel that crosses it, enabling rebel commandos to get past our patrols, right into the center of town.

As in the Casbah, where the houses rise one on top of another, the hovels of Constantine are so closely wedged together that only a few winding passages make it possible to get through between them. To venture in is to take a leap in the dark. But what fun it is, alone and in full uniform, to saunter slowly in this perilous coolness! How intoxicating to shut one's eyes and give oneself up to the rare happiness of pure danger!

It is into these little passages that the terrorists rush like a whirlwind after committing some outrage. They lead to secret entrances into the labyrinth of caves through which it is possible to reach the bottoms of the gorges, and safety. Heaven help a lone paratrooper who might happen to be in their path! The rebels would pick up his submachine gun and his beret, and that would be that. The red beret has in fact become the rebels' prize trophy. They carry it proudly about with them, much as the Jivaro Indians lovingly keep the shrunken heads of their slaughtered enemies. In the Chenoua mountains one day we found three on a detachment leader's dead body, one of them still soiled with blood.

Three minutes after getting past the sentries guarding the entrances to the Médina, I have absolutely no idea where I am, or even in which direction I would have to flee, if attacked, to get back to the European part of the city. And that's all I ask for. These secret perambulations are delightful, and so restful! Today I want something more than the danger of a deadly bullet in a skirmish, I want danger for its own sake.

I am thirsty. At the counter of a fat storekeeper almost invisible behind swarms of flies, I buy an enormous, juicy watermelon, and I walk on with it under my arm, like a football.

One tires quickly of winding stairways. They are very numerous in the Médina. A European foot has trouble getting used to them. I come to a dirty little Arab café, with benches along narrow wooden tables. I sit down wearily. A few young Algerians in their twenties are already seated there, and among them some fierce-eyed old men. They are relaxed and in no hurry. From time to time they sip their mint tea or take a pinch of their Indian hemp.

As I expected, the conversations stop dead as soon as they see me. I pretend not to notice. I lay my P.M. on the table. And I wait. They are waiting too. But for what? What do they take me for? For an agent provocateur? A deserter? For a rebel disguised as a paratrooper, or for a rebel "para"?

Do they think I am waiting for one of their leaders, and about to arrange some act of high treason with him? Or that I have come to auction my weapon? Or that I am just an advance element, and that from the neighboring alleys there will suddenly appear a party of furious paratroopers armed with F.M.'s and with knives between their teeth? Or do they think that I am crazy and that I am going to get up on their table and make them a speech about peace? They are waiting. So am I.

Back in his little room, the proprietor doesn't know what to do. And neither do I, really... "Garçon, if you please!" I finally say, as if I were in Paris. "Garçon, garçon! Asma, asma! Aroua mena fissa!" He finally comes over in despair. No doubt he already sees his shop collapsing in flames. "If you please, will you kindly bring me a glass of mint tea... like that," I say to him with the utmost courtesy, pointing to the glasses of the Arabs.

"All right! Yes, yes! All right, all right, sir," he replies, bustling about as if I were angry, and stumbles back, glass in hand. I give him a hundred francs. The tea is worth five. "For your poor," I tell him. He very likely doesn't understand me, but he takes the money.

Some of the Arabs leave, as though insulted by my presence. A number of others, however, in the very back of the room, draw together for a whispered consultation. This is bad. They glance at me out of the corners of their eyes, gesticulate and exchange piercing looks. I stare at them one by one as boldly as I can. They look away. I keep thinking: Now, what about that one? Could I get the better of him in a hand to hand fight? My hand instinctively steals toward my P.M. "But this is enough for today," I say to myself. "Better go back." I remember being told as a child: "If you're afraid of a dog, be sure not to run: he'd chase you!" I go away slowly, very slowly, as politely as I can. But by now, I am scared, good and scared!

The battalion left for Batna during our absence. Our comrades are sitting in the straw of an immense shed, waiting for us; they are in full equipment. El Madher has just been attacked. We don't even have time to sit down. On the way, I learn that the caïd of T'Kout had his throat cut yesterday by some rebels. "Good news at last!" says somebody.

We are leaving N'Gaous tonight for good. For the last time, we follow the path under the mulberry trees. The heat has loosened their scarlet berries, which keep dropping on our bare backs, making spots of mock blood. It's hard to leave . . . As for Captain D., he lingers a while in the one little street. He suddenly finds himself being vigorously stoned. The villagers are taking a few parting shots to express their real feelings toward us. But the captain is quite a direct person himself. He doesn't like being hit in the face with stones. It hurts, and it's insulting. Without a moment's hesitation, he pulls the safety catch of the incendiary grenade he always carries on his belt and tosses it at his assailants like a bouquet. Tremendous explosion. Without even deigning to turn around, Captain D. walks calmly back into camp. The old school.

The last Indochina regiments are coming back into Algeria this week. There is going to be a big redistribution of all paratroops. We are the first to move with arms and baggage into the magnificent Sidi-Mabrouk racetrack, five kilometers from Constantine, where an immense camp is rising like a city.

Autumn is beginning. The continual tramping of thousands of men soon turns the camp into a muddy swamp. The heavy tents have to be hauled through this mire, and the iron tent poles have to be set up. The thousands of guy ropes criss-crossing each other at ground level are so many pitfalls for the unwary. Hundreds of "marabouts" will cover this great field.

We find comrades we'd been out of touch with for two years. Old sergeants fall into each other's arms. The army is still a club, where one talks "man to man," far from the enticing, trifling women, the cowardly, boastful little men of the big cities, all the people who for professional soldiers represent nothing but incompetence and debility. In this cleansing golden sunset endless confidences are exchanged.

Regulations are sufficiently lenient to allow a little strolling about in the evenings. But every day at least one soldier manages to get himself murdered in town. Consequently, it is forbidden to go out unarmed and in less than threes.

On September 28th, we solemnly turn in our weapons to the quartermaster. The 8th Battalion of Coloniel Paratroops, the "blizzard" battalion of the 1st Colonial demi-brigade of paratroop commandos, is no more. End of an adventure.

"Ce que c'est que de nous,"* says someone as he turns in his gun. I turn around. It was a peasant from the North, usually far from loquacious, whose emotion had brought back to him the old colloquialisms of his ancestors.

The 8th B.P.C. had in recent days amounted to no more than half its original strength. Some really were killed in action. Others had disappeared for incidental reasons. Still others, the sick, the wounded, had had to be sent home. And here we are, the last square, thinking it's perhaps time to catch our breath a little. We are tired! But, this time again, our rest does not exceed four days.

Excursion with my friend Marc R. into Constantine. We sit down on a terrace. Young girls go by, wonderfully youthful and care-free. Pink dresses, golden shoulders, black hair. Their walk is like a dance, and they look at us and smile imperceptibly. Their charm goes straight to our hearts.

As we walk about the European city, we breathe the atmosphere of a world about to end.

## 34

September 29th, the feast of St. Michael, the patron saint of paratroopers. Why St. Michael? Could it be because of the wings supposed to adorn us, like the most famous of the archangels? But then why does the badge on our sleeve represent a horrible red dragon, just like the one he cast down to earth? Shall we ever know whose side we are on: the Devil's on our sleeve, or the Good Lord's?

On this anniversary there is usually an outdoor mass, followed by a tremendous feast that continues late into the

---

*"We are so unimportant in this world"

night. This year we have neither. Instead, we go out on an operation at three in the morning and don't get back till the following night.

As compensation, we are off duty all the next day, a very rare favor.

I start off immediately for the Arab quarter. Before I have gone ten steps, an old fatma says to me with the overflowing kindliness of grandmothers the world over: "Don't go in there, monsieur, don't go in there! It's dangerous!" The little street I am entering is dark as a cellar.

I smile at the friendly old lady and, not to vex her, I stop. But the moment she's gone, I continue on my way. Whatever happens, I at least have a brand-new offensive grenade in my pocket.

The wise old grandmother knew what she was talking about. An M.P. will be murdered in this same street two hours later . . .

In the course of a gigantic parade, the battalion is again dissolved, but this time officially. We are in full dress uniform, with polished boots, braid and tie, all the regalia for the "Present arms, ground arms," the clicking of heels in the spurting mud, the waving of flags in the stiff breeze. All this punctuated here and there by bugle blasts.

I hand in my automatic rifle. I've been promoted to lead man of the 3rd Combat Company, 2nd Regiment of Colonial Paratroops.

They combine us with what is left of the Indochina regiments, who have only three more months to go. But neither the weapons nor the uniforms are the same. Each battalion clings to its own peculiarities.

While getting our new clothing—amid indescribable confusion—we are confidentially informed by a staff secretary that there is something going on in Morocco. Two hours later, we are confined to barracks.

State of alert. We're going to parachute into Morocco. We prepare our packs and weapons. Then we wait. Heavy rain has just started. We're forbidden to open our packs. The company must be prepared to line up at a moment's notice in battle readiness in front of the tents. We can't even read or write.

A day, two days, three days go by, four, five. It rains, and

rains, and rains. Bored and irritable, we occasionally walk
over to the edge of the camp, in spite of the deluge. But one
has to be careful. Rebels are prowling about. One day we find
a Colonial Army sergeant and an M.P. hidden in some
bushes, shot through the head and covered with mud.

We learn that large-scale trafficking in weapons and
ammunition has started in our new regiment.

During the reorganization, thousands of cartridges and a
certain number of weapons were more or less carelessly left
lying around. The cartridges are everywhere: in the pockets
of uniforms, in the bottoms of packs, and even in the mud,
where they sink out of sight. After we leave the camp, Arab
children pick up quantities of them. Meanwhile, the traffick-
ers are right among us. The customers are not only the
Europeans of the city, most of whom are armed, but also the
Arabs. Cartridges bring their highest price in the brothels of
Constantine. They have become a medium of exchange.

New operations in the Constantine sector: we are going
to surround the villages where the terrorists from the mountains take refuge after striking their blow in the city.

In the Aurès mechtas, we used to find wooden chests,
piles of blankets, and a few jugs. That was all there was. Here
there is more decoration. Sometimes it is passages from the
Koran with the characters intertwined in wild flourishes,
sometimes crude chromos of Arab legends, depicting muscular horsemen carrying off lachrymose, well-developed maid-
ens. We find pages from *Paris-Match* tacked up with great
care, and even from the Nazi *Signal*. Sexy pinups display
their luscious charms. Quite enough to stir the imaginations
of Arabs unable to afford more than one wife.

Sometimes we also find magnificent radio sets. These we
systematically destroy. Radio Cairo slyly murmurs its propaganda over them every evening, and the whole village gath-
ers to listen.

Occasionally, too, even in mechtas way up in the mountains, we find European furniture of the purest 1930 style.
Enormous ugly beds with carved flowers on their wooden
headboards. A bed, what luxury for these poor people who in
most places sleep on the floor in their goatskin robes. What
privations must have been the price. And there's often no
road leading to these villages. You wonder how such things

could get there. On muleback? In sections? On the backs of men?

We break into these dwellings like robbers, generally at dawn. Quite often we find the people still in bed. It's indecent.

"Time to get up!" shout those who think you can be funny with a submachine gun in your hand. Everything has to be searched. If there are bureaus, the drawers are yanked out and tossed up in the air. Whatever is in them lands on the floor amid roars of laughter. Linen and clothing are shaken, torn, trampled and muddied. Bright silk kerchiefs gleam and sparkle on arms fumbling in the chests where the women kept their pathetic little treasures. The heartbroken, terrified fatmas don't dare complain. The men have been rounded up in the square. They don't have to watch the searching of their homes.

Then comes the looting. The soldiers back from Indochina are expert at this. They even quietly make off with things for which they could not possibly have any use—for example, those heavy copper mortars in which the Arabs mash their couscous.

We do not let the men go till we are about to leave. They rush to their mechtas to see what has been taken. Usually none dares complain. But once one did. He came running up with tears streaming out of his eyes and seized the captain by the sleeve. "Monsieur le Capitaine! Monsieur le Capitaine!" he shouted in front of the whole battalion. "Monsieur le Capitaine, they've stolen my alarm clock!" Stolen? The ugly word. And the honor of the army? Exclamations and loud laughter in the ranks. "His alarm clock! He's been wronged, he's been robbed! Poor fellow, poor fellow." But the laughter doesn't ring true.

The captain is in no hurry. There happen to be gendarmes with us. "Have all the packs opened," he shouts to his officers. The platoon leaders walk perfunctorily through the ranks. They glance at the open packs. All sorts of strange objects are shining in them, but they don't see them. They don't care for this sort of work. That alarm clock, however, has to be found. We are all getting impatient. Finally the captain himself inspects the team that searched the plaintiff's house. A magnificent alarm clock, deep blue, enormous, shining, is extracted from the culprit's pack. It has a loud tick. Embarrassment and once more general laughter. The alarm suddenly goes off with tremendous noise. The thief gets two weeks' prison.

But everybody else keeps his loot.

Whenever I have time off, I stop the first car that comes along and go to Constantine. Sometimes the drivers are Arabs in burnouses. One evening, there are four of them crowded together in an old car. They give me encouraging looks and finally invite me to get in. I sit down next the driver. If one of the three behind me should fire that little bullet into the back of my neck, there just would be one less paratrooper in Algeria tomorrow. They can't take their eyes off the submachine gun I am holding in my lap. Is it covetousness, or fear? Maybe they are rebels? And maybe they are on leave, like me? I offer them cigarettes. Three minutes later, each has his little cloud of smoke about his lips.

I try talking about France. At first, they say nothing. Then one of them brightens up: France? He knows it very well. Why, of course. Especially Paris. And off he goes, on and on: the Boulevards Barbès and Rochechouart, where there are such wonderful shops, and such marvelous women, so tall, so attractive, so agreeable. But also, unfortunately, so much dust. Then, like everybody in this country where water is so precious, he raves about the Seine. "The world's largest oued . . . In the evening," he tells his friends, "you see the trees bend down toward the water." I listen in silence . . . "And it never runs dry," states the Arab authoritatively. Respectful admiration from the others, who nevertheless cannot quite believe him.

We stop at the Place du Gouvernement, shake hands heartily and unaffectedly under the eyes of the astonished sentries, and go our separate ways, followed by disapproving glances. Some day, perhaps, these four men will have me in their sights, unless it's the other way round.

# 35

A vast offensive is being prepared in Kabylia. Our first stop is the port of Bougie, where we arrive after an exhausting journey in cattle cars. We are billeted in a sardine factory. After the straw and rations have been distributed we spread out through the town. But not for long. By noon we are confined to barracks for bad behavior. And here we are once again shut up, this time behind the bars of a factory. All we can do is to take greedy breaths of sea air.

But from time to time, coming from some school or office, young women pass by on the road. And then it is an absolute concert of fierce and delighted howls, a shower of more or less indecent calls and comments. Accustomed as they are to this undisciplined soldiery, the little ladies go by without turning their heads, but without ceasing to smile either. They are escorted by some pretty dreadful songs. All dignity is dead. This, to be sure, is far from new. Still, what a strange phenomenon that men who as civilians would never so forget themselves as to approach a strange woman in the street, were she the most beautiful creature in the world, are now reduced to jabbering at passing girls from behind bars like raging apes.

In the afternoon, a wash in the sea for the entire regiment, colonel included. We needed it. It's December, but the water is warm and calm.

In the evening we finally get town leave. Several of us remain until midnight on one of the terraces overlooking the sea, quietly talking among ourselves while gazing to the right at the city with its lights cascading down toward the harbor, to the left at the people passing by. Smiling old men in straw boaters of the 1900's lean on the arms of charming old ladies in mauve and white; behind them come young girls in multicolored dresses, all pretty, graceful and gay. Charming hours. But we would need three months here. Our hearts, momentarily softened, will soon return to normal.

We leave the next morning, heavy with regret. The road runs along the shore, which the sea is licking with a thousand little blue tongues. Pure air and dazzling light. We begin singing in our trucks.

At two o'clock the convoy stops. We take our canned rations and sit on the yellow sand. We stay here till night. More swimming and loafing. Some go blissfully to sleep. We can sleep any time now, anywhere, under any circumstances.

# 36

We do not move till nine o'clock.

The enormous convoy drives on a few more hours in the dark. Djidjelli is sleeping when we go through. Not a sound, except the tramp of the patrols echoing in the darkness. Fog has settled down over the city. At daybreak we halt opposite El Milia. Here's where we start work.

We first cross a wide stream on a broad pontoon bridge the engineers have just built in great secrecy, and then climb straight up onto the rebel maquis. The artillery follows.

Day is breaking. The surprise is to be complete.

Within a few hundred yards of the far shore brisk firing begins, quite a lot of it. But these first rebels, who shoot without waiting for us to discover them, are only here to delay us. We must not bother with them. Our objective is the main body of the F.L.N. regiments that have been occupying this Collo peninsula with complete impunity for months. We have to catch them before they melt into the landscape. We therefore at first fire only to reply to too insistent shooting, and keep right on. The important thing is to reach the summits.

Five o'clock. My morning vigilance has relaxed. I am marching thirty yards ahead of the rest, calmly, unsuspectingly. I am even a little bored.

Suddenly, on the same trail, but going the opposite way, a rebel. "Oh!" says he. "Oh!" say I.

Very slowly, a quarter of a second goes by. He looks at me. I look at him. We're alone, we're the same height, probably the same age, and in almost the same uniform.

... Tac, tac, tac, tac ... tac ...! I fired first. My submachine gun was cocked, contrary to usual practice—the least jar, catching a branch, may make it go off—and that saved me: I had only to pull the trigger. He had barely time for one shot, which went wild, whereas at least a dozen of my bullets hit him. For one more instant he stares at me with wide open eyes, then bends at the knees and rolls to the ground, his gun making a great noise as it strikes the stones.

The men behind me come running up. "Not bad! Not bad!" says the corporal. He thinks I am pleased with myself. He doesn't realize that though a moment ago I saw in this man nothing but a threatening target, now I see in him something very different, and that this outstretched body fills me with shame.

The dead man still has his big hunting gun slung from his shoulder. His hand has let go the regulation revolver with which he had at least managed to fire one shot. I shall keep that empty shell a long time and also the white and green badge from his cap, which dropped off his head as he fell.

We pick up his weapons, make sure he is really dead, and leave him there without even the usual tent cloth over him. We have to go on. When the operation is over, some Arab will come and bury him where he is. No one will ever know whether he gave his life for his country or just disappeared— for, like his comrades, he has no papers on him.

In a small wood, we find some corrugated iron shacks, with big tables in them, and several dozen tin army plates lying about, some still full of couscous.

Near the shacks we discover three automobiles concealed in the brush, out

MAS 49, 7.5 mm.

of sight of the air force. So much organization makes us uneasy. How could these vehicles have been driven in here, over these trails? We burn two of them, as well as the shacks. The third car, a very fine light gray four-wheel drive, is reserved by the colonel for himself.

Farther on, we find an abandoned makeshift infirmary, full of medical supplies. We have still seen very few rebels, though.

To avoid a surprise attack, we choose the highest and most deserted of the villages to spend the night in. There are things to eat and drink in the mechtas, and also woolen blankets, very dirty, it's true, but we're past worrying about that. The region is so unsafe that everyone, NCO's included, has to stand guard. No one gets more than a few hours' sleep.

We've no rations left and shall have to live off the country. Early next morning, we go all over the village and round up the abandoned little half-wild goats that are drearily bleating behind the mechtas. We milk them as best we can. But we don't average more than a cup per goat: rich milk, but odoriferous and full of black hairs. We finally give it up, and slaughter them for their meat instead. For breakfast we also have old pieces of kessra we find in the mechtas, an unleavened wheat cake that is much better than the army biscuits.

We spend the whole day marching through the wooded mountains, stopping only now and then, for a quarter of an hour at the most, to check our position. There are a great many violent little skirmishes. We are in such constant danger that we have no time to feel tired. The woods are full of watchful men, who stealthily retreat as we approach. For the first time, we get orders to fire—though it's broad daylight—without warning, at anything that moves.

The country becomes more and more wooded. Impossible to make out anything at all. The solitary guerrillas seem to have orders never to break contact without firing at least four or five shots. We probably do more shooting than they, but mostly by guess work. Our nerves are beginning to fray. What a symphony. Shotguns, submachine guns, pistols, rifles, Mas 36's and 49's. A musical ear can identify every one of them. All this in the end produces dead and wounded. The rebels are never the only ones left on the field, contrary to what the newspapers often suggest.

There are other people in these mountains besides rebels. The wild thickets are also full of terrified women and children who have taken refuge here. When caught in direct fire, they crouch awkwardly behind rocks or branches, or run screaming down the bullet-swept trails.

Heavy fire greets them when they appear, and follows them till they are lying motionless with their faces in the dirt. Many foolishly lose their lives this way, while the rebels are escaping behind the screen they form.

"For God's sake stop!" finally shouts an NCO in spite of the orders. "Don't you see they're women and children!"

No, no one had seen. To be sure, some—for example men firing automatic rifles at five or six hundred yards—really can't see whether a person rising from a bush is a man or woman, especially as many fellaghas here still wear jellabahs. But here's a ten-year-old child that lies gasping in the path with a broken leg. Can the man I just saw hit him at thirty-yards with a submachine gun say he didn't see?

And what's to be done about the wounded? They ought immediately to be taken to a hospital in helicopters. But what if they told what they've seen? Besides, there isn't time. Nor are there helicopters. Or gasoline. "Let them look out for themselves." So, off we go, leaving these people to suffer, or die. Off we go. That suits the rebels perfectly.

At nightfall, we reach a village way off from anywhere and completely deserted. Just what we wanted. Joyfully, having forgotten everything, each man chooses a mechta and takes possession of it. We stay here several days.

All these villages are poor. But even among the poor there is hierarchy, and no two mechtas are the same. The one most sought after is the grocer's. Lucky the man who finds it first. He will have plenty of eggs, sugar, chocolate, and sometimes even a bit of cash, if our arrival has been unexpected.

The next order of business is foraging. The chickens have made their last desperate flight to the roofs. They are soon spotted, strangled, plucked, roasted and eaten. By then it's almost dark. We have to retire into the mechtas and stay there till dawn, protected by the sentries, who are already stamping their feet to keep warm. We lie down in the warm, but very buggy hay. I stare at the mud wall slowly vanishing in the darkness and think of the old woman whose crumpled, yellow corpse I had to step over in the path a little while ago.

* * *

Three days later, we descend upon El Merba, in the Beni Belaïd Section, a rich village of more than a thousand inhabitants.

Except for bewildered animals, we find no one there except a crazy man who comes and laughs in the colonel's face (at the risk of being shot) and a poor little wrinkled old fatma who couldn't or wouldn't follow the general exodus. We settle down. El Merba will be our rear base for a week.

The usual sack begins. Everything edible—dried fruit, onions, animals alive or dead—is systematically pillaged. Every mechta is ransacked from top to bottom. All the chests are full of materials and food, every bit of which is hurled outdoors. A number of men find coins and jewels and all sorts of bracelets, and as a result, the search, which was about to end in mere horseplay, continues in dead earnest. Solidly built mechtas are completely demolished: big silver, and even gold coins are found in their roofs, carefully wrapped in old pieces of gray paper.

We find a few weapons too. After all, that's what we're supposed to be looking for. And quantities of ammunition.

We turn the village over as though spading a garden. When we can't find anything more, we start breaking everything, just for the joy of destruction. In nearly all the chests we find old wedding dresses: these we hang on the trees in ridiculous poses; then we drag them through the mud. Some dress up in them. We strangle wretched yellow cats, for the fun of it, because they are ugly. By the end of the second day, this prosperous village is a heap of foul uninhabitable ruins, so utterly devastated that there is nothing left to eat. Scene of other times! But war is timeless.

The second evening, when there's nothing more to destroy, our sentries notice strange processions approaching. Led by old men waving white flags, long columns of women and children are advancing to the accompaniment of some religous chant. The first ones are received with long bursts of fire from our lookouts, who, having had no new orders, are still firing on anything that moves. But the columns keep on coming, uttering mournful cries. The shooting stops.

We send out a patrol to make sure it really is just women, children and old men, and not rebels dressed up as fatmas, as has happened before; and, after a long parley, we finally decide that these people, the inhabitants of the village, can come back to their homes.

Surrounded by poor little children in rags, the half-starved fatmas return one by one, convulsively hugging their hungry, crying babies to their thin chests. We question these poor women. They have had practically nothing to eat or drink for three days. They and their children have spent the last three nights among the rocks. The rebels had convinced them that we would kill them all. It was hunger, stronger than fear, that induced them to return to the village.

But what a homecoming. We see them search with trembling hands among the ruins of their houses and possessions. Many are crying quietly. Others shriek hysterically and tear their clothes. The scene becomes unbearable.

None of us says a word. We'd never imagined this. "We're criminals," mutters Grand-père—the old soldier who shot at the stars at T'Kout. "We're filthy, all of us!" A woman sits down in front of her house, uncovers her breast in front of us, and tries to feed the youngest of her children. But there's no milk, not a drop.

We organize small patrols to probe the territory around the village. On one of these, I happen by mere chance to glance into a dense thicket on the embankment of a sunken road. I notice a hole. It is like any other hole, but, again by mere chance, I poke my foot into the brush that partly covers it. The brush rolls away: it was a pile of dead branches. A hiding place? I aim my submachine gun at the hole and bend over, a bit nervously. I see two pairs of eyes watching me, blazing eyes like hunted animals'. Two men are sitting in there. I keep my gun aimed and watch their hands (a grenade doesn't take long to throw). I beckon to them: "Come, come, asma! Out of there. You're caught, get up!"

Two powerfully built young men come up out of the hole. They are covered with dirt. Apparently they have no weapons. Are they rebels? One of my comrades takes them to the lieutenant.

I go down into their hiding place and in the back of it find a few biscuits, some clothing, and two enormous army packs crammed with cartridges. They certainly are fellaghas, but where are their guns?

We intend to find out. The interrogation begins. "Gun?" says the lieutenant (he's Count M. de V. de L.). No answer.

Perhaps they don't know French. "Boukala?" he continues. Still no answer.

Near the lieutenant, Corporal S. is waiting to play his part. "Where are the others?" asks the lieutenant. Silence. "All right, go to work, S."

And S., the blond Alsatian with the big baby face, S., the ex-amateur boxer very proud of his heavy white fists, S., the poor big stupid beast, strikes. In the eye, on the nose, on the mouth. A rain of blows. He is working himself up, beginning to enjoy himself.

"Where did you come from?" Again silence. S. goes to work again. At each punch, the two men's hands instinctively go up to their faces. We tie them.

At the end of five minutes, both their faces are covered with blood. S. wipes his hands. A few minutes go by. Heavy breathing. A few more blows. "Stop!" finally says the lieutenant, with affected calm. "Let them get their breath."

Another volley of questions. Still no answer. Another shower of blows, harder and harder. S. has worked himself up into a real rage now. He is being resisted—passively, of course, but resisted. His fists are tired, so he kicks the men in the shins and in the belly with his heavy jump boots. The lieutenant seems to think this in poor taste. But we are watching, and he has to convince us that he's tough.

One of the prisoners falls. A few cries of pain have escaped them, but neither has said a word. With a kick in the groin, S. finally downs the man who was still on his feet. He then turns to the other one, who has remained flat on the ground.

"Yeutenant, yeutenant!" finally shouts the younger of the two prisoners.

"Stop!" shouts the lieutenant to S. "You're overdoing it. They're going to talk."

We restrain S. The men are talking. "Over there," they say, pointing to the horizon, "a cave full of weapons and ammunition. That's where the guns are."

The platoon sets out at once, with the two rebels staggering in the lead.

As we march, the lieutenant calls the two men assigned to guard the prisoners. He speaks to them in a low voice. They smile and even laugh a little.

Thirty yards farther on, I see my two comrades silently

cock their submachine guns, holding back the trigger. One of the rebels senses, or possibly hears, something and turns around, wild-eyed with fear. One burst knocks him down. A second finishes him. His comrade doesn't have time to turn around. Blasted in the back at a yard's distance, he is flung forward on his face and killed by a second burst which sprays him from head to foot.

About face. We go back to camp. Did our lieutenant not believe his suddenly overtalkative prisoners, or was he perhaps afraid to venture with his platoon into a place where he might have been outnumbered? Anyway, he can always say they tried to escape.

Next morning, a woman in the village recognizes one of the two rebels as her husband. Just when we are about to bury them, she rushes boldly into our camp, weeping, shouting, and insulting us. She threatens us a long time with her thin little fist. All the other women come to her support. We have to take the poor creature back to her mechta by main force and keep her there till we have finished burying her husband.

After a few days, we find ourselves without a thing to eat. We now regret the sacks of wheat we ripped open with bayonets, the crocks of butter we smashed against the rocks. A platoon is sent down to get supplies on the plain where the engineers, the infantry and the mule drivers are encamped.

It returns in the afternoon, but with meager loads. There are several units of paratroops and legionnaires camping out like us in the mountains, and the quartermaster, not having forseen such a long operaton, has run short.

We each get a few raw carrots, like donkeys—to give us fresh vitamins. A few potatoes and onions, and some fruit arrive by helicopter. We're also given a little meat, but frozen and therefore practically inedible in this climate.

One of the women of the village, attracted by the provisions that have just reached us, manages to remember some of the French she learned years ago at the convent school. We learn many interesting things from her, for example that the village had forty-five rebels in uniform living in it till twenty-four hours before we arrived. The white and green flag of the "National Liberation" had waved for weeks from the little mosque, in full view, without any plane's ever spotting it. When they left, the rebels had taken with them all the men between fourteen and sixty, whether they volunteered or not. They had said they would return as usual as soon as the operation was finished. "They aren't mean," adds the woman. "But they make everybody find them food, even when there's none left. They sleep in the houses and make the men of the village keep watch. They don't spend the night outdoors till word that the French are coming is relayed to them by fire signals from the lookouts on the plain. They never say their prayers. And they don't like the rich!"

We continue reconnaissance in wider and wider orbits around the village. The maquis consists of very low brush, but it is so thick and thorny that it often takes an hour to go five hundred yards. One day an enormous wild boar, very black and bristly, gets up right in front of us on his thin, muscular little legs. He sniffs peevishly, furious at being routed out of the thicket where he was sleeping. The first burst of fire hardly bothers him: he charges the man that shot at him. It takes six simultaneous bursts to bring him to his knees, and he has to be finished with a knife. We cut up the carcass on the spot. It would be impossible to carry such a mass of meat. Long red slices disappear into our packs. An ex-butcher does the skinning and keeps the best pieces for himself. At last a morning not completely wasted.

One day one of us climbs for fun into one of the olive trees that surround the village, and we soon find that most of these innocent symbols of peace are hollow, and absolutely full of weapons. Just put your arm in and you can pull out magnificent guns, all carefully wrapped and most of them brand-new. A great deal of matériel is coming in by sea in spite of our patrols, and this region is a veritable supply base. Seventeen weapons are found this way.

Since we are promised a reward of 5000 francs a gun, we go at this work with a will. All the trees are taken apart. We also find cartridges, ammunition belts, clothing, and sacks of beans and wheat. It's the enchanted forest.

As for the rebels, they've disappeared. Not a shot has been fired for four days. Where are they? They can't have fled. We are on a peninsula. The cruisers have been watching the sea night and day since we arrived. They sweep the beaches all night with their searchlights. Everywhere else, we've spread a net so fine that an eel could not get through.

Perhaps a fellagha could, though. A man in danger will think of the most extraordinary tricks.

On free afternoons, we take hilarious mule and donkeyback rides through the paths of the topsy turvy village. There is other recreation too. Some are by this time on very good terms with the women, a number of whom are young and pretty. Biscuits and tins of beef are traded for seductive charms—soon on such a scale that the village has to be divided into two zones, with sentinels posted on the boundary, or every evening as soon as it's dark the whole platoon would disappear into the mechtas one by one.

The night before we left, my squad mate Bernard was out unarmed from one to three-thirty in the morning. There were a few shots exchanged that night, but he had the luck not to be hit either by one of us or by one of the rebels, who also come to see the women at night, not three hundred yards from where we sleep.

Next morning, as we march back to the sea, Bernard tells me all about it.

"The hardest thing was to get across the boundary without being spotted. But I managed to crawl through between F. and V. on my knees and elbows. Neither saw me.

"I had trouble finding the right mechta, where I'd noticed a pretty fatma that smiled at me, the day before. All those shacks look the same in the dark. I finally found it, because a lot of its roof has fallen in. The door's broken too, so I had no trouble getting in. I just slipped through without knocking, my heart pounding with fear but also with pleasure.

"At first I couldn't see a thing. I struck a match. Nobody was asleep. I saw the girl. The dark made her look like a ghost. There were other women there, all very old and huddled together in their rags. They gave me a funny look. Right away, I gave them the food I'd brought, and they took it. Then I took my girl's hand and started for a dark corner. She followed without a word. We lay down. And activities began, and sighs...Then, what do you think, she suddenly seized my hand and kissed it wildly.

"This went on for two or three hours. What a night! It was wonderful. And do you know what my little fatma was doing all this time? She was squeezing me and patting me and putting both arms round my neck and speaking softly in

my ear—in Arab, of course, but in such a sweet, gentle voice
that I understood most of what she was trying to say: 'I love
you, my dear, I love you!'

"And then, she kissed me so wholeheartedly. Imagine!
Like a young girl. She kept kissing me. Now I ask you, have I
got a face to be kissed that way? I was nearly crazy. I was
drunk, dazed. She kept on kissing me, really kissing me. It's
that that I won't ever be able to forget!"

## 37

We are stranded in Boufarik, forty-eight hours before Christmas. There were parcels, letters from the family, love letters,
letters from people we care nothing about—nearly everybody
writes, because it's the thing to do. But we've read our mail
and rested, and are so bored that we even regret El Merba
and the mud.

The colonel sends a message: "Volunteers are urgently
wanted to form airborne anti-guerilla commando groups . . ." I
apply. Anything's better than the boredom of this semi-
garrison. To my surprise, by no means everybody signs up.

Next morning, we are in a state of alert, and the regiment is confined to barracks. Those invited to spend Christmas in a "family atmosphere" have to send word they can't
come. Great disappointment.

We do not go out till Christmas Eve and then only from
four to eight in the evening to reinforce the gendarmes' road
block at the "Quatre-chemins." A rebel truck was expected to
come through here.

When we return, it is only to spend the rest of Christmas Eve in the sheds. A cold wind blows through them all
night and makes our hearts even heavier. We are crowded
together, but each feels alone. Most lie on their beds, miserable because they can neither go out nor sleep; and they argue
and quarrel, prisoners of themselves. Others keep haughtily

apart and quietly ponder the futility of life. Still others, with
bottles in their hands, sing they hardly know what, a sad and
savage mixture of barrack room refrains and half-forgotten
carols, that reverberates under the high rusty iron beams
shaking in the wind.

Then over this confusion there rises another voice:

> *Partir, c'est mourir un peu . . .*
> *A la guerre, a la guerre!*
> *C'est un drôle de petit jeu!*
> *Qui n'va guère*
> *Aux a-mou-reux!*

> To leave is to die a little . . .
> To war, to war!
> That's a funny little game
> That doesn't please
> Lovers!

One of the veterans, in his weariness and boredom, has
begun this old song of the soldier's resignation to his fate, a
song so despairing that we are forbidden to sing it. He is not
at all drunk, but just cannot keep quiet any longer. So, he
sings. He is ugly, tired, taciturn, and irritable, perhaps
stupid, quite without charm. But his voice is beautiful, and
that is enough.

The coarse and silly songs die out. The shed shakes in
the wind, and the old soldier sings on alone.

> *. . . Pourtant c'est presque toujours*
> *Quand revient l'été*
> *Qu'il faut s'en aller!*
> *Le ciel regarde partir*
> *Ceux qui vont mourir*
> *Au pas cadencé . . .*

> . . . And yet it is almost always
> When the summer returns
> That one has to leave!
> The sky looks down
> On those who are going,
> Going to die
> In step . . .

At the word "mourir," the corporal comes in. The deep voice must have carried all the way to the mess and vexed his little martinet soul. But the song continues:

> ...*Quand un soldat revient de la guerre, il a,*
> *Quand un soldat revient de la guerre, il a* ...

> When a soldier returns from the war, he's got,
> When a soldier returns from the war, he's got...

"Quiet! For heaven's sake, quiet!" shouts the NCO in a fearful voice, wild with rage. "Quiet, or I'll give you two weeks! What's the matter with you?"

Two weeks? The old soldier looks the corporal in the eye, very deliberately, and then, even more deliberately, he finishes his song:

> *Dans sa musette un peu de linge sale*
> *Un peu de linge sale, et puis voilà.*

> In his musette some dirty clothes
> Some dirty clothes, and that is all.

Next morning, for Christmas, we see our old comrade come back from the barber with his head shaved.

From the 25th of December to the 1st of January, still in a state of alert, we spend most of our time at the Blida airfield. In spite of the violent wind that comes down from the Tellien Atlas, we manage to jump three more times. A few broken legs... We have to finish our eight annual jumps before New Year's if we want to go on drawing the jump bonus, the "air pay," symbolic "salary of fear."

# 38

There are two things I remember about the 1st of January of this new year: sadness, and rain. If happiness, as Giraudoux says, is "feeling one's soul immense and one's body very small in the middle, like a kernel," our unhappiness is feeling our soul a wretched little thing that we torment without even telling it why. The barracks, this 1st of January, intensifies our wretchedness. Sadness has accumulated here, ugly and dirty like gray dust in neglected corners. The atmosphere is so heavy with boredom that we sicken in it like caged animals.

On the 2nd of January, we are back on our old mountain roads. Once more we throw the heavy ammunition packs into the trucks and doze till dawn, half frozen, on the icy benches. Again it's night convoys, night-long thirst in the fog, and that cold that starts in your legs and soon grips your whole body in a painful icy sheath.

At one in the morning, the trucks stop between two dimly seen mountaintops. A frozen mist is slowly melting, blotting out everything. We set off on foot in the dark.

We are greeted by a patrol of a dozen men with knitted scarves under their helmets, armed with submachine guns: the Alpine Chasseurs. Without saying a word, they lead us to their mountain post surrounded by a barbed wire fence. We go in one by one through a zigzag passage, at the entrance to which is a big machine gun covered with black and green plants.

This post is just a little forest farm, but it has become a sensitive point. Last week, a company of Algerian infantry was camped there. It disappeared. Ninety men and all their equipment vanished into thin air. Only their officers, all of them native-born Frenchmen, remained. That is, their bullet-riddled bodies were found in the wrecked house; one had his eyes put out. The Arabs had carried off everything they could

151

and burned the rest, even the armored car. It all reeks of treachery.

We go off in pursuit of the rebel band, which, in a previous engagement, had also captured fourteen of our fellow paratroopers. They absolutely must be found, alive or dead.

We overtake a few of the infantrymen next day. They had no choice, they say, but to follow the rebel band, which was much more numerous than they—three hundred, it seems. But, with ninety men, can't you defend a fortified farmhouse against even three hundred attackers?

Three months later, one of these infantrymen comes to us of his own free will and volunteers to guide us to the rebel battalion that had been keeping him prisoner. All we find is indistinct signs of a camp.

We keep this man with us a long time. He may well be just a deserter sent by the rebels to watch us, while waiting for a chance to desert a second time. He is sometimes useful as an interpreter. But being an Arab, he does not understand the Berbers of Kabylia, or so he says—though he occasionally tries to ingratiate himself with us by maltreating them. When the gendarmerie at Duvivier lays claim to him, we relinquish him with no regret.

An ambush keeps us crouched motionless till four in the morning in some clumps of oleander, with our feet in icy water. We shiver in the silence, the vast mountain silence unbroken except by the sinister, monotonous croaking of frogs and from time to time a little cough from one of our comrades. In the morning our cheeks are smarting with the frost. A new man, from Toulon and only eighteen, cries about it all day, chilled to the heart. Finally he quiets down, the way we all did after our first operation.

The next day we discover fourteen naked corpses, seven in one ravine and seven more in another. Now we can go back: the general commanding the operation had sworn it would not end till we had found our comrades. The day after we return, we learn that these corpses were not theirs.

We go through Palestro. The little town has become an immense camp. In great confusion, the tents now house whole villages claiming to have come over to our side, as well as our own rear units, amounting in numbers to a division: signal corps, engineers, transport, staff, etc. They're not having such a bad time here. But we can't even stop.

# 39

One morning, we notice some long white buildings on the top of a very high hill. They are partly hidden by thick olive trees and have tile roofs like the farmhouses in Provence. From the moment we see them, we are also aware of a low but continuous murmur that the wind brings to us in gusts. We deploy and approach as quietly as possible. They can't have seen us yet. From inside the buildings the mysterious murmur continues to rise into the cold air like a religious chant.

Being in the lead patrol, I am one of the first to enter these strange buildings. While one of my comrades covers me, I skirt the wall with my submachine gun cocked till I reach a very thick wooden door surmounted by a crescent. I strike the door with the barrel of my P.M. and as usual shout: "Open! Asma!" Then I wait, keeping prudently to one side... No response. The chanting has not stopped for a moment. "Do you think they're crazy, or what?" whispers my comrade. This is certainly not usual. Generally you get a response, if only a burst of fire through the door. Could this be a trick? Let's break down the door.

One good shove is enough. The lock, which was nothing but a wooden hasp, gives way, and I land inside practically on my face, with my P.M. still horizontal, however, and ready to fire, and with my comrade and the rest of the lead patrol right behind me.

We stop, amazed. About a hundred young men, barefoot and dressed entirely in white, are facing the sunrise and chanting responsively in the already warm light. Their deep solemn song is like a Gregorian hymn; their attitude is that of sun worshipers. They are clearly praying. What can they be saying to God, at this hour, in this place, and in so full a voice?

We are in one of the oldest and most famous of Arab monasteries. After a moment of surpirse, the search begins, as anywhere else. As we go about, mud-stained and dirty-faced, with our submachine guns in our hands, among these ascetics devoutly kneeling in the morning light, we all feel embarrassed and ashamed.

There is nothing in the spotlessly clean courtyards, not even a speck of straw. But a quick inspection has to be made. Around the courtyards, in addition to a vast oratory, a mosque, and refectories, there are several tiers of cells, all perfectly whitewashed.

Meanwhile, the young monks go right on with their prayers. Their calm, deep voices contrast with the shouts of the vandal horde that has invaded their domain.

An old man with a long white beard finally gets up. In the name of his community, he comes and explains to the captains, who hardly know what attitude to assume, where it is that they are. The men who meditate here do not make war in any way on anyone, and wish that Allah may be with us, as with everyone else. "Have the rebels been here?" asks one of the captains roughly. No answer. "Have you harbored any wounded?" (We had found some suspicious bloodstains.) No answer.

We know that a powerful band went through the region recently. But probably it has not stayed here. They would undoubtedly have taken along all these strong young men, most of them Kabyle peasants. No, they must, like us, have felt intruders in this holy place. If only for political reasons, they must simply have reprovisioned themselves, hurriedly bandaged a few of their wounded, and gone away. These men have the faces of mystics and are not the sort to make soldiers.

"Search everything." We rush into the cells, into the out-buildings, into the chapel. Everybody hopes to find, if not weapons, at least curiosities, what we call "bricoles": Arab rosaries, little rugs, amulets, verses from the Koran on little panels of wood—all those trifles we usually throw away at the next village.

Some, vexed at having so far failed to disturb the calm of

these young monks exactly their own age, begin to lay hold of them, pull them up, speak to them roughly: "Quick there. On your feet!" The Arabs obey, without seeming to notice this anger.

By dint of kicks and clubbing, about a hundred monks are assembled on the road. For fun, we line them up three abreast. We even try to make them march in step, but they are barefoot, the road is much too narrow, and we have to give it up. Finally, we all load our packs onto the novices, and even onto the old men with white beards.

Aren't our orders to leave no one behind us, guilty or not? The mere fact that they could live in the heart of this insecure area makes them suspect. Faster! Faster! Along the stony path, young men in uniform jab their bayonets into the legs of the tall, bent old men, while others, in a frenzy of stupidity and cruelty, violently slap the faces of sick men limping in the rear. We finally turn over this cumbersome mass of prisoners to the gendarmes. They will do what they please with them.

We continue on our way at a faster pace, miserable and half blind for lack of sleep. The youngest of us are staggering. I march with my eyes almost closed, thinking of my comrades grown cruel because of their unhappiness.

Of the fourteen men captured by the rebels, we find three on a path not far from Noalla, with their throats cut from ear to ear. Later we find some of the others still alive after their escape. They had seen us go by within five hundred meters of their guards. But they all had submachine guns pressed against their backs and could not do a thing. As for their three comrades, they had been slaughtered before their eyes for refusing to run.

We march another whole day and night, searching every village from top to bottom. All the doors are padlocked. But we find no one inside except terrified women, children and animals all piled on top of each other in the dark.

We spend the night in a village that is still completely inhabited. The rebels can't have been here yet. We are so tired that no one thinks of going after the women, the way they did at El Merba. Besides, last week a man in the 2nd Company set off on one of these expeditions and never came back. They think he was probably mutilated and massacred by the women themselves. His parents will never know how he died. He will have his cross, his citation, and a tricolor flag for winding sheet, for the glory of France, but his coffin will be empty.

Marc, Bernard and I are invited to coffee by the Arab family in whose house we spent the night. Is it for fear we'll ransack everything before we leave, as so many of our comrades do, or simply out of kindness?

Greatly surprised, we sit down cross-legged on the floor in front of the little cups that are being set for us. Our faces are a sad and horrible sight—filthy beards, hollow cheeks, inflamed eyes. But our hosts are also ill-fed, unshaved, and careworn, and we are alike as brothers this morning, we paratroopers and mountaineers!

Into the microscopic little pink and white china cups is poured the most unctuous coffee, velvety and heavily aromatic. Dead silence: this is a ceremony, almost a rite. A drop spilled is an insult, a cup broken means war. We muster on our faces all the dignity we have left.

We drink slowly, ever so slowly. Opposite me, the old head of the family smiles ever so faintly in his beard, delighted. The women, the only sign of whom had been the sound of bare feet, begin to appear out of dark corners. They come forward, steal a look at us, disappear shyly into the shadows, and come back. Of course they're not going to drink coffee with us. That would be highly improper. But we all three smile at them together, with the very best grace we can.

As usual we give the children all our chocolate and sugar, and we leave, this time with regret.

## 40

Marc and I have a twenty-four hour leave which we spend like tourists in Algiers. We pay a call on some old scholars who have been living for several years in the Upper Town.

"Aren't you afraid?" we ask.

"No. Life goes on. We could go back to France, but we're too fond of this sea air, of these pure, unspoiled Algerian landscapes. And then we have several Arabs among our best friends. Leave all this? No!"

Next morning, excursion to Blida, a paradise of a city, with thousands of orange trees. Paradise at the Gates of Hell, though, for, just beyond the first pass of the blue and white mountains that tower above it, rebels are waiting to come down and spread death.

A glance at Chréa, the Algerian Chamonix, under whose blue cedars are immense ski trails for the tourists. But today the only tourists, like us, are in uniform and armed with submachine guns. This is now just a stopping place for convoys on their way to operations. Quite a curious place too. From a long way off, you hear shouting, in a perfectly incomprehensible language. It is the tribes of half-tame monkeys who spend their days screeching in the city's tall trees and go back into their cage at night. They are sad-eyed, peevish, and bored, or there's no one to entertain them any more, except occasional soldiers who offer them things they don't like, even lighted cigarettes.

We return to Boufarik to learn that a policeman has just been stabbed in the middle of the street. Two days later, a pineapple grenade is thrown into the NCO's mess and wounds several men. Boufarik once was one of the safest cities in Algeria.

## 41

Big event this morning. A special platoon of NCO trainees is being formed with thirty men from the regiment. My name figures among the "designated volunteers." We get the news at ten o'clock, and at noon set out for an isolated farm in the Mitidja.

The moment we arrive, we have an assembly. In the

filthy barnyard we stand stiffly at attention as our new chief, Lieutenant T., makes his first appearance, with three NCO's trotting at his heels. Tall and thin, but very broad-shouldered, with fiercely energetic eyes, the man makes a strong impression. From the start, his severity toward others, and toward himself as well, seems boundless. He worked so hard to make himself an officer that he has a horror of any sort of relaxation or pleasure. All through the next three months he works us so mercilessly that several men finally give up in discouragement, preferring to remain privates the rest of their years in the army.

What he wants to make of us, and does in fact make of most of us, is a special corps of stiff, strict little martinets, devoted to the army, body and soul. His methods are those of the S.S., whose roughness and ferocity he admires, although, he says, the S.S. were never, after all, but "nice little boys" to him.

A week goes by. Eleven of our group return to their platoons, discharged as unqualified; that is, too slack, too ignorant, or a little too fond of a good time. They are delighted to leave.

\* \* \*

**Browning .50 Cal. H.M.G.**

A week later, in near-zero weather, four others are locked in a dungeonlike grape silo, head shaved to within a millimeter and no blankets—for staying in bed four minutes after reveille.

This lieutenant keeps us on the stretch for ninety days with a skillful mixture of mental and physical labor. Marches by compass, maneuvers in which we have to stand still for hours in the frozen vineyards, follow each other in uninterrupted succession. Nor does this prevent our participating in all the operations executed by the regiment during the same period. The only difference between us and the others is that the moment they return they can rest, whereas we have no sooner taken off our packs than we have to get back to our notebooks—those notebooks in which we had been taking down outlines of the firing mechanism of the .50-caliber machine gun, or similar frivolities, when we left.

As a chemist studies the resistance of metals, so this lieutenant used to experiment on us to see how much we could stand. Though he was not easily impressed, I think that in the end we did astonish him. Just to show him we could be as tough as he, we did in fact become almost as hard as metal.

There was, I think, no room in this fanatic's head for doubt, and perhaps even less for truth. Many of us wished him dead. I loathed him. He, however, liked me very much. Queer thing.

What an infernal period of our lives it was for all of us. While men of our age in the warm, luxurious cities of Europe had nothing on their minds but dancing with silly little girls and clowning to be popular, we, in the cold of that atrocious winter, were studiously perfecting ourselves in the art of killing. We were learning to blow up railroads and bridges, to kill with knives, even to use flamethrowers.

A truly astonishing beast, this lieutenant. As he himself frankly boasted one day, he would unhesitatingly have machine-gunned his father, his mother, his wife and children, simply at an order from his colonel. No problem. It takes this sort of creature to make good armies, really professional armies, with nerves of steel.

Training at the Commando School in Soumma. On the walls here, we are faced with enormous hand-painted letters that convey such precepts as "If you are outnumbered, run!" or "Attack from behind!" A new chivalry is being born.

Two more men leave the platoon for the hospital in Boufarik. One is suffering from complete exhaustion, the other has a nervous breakdown. We are barely half our original number.

Target practice with various weapons in combination, sham battles, field maneuvers, counterguerrilla training, handling of explosives, marches to the sea by compass across the flooded plain, are succeeding each other at a more and more accelerated rhythm.

Mail is forbidden. We have to wash our brains of everything not strictly military.

March 9th. The regiment leaves Boufarik for Tebessa, on the Tunisian frontier. Three squalid days in the straw of a cattle car that takes us very slowly from Sétif to Constantine, then from Guelma to Souk-Ahras and Tebessa.

From the train, we study this region where we shall have to operate. Our first surprise is to discover that over hundreds of kilometers there is not a single telegraph pole left standing. Everything has been cut down, sabotaged, and so far as possible made permanently unusable. Dozens of big farms have been burned. Thousands of trees have been felled. Scorched earth.

Just before getting to Tebessa we see an entire train lying along the road bed, riddled with bullets. A little farther on, we have to wait for a company of engineers: the track has just been cut, this very afternoon. Right in front of us. The engineers don't seem at all surprised. They tell us this happens nearly every day.

Rather long stop in the Souk-Ahras station. A ragged little Arab is selling dates along the cars. A group of "paras" steal a few of his boxes. Childlike, he goes and complains in tears to the two tall policemen on duty in front of the waiting room. The cops—Arabs—listen to his lamentations in silence. He looks up at them confidingly. A minute goes by. Nothing happens. He insists. Whereupon they calmly proceed to thrash him most thoroughly with their rubber clubs. The little boy is knocked flat. They keep right on, almost mechanically. The child finally gets up and starts to run away, robbed and beaten.

But that is not enough for the policemen. They go running after him and escort him with a rain of blows, amid loud laughter and applause from almost all the soldiers.

We have come to relieve the 1st R.E.P. After a certain percentage of deaths in a regiment—33 percent, I think—relief is automatic. But there is another reason for the departure of these legionnaires—their last Sunday in town.

That Sunday they had leave. A corporal ventured alone into the Arab quarter. Some Arabs knifed him in the middle of the street. Later, a legionnaire came by and found his corporal stretched dead on the pavement, with a dog circling about him. Furious, he lifted up the body, which was still warm, carried it on his back across practically the whole city, and laid it at the feet of his comrades.

A quarter of an hour later, the whole company of the day (the rest were in the mountains) descended on the city, began demolishing the Arab quarter, and started a fire which completely destroyed it. Sixty-four people, mostly men, were killed with P.M.'s or bayonets in less than an hour.

## 42

Tebessa's Roman walls have been dismantled many times, following conquests and reconquests, but they remain today even more beautiful than when they were new. Flanked by their immense square towers, they sparkle like gold in the evening sunlight as they did centuries ago. We enter the city by the Gate of Caracalla, the Roman arch of triumph. The Gate of the South, known as Solomon's, is the outlet through which the Arab city has spread like a river over the sterile plain. Within, and sheltered from the sand which blows outside like a tornado, there are a few Roman temples, some huge ancient barracks, and a multitude of little houses all huddled together. The city is surrounded by the absolute silence of the desert, where nothing has been secure for centuries.

In Roman times Tebessa the Proud was, like Timgad, wrapped in a green robe of olive trees. Now it's just an enormous sandstone mass abandoned in mid-desert and being slowly swallowed by the sand. We experience our severest heat and cold here, and even in the streets, the sand gets in our eyes, plugs our ears, sticks to the roofs of our mouths, and gives us gray hair.

The platoon pitches its tents near the Gate of Caracalla around a particularly dry spot known as the "Watering Place."

On April 14th, at 7:30 in the evening, the time when soldiers on leave are all over the city, thirteen bombs and grenades go off simultaneously in thirteen widely separated places, to the accompaniment of long bursts from the submachine guns that the rebels in the streets suddenly produce from under their jellabahs.

At the same moment a fire breaks out, similar to the one started by the legionnaires. Night falls. Smoke clouds the darkening streets. Indescribable confusion. The outlaws boldly attack all European civilians and even the patrols in the rues Solomon and Caracalla.

I was in the street. At first the delirious, howling mob does not notice that I am alone and unarmed. It is too busy watching the death agonies of two policemen just shot down by a rebel commando. As soon as they are dead, the mob begins to stir and takes account of my presence. All I can do is try to escape. I run close along the gray walls of the little streets, with my beret in my pocket. My heart pounds, and I feel Death himself running full speed behind me. Finally, I meet some of my comrades. The shouting mob begins to surround us. "They're going to get us," stammers an engineer, pale as death. But legionnaires and colonials, alerted by the flames and the uproar, rush up, gun in hand. A violent melee follows. Bullets whistle in every direction. It's soon impossible to tell where they are coming from. Twenty-seven Arabs are shot down right there. Violence breeds violence.

It's now the Arabs' turn to retreat shouting. The rebels in uniform have already made off by a back road under the ramparts. And, though all the exits were immediately blocked, very few are caught with weapons in their hands. Those who are will pay.

Meanwhile, the fire roars in both the Arab quarter and the European city. Tremendous explosions, apparently underground, begin to blow out windows of stores disappearing in cottony spirals of smoke. The fire is said to have reached a supply of bombs. This has all been going on less than an hour, but already some of the smaller houses are falling in, completely burned out. The crowd is disappearing.

The real repression now begins. Systematically, the police company quartered in the city act with utter, and open, ferocity, even outdoing the Legion. The sight of their two comrades shot down like dogs in the street has infuriated them. Butchery begins, while far into the sky the lurid air carries black particles of wood and paper.

And today is Easter.

# 43

Next day, the first of the big Djeurf and Guentis operations.

Two hundred rebels who arrived from Tunisia Easter night have been located by the air force in the neighboring mountains. Was the Tebessa insurrection only a maneuver to keep us in the city while they were coming in?

When we arrive, the captain tells us: "There are two hundred men here, well armed and well equipped. Yes, there, in front of you." We are on a high trail, ringed about by eroded mountains, the giant striations of whose cirques stretch parallel to each other as far as the eye can reach, white, gray, or yellow, according to the rocks composing them. All this is bare of any sort of life. From above, these old ruined mountains, these jagged masses that millennia of alternate frost and sun have broken into millions of disintegrating fallen rocks, seem but a succession of great round holes, craters of the moon, a world where men must die of thirst, fear and despair.

An hour ago, two hundred rebels were marching here. But where in the name of heaven are they now? We can see absolutely nothing. They've fooled us again, we think, or else they're already so far off that we'd better go back, instead of roasting here like rats.

We are now on the rim of a crater at least five kilometers in diameter and perfectly round. Under the blazing sun, it seems an enormous trap opened like a mouth. The white light condenses in it as in a mirror and makes you squint. Five o'clock. We begin to go down, in silence.

Suddenly, a shot rings out. Then two, then three, ten. Instinctively and as one man, we all throw ourselves on the ground.

Then, as we raise our heads, we see that the rocky walls are pierced by a thousand flaws. Over a distance of several kilometers, the enemy has occupied hundreds of caves, invisible from the outside, and for three days these caves will exude the black poison of death.

The first shots, which came from the side, had hit no one. We wait with our noses in the rocks. Nothing happens. But the rebels are obviously there, on the same cliff as we, lurking in these cracks like rats. The shots came from the right. But there must be men concealed on the left too. We're not sure whether we're surrounding them, or being surrounded.

The platoon's lead section starts creeping slowly forward. They all adapt themselves so perfectly to the terrain and stick so close to the rock that we soon have trouble keeping sight of them. But with our naked eyes we can see the dull black barrels of the rebel guns protruding out of the holes the first shots came from, and moving almost imperceptibly to follow the movements of our comrades. No doubt it's useless to try to cover them by firing F.M.'s and machine guns at the cave openings. But we shoot anyway, for war is above all a psychological game in which the most important thing is to cause fear. Our somewhat random volleys spatter and splinter the most menacing of the rocky walls. But the invisible killers do not even draw in their guns. All we've done is to give away the exact positions of our F.M.'s, which we now have to move.

Ten yards from the nearest cave, one of our lead men lifts his chest a little to throw a grenade. He swings his arm in a wide, majestic gesture... But his motion reveals the flash of the metal canteen shining like silver on his belt. He has

just time to shout "Ah!"—an "ah!" we all hear—and falls
forward, face down. Dead. A bullet square in the forehead. A
few seconds later his grenade goes off in his hand, tearing his
body to pieces and covering us with a hail of stone fragments.

There must be at least twenty rebels in the rocks right
around us.

Some of us run under fire and take position above the
ones we have spotted so far. After a while, very slowly, like
spiders paying out threads from their stomachs, we lower
grenades on the ends of long strings. When they are level
with the openings from which the rebels are firing, we give a
sharp pull. The grenade, freed of its arming device, immediately explodes (we had shortened the detonators) and at least
destroys the enemy weapon.

One rebel snatched one of these unpinned grenades as it
went past him and threw it back, laughing. That was the only
time I ever saw a rebel laugh. He was killed a half hour later,
by a rocket shell that blew him to pieces just as he put his
head out to take aim.

From time to time, the air force circles over us. To avoid
confusion, we mark our positions with white material. But
these markers also indicate our positions to the rebels.

We have been here several hours. Our arms and legs are
cramped and our heads ache. We make a second attempt to
crawl up to their positions. But even our boldest have to stop
at the point where the terrain becomes completely bare. Any
rush beyond there would be madness.

Toward evening, our fighters come back for a final strafing before dark. At great risk, they almost graze the cliffs and
again machine-gun all the caves. But their big 20-mm. bullets
ricochet perfectly uselessly. Even bombs wouldn't do any
good. In spite of the avalanche of fire, some rebels blast away
at the silvery fuselages with their F.M.'s. They will shoot
down three big Sikorsky helicopters in three days.

Other troops, legionnaires, Bérets bleus, and colonials,
come by helicopter to reinforce us. They take position to our
right, left and rear. There are more than two hundred rebels
in this crater of ours, like bees in a hive. Those we have
encountered so far are just a handful under orders to keep us
busy.

Four long days go by this way, in semi-expectancy. All we can do is improve our positions a little by rolling big pieces of loose rock in front of us. The rebels don't have to do anything. They might as well be at home, so impregnable are their caves. After dark they hurl insults at us, along with their empty sardine cans—the only entertainment of the whole day.

For four days, we practically never sleep. How can you, when you know that within twenty yards is a man, or two or three men, watching you from a hole in the rocks? All the the same, we do try to set up a system of sleeping by turns.

The third night heavy snow begins to fall, freezing us in our holes, paralyzing us in body and mind. The big whirling flakes extinguish our rocket flares. A number of captains give orders to stop firing. They would rather let the rebels escape than have their men shoot each other.

That very night, about one o'clock, the hour when

**Sikorsky Helicopter**

sentinels are at their weariest, the rebels rush silently upon us.

Screened by heavy, acrid smoke, they head for our neighbors, the 2nd R.I.C.,[1] where the way through is the easiest. We see them coming down like threatening ghosts on our right. But, being under orders not to take our eyes off our sector of surveillance, we can hardly fire at them at all. No matter what happens, we are not to let ourselves be hoodwinked by a diversion, even a massive one. Only a handful of rebels reach us by mistake, five or six at the most. Of these, not one gets through. They fall between us and their comrades in the cliffs, and their corpses remain there to the end of the operation.

Some of the Colonials of the 2nd R.I.C. give way in their surprise. Their losses are heavy. Many rebel commando groups escape, this third night, and probably get back over the Tunisian frontier.

The 2nd R.I.C. picks up its dead and evacuates them in helicopter ambulances. We still do not move, but continue waiting, as do those we are watching, and who are watching us.

During the fourth night, the last twenty rebels, who are probably as exhausted as we, also try to escape. Like their comrades the night before, they do it at about one in the morning. But this time there are fewer of them, and there is no surprise. Tactical error, or concerted suicide?

We open fire at once, chiefly with machine guns. Seven of them fall, almost into our arms: four dead, three wounded. The others get through us without firing a single shot, by running like mad. Only the very last ones use their weapons, killing two of our comrades, almost hand to hand!

They scatter in the bottom of the crater, trying to find the way out. But they are given away by our flares, which go up easily tonight in the absolutely clear sky. Some Legion elements posted behind us as a "cork" open fire, at the risk of hitting us, and shoot them down one after another. Not one escapes. Not one was more than tewnty-five. Are there not always young men like them, in all the armies of the world,

---

[1]Régiment d'Infanterie Coloniale.

who die in place of others—bravely, say some; stupidly, say others?

At dawn we begin a systematic search of the caves and find three badly wounded Arabs, all of them armed and savage as animals at bay. They have to be "neutralized" with grenades.

Some of the caves are mere fissures between giant boulders leaning against each other, and you wonder how a human being could have crouched in there so long. But others are as high as houses. They communicate with each other through numerous passageways and have several stories of well-constructed platforms. The floor is covered with thick straw, with sheepskins, sometimes even with rugs. Hundred-pound bags of couscous—one wonders if they were dropped by planes—water in goatskin bottles, sugar, and even live goats and sheep, have been stockpiled here on a very large scale. There are storerooms cut in the rock where, besides equipment and piles of new uniforms of Egyptian make, we find quantities of leaflets and documents (most of which we burn), portable typewriters, Red Cross boxes with syringes, packages of bandages, etc., and blankets much like ours, together with army cots.

As we are advancing into the biggest of these rooms, we have a final bit of action, and still another casualty. A fellagha who had stayed behind for some reason or other shoots the moment we come into his line of fire and wounds S. We drop to the floor and lie flat. But we still can't see him, even with flashlights, though we hear him reload his gun. A flare finally reveals him lying on one of the platforms built along the sides of the cave. We have just time to see his head and his gun sticking out over the edge. We fire. He's hit, and his gun tumbles down almost on top of us. We rush for the gun, and the man. He's alone, and not badly wounded, but in the hand. Probably he's no more than eighteen—not a sign of a beard.

We quickly beat him off his perch, and the captain, in a fury, gives him a slap in the face that nearly takes his head off, then has us tie his hands, even the bleeding one. But the man is supple as a cat and makes several attempts to get away from us. We beat him half to death, and ship him by helicopter to Tebessa, where he can be properly interrogated.

* * *

We load ourselves with booty that is on the whole more cumbersome than interesting. The stocks of food and clothing have been burned where we found them. Tomorrow the engineers will come and do what they can to blow up the principal entrances. Our work is finished.

We had not known how tired we were. The dull fatigue building up in us hour by hour is intensified by cold and thirst, and now, with nothing else to occupy us, we are alone with it. We feel the whole weight of our bodies, those obedient bodies that do not complain till action is over. Haggard and red-eyed, we stagger up out of the crater like drunken old men. Ten yards from the trucks, one man falls in a dead faint.

We climb almost unconscious into the waiting trucks. An icy wind whips the tent cloths we wrap about ourselves to try to keep out the cold. We are given bread, wine, cigarettes. Few make use of them. I want to think about my dead comrades, but am already being jolted to sleep.

At Tebessa the next day, we do not get up till noon. Then we dig a row of graves in the town's already crowded cemetery. All the hospital's refrigerators are full, and the weather has once more turned hot.

Except for a few rich Europeans who lived to a good age, say eighty, hardly anybody is buried in this cemetery but young men in their twenties. Some graves date from the Conquest. In rows of ten, they tell of Corporal R., aged 23, killed in action; of Hussard V., aged 21, killed in action; of Chaseur A., aged 20, killed in action . . . This will be a year of paratroopers and legionnaires.

In the gray dirt, which is full of scorpions, our spades uncover heads still entire and bones mixed with old pieces of coffins. The returning sun is melting the last patches of snow. And bones yellowed by earth and sand, washed clean, are shining in the bright light.

The graves—two yards in depth—are very quickly dug. Of course we're used to this work: we do it for ourselves every evening. They're just the size of a foxhole.

The burial takes place the next morning at seven o'clock.
The first corpses are taken from the hospital refrigerators. Then begins the awkward procession of coffins, which go

sadly by, covered by the blue, white and red, side by side on the G.M.C.'s and the 6 x 6's. The drivers have scrubbed their trucks for the occasion and painted the tires white.

First the Colonials. The 2nd R.I.C. had twenty-two dead, as well as eight missing (along with their 60-mm. mortar) and twelve wounded. The Colonials cross the city, keeping time in widely spaced ranks on either side of the coffins. Not an Arab in the streets. European civilians and territorial auxiliaries in treillis are the only spectators. A few women are crying, and this ridiculous noise, along with that of the throttled-down motors, is all that breaks the silence.

Then comes the Legion's turn. It had contributed only one company and this time had but two dead. The legionnaires are in full dress uniform. Their famous stride is slower than ever this morning. On the two coffins, those of a corporal and a private, they have added their own green and red flag to the indispensable tricolor. An old legionnaire is weeping in the ranks, yes, like a woman, and big, silent tears fall heavy as blood on his green tie. Not one of his comrades turns around. We pretend not to see.

Finally, closing the procession, come our six comrades. A few civilians follow timidly at a distance.

We enter the cemetery, which is as bustling as a fair this morning.

The long oval boxes are lowered with ropes. A few officers, including, I think, some sort of general, stand stiffly at the edge of the graves. They make no speeches, nor does the chaplain.

The earth is shoveled back. We tramp it firm. Then we set the painted wood crosses, like stakes. The Djeurf operation is concluded.

I don't know what was done with the rebels' bodies.

## 44

May 8th, 1956: third anniversary of Dien Bien Phu. The rebels are sure to be planning a big blow for the occasion, but this time the staff decides to set a trap for them. At five o'clock on the evening of May 7th, we leave the city as noisily and conspicuously as possible. The rebels needn't worry, we won't be in Tebessa on the 8th. We drive away in the gathering dusk. At low speed, we go as far as Youks-les-Bains (so named, probably, because we can't get enough water at the fountains to fill even our canteens). Then we all turn around and come back full speed toward Tebessa to catch the simple-minded outlaws who won't have failed to seize the city in our absence.

Near the ramparts, we hide the hills to wait for the dawn and the big suprise counterattack. Half frozen, with no blankets and no wine, we stamp around for hours in the rain. H-hour finally comes, and in five minutes the whole of Tebessa is encircled by the unbroken chain of our five companies.

We re-enter the city in a torrential downpour, ready for anything—except what we find, which is nothing at all!

We get back into our barracks at noon, very depressed, without having fired a single shot.

A few days later, in the course of a march in the vicinity of Tebessa, we stop at evening in one of those heaps of Roman ruins with which the region is strewn. It is beautiful weather. At peace with the world, each man, shovel in hand, absentmindedly digs his hole for the night as he watches the sun stretching its light far and wide over the great fallen stones.

I have dug my last shovelful, but before laying out my tent cloth and my pack in the bottom of my hole, I want to flatten out the earth I have dug, to prevent its falling back in. While so doing, I suddenly notice a very small faintly shining bit of metal. I lean down, expecting to find it's a cartridge, or a uniform button. It's a disk, polished and perfectly round. I rub it gently on my beret. Lying in my dirty, callaused palm is a delicate Roman gold coin.

Under a very fine and pure profile, I read: Constantinus. At least sixteen hundred years separate me from the man who dropped this coin here. I wonder who he was: perhaps just a soldier, like me, some legionary tired from marching all day, as I am, without seeking to understand. Maybe he dropped his coin as he was stooping to stretch out on the very spot where I am going to sleep.

A few days later, accompanied by a comrade, I call on the curator of the Tebessa museum.

I tell him all about my adventure and show him my find. "Yes, it's a pretty coin," says he, touching it. "A very pretty little coin," he continues, the way one says: a very pretty woman. "But, they're found everywhere in this region, these coins. Perhaps not as fine, it's true . . . Just look, though . . ." And, moving away a curtain, he shows us into his little private museum.

On the walls, all the way to the ceiling, are a multitude of carefully labeled Roman relics, the fruit of years of ardent search: lamps, fragments of vases, statuettes, ewers. And, in among all these things, flowers, living ones, hundreds of flowers of all sorts. "On account of the goings-on," explains the curator, "digging has been interrupted since 1954, but there's still much to be discovered, particularly in the ruins where you found your coin."

He gives us tea. Reminiscences of Paris, which he left in 1920. We part old friends. "Hold on," he says as we're saying goodbye, afraid of missing roll call. He plunges his hand into a big bronze vase and gives us each a whole handful of his ancient coins.

We almost throw our arms around the good old man.

# 45

June 18th. Departure for a second operation in the Djeurf sector.

This affair begins with the recall of all the men spread around the town on leave. At about 8 P.M., trucks come and pick us up in the streets. We rush for our equipment and weapons, leave the base at 8:30, and drive through the southern night fifty miles an hour with all lights out. At three in the morning, in Chéria, we meet the Bérets bleus from Khenchela.

At 5:10, just as day is breaking, a Piper reports a big rebel band that has been maneuvering around Djeurf since the last engagement.

We get off the trucks, full of fear and hope. Ten minutes later, on reaching the top of the first peak, we hear the first bullets whistle.

"There they are, boys!" suddenly shouts Chief Corporal C. at the top of his lungs—a Breton, obstinate as they come, who always insists on scouting by himself, ten yards ahead of anybody else... "Hit the dirt!" Those are his last words. He falls, killed outright by a bullet in the forehead.

We can't stay on this peak. We look at each other. "What do we do now?" The fellaghas are within a hundred and fifty or two hundred yards, some probably nearer—a few are clearly visible in the valley, at our feet.

The Piper, which has already got one F.M. bullet in a gas tank, shows us the way. Its two escorts drop a grenade on every rebel they see, and thus let us know their positions.

All the companies are already engaged. Never have we made contact so quickly. This time as last, there must be more than a hundred rebels, very well protected and firing only when sure.

At nine o'clock, we already have four wounded, as well

as the chief corporal killed. They fell while walking a hundred
yards ahead of us and it is almost impossible to reach them,
for the rebels are firing at anything that moves, even the
medics with armbands. We nevertheless succeed in carrying
away L., the worst wounded (hit in a lung), and in evacuating
him in the staff's Bell. Gasping and choking, he has to sit next
the pilot, for there is no other seat.

The companies cease their advance. As the air force has
had to stop strafing in front of us in order to support other
units, we send out a patrol to reconnoiter, supported by our
two remaining F.M.'s, which keep up a steady fire to create a
diversion. But one of the F.M. men, exhausted by heat and
thirst, suddenly stalls like an overtaxed motor and falls in a
faint over his gun.

The situation is critical. The fellaghas, observing that one
of our F.M.'s has stopped firing, concentrate furiously on the
other, which performs magnificently in the  risis—until it
james.

The jamming of an automatic rifle is, to be sure, never
very serious. All you have to do is quickly run a ramrod down
the burning barrel. At least that's what the instructors say.
But under fire it's not quite so simple. Our automatic rifleman, W., tries to detach his barrel, as he must have done
many times on the range. But, to get his ramrod, he
unthinkingly raises himself on his forearms. Immediately, a
bullet hits him full in the body. He drops everything, and the
fellagha who fired the shot leaves the caves and rushes
forward to seize the weapon he supposes abandoned. The
wounded man's loader sees him, however, and opens fire
with his carbine. The fellagha is killed.

We drag the poor automatic rifleman's corpse to the rear
by the feet—much as they drag the picadors' disemboweled
horses out of the arena. Had the rebels attacked then, they
might well have broken through.

While we are hurriedly taking apart his F.M., which is
still burning, W., who is not dead at all, comes to. In spite of
the bullet in his body, he tries to get up, and even flies into a
rage, insisting that we give him back his "big gun," as he calls
it. He claims he's the only one who can work it. The medic
has to give him a shot to quiet him.

The rebels keep on firing. The patrol comes back and
reports that they are "everywhere." We have to crawl to make

contact with the next company, which is also under heavy attack.

The fighter planes come back. But their machine guns are now useless. Even the rebels farthest from the cliffs have been able to take cover. They are lying under wide flat stones and have nothing to fear from the air.

An hour goes by. Then we move again. This time, at a given signal, we run straight ahead and get over the last summit. The receding slope is completely bare for several hundred yards. We make it. The bullets whistle from every direction, but not one hits anybody. Even for a good shot, it's very hard to bring down a man racing against death.

We reach our new positions. "I think I'm wounded," says a sergeant in a thoughtful voice. He is: a bullet through both legs. He says no more, and posts himself behind a rock, like the others. Not till evening, when he is writhing in pain, does he finally call a medic, and faint in his arms. He has to wait four more hours before being evacuated by helicopter, four hours that he spends close behind us, with clenched teeth and never a moan. He won't even give us his carbine, though he can't use it. And, to the end, he is interested in everything and ashamed at being out of the fight.

Captain V. is famous in the regiment for his mania of always staying on his feet, whether the bullets are whistling or not. He must think it plebeian to lie down in the daytime. He is an authentic marquis. For fear of dirtying his hands, he doesn't take off his big leather gloves except at night, if then.

Today he stands conspicuously on the very tip of the last summit, absolutely alone, looking through his binoculars and trying to spot the exact location of a particularly virulent nest of rebels. "Why, yes, you can see them, you can see them very well. There are four of them," he shouts—and lands in a heap, breaking his fine binoculars! A bullet in the foot. The rebels could see him very well too.

In the afternoon, the planes come back and strafe the cliffs. The rebels seem to be more strongly ensconced than ever. They don't even draw in their heads, but keep right on firing at the fighters, at the helicopters, at us, at anything that moves, at anything that shines.

While waiting for the planes to finish their act, we settle ourselves in a sheltered hollow. In front of us is a oued, on the other side are the rebels in their cliffs. The heat is frightful. No more water, no air. B. scrambles forward a little way to get a more advanced position, and he gets shot in the foot too. Then he faints like a baby going to sleep. "It wasn't on account of my foot that I passed out," he explains to us later in the hospital, ashamed of what he considers weakness, "but from thirst. I hadn't had any water since morning. I lost my canteen when I jumped from the helicopter."

Our thirst does become really terrible. Down in the oued, of course, there probably still is a little water. But there's no cover; it's very dangerous . . . All the same we try it, protected by mortar fire. Volunteers go down, one by one. But each time, two bullets in quick succession prohibit these attempts. The moment a man takes a canteen out of its felt cover to sink it in a puddle, the metal catches a ray of sunlight and makes a perfect mark. Someone gets the idea of wrapping them in berets turned inside out. And we get a little water, hot from stagnating in the sun, dirty, and green. We drink it without looking.

Late in the afternoon, a helicopter arrives in a crashing volley of bullets and lands behind us. Crates of rations, ammunition, cans of water, are tossed out to us in great confusion. This means we are here for the night. Before it gets completely dark, we crawl out and mark our advanced positions with squares of white material, to avoid killing each other during the night. At seven, the order is given to make no further advance anywhere. There is now silence, broken only by the cry of a jackal who must be prowling between the lines.

Two hundred yards beyond us, halfway between our foremost elements and the rebels, two of our men have remained on the field. One is Sergeant A., whose field glasses and fine American carbine must have been noticed by the rebels who shot him down. The other is V., from our platoon.

Three of us have already tried to recover, if not their useless dead bodies, at least their weapons. The captain forbids any further attempt. The dead are dead . . .

Not until the operation is over do we realize that it was not a jackal we heard crying till the morning.

V. was not dead, though seriously wounded. The coolness of the night caused him to regain consciousness soon after dark. Being half paralyzed, alone, and unable even to reach his first-aid kit, he kept calling to us desperately, but in so broken a voice that we did not recognize it as his, or even as human.

Until the morning, V., my poor comrade, continued to cry in agony from his bed of stones. Until the morning! Delivered in mind and body to the extremity of terror, he suffered past anyone's imagining. His hoarse cries did not finally cease till dawn.

In the darkness, a rebel crept slowly toward him, whom he very likely saw coming for a long time. There he is! He touches V.'s body, takes his weapons from his hands, and then puts out his eyes and cuts his Achilles tendons. But he doesn't kill him. He wants to make him suffer, and to prevent his coming to die among us. A hundred yards from him, his comrade, Sergeant A., a little later dies in the same way, blinded and hamstrung, very slowly, while we are waiting for the dawn.

V. was a very tall fellow, slightly stooped, always happy as a child when an operation promised to be at all exciting. He was madly fond of war. For him, it had never been anything but a great marvelous game. When we set out for this operation yesterday, he was, as usual, laughing over it joyously. It was his way of loving life.

Daylight comes. Renewed bombardment of the enemy positions. Very few rebels will escape this time. Two of their

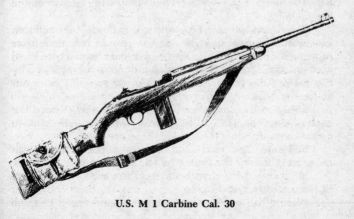

U.S. M 1 Carbine Cal. 30

leaders were caught yesterday by a sentinel in the bottom of the oued: one killed before he could turn around, the other so badly wounded that he died during the night.

The bombardment fills all the hollows, particularly the one we are in, with dust as yellow as sulphur. Fragments of rock come down like rain. An enormous mass breaks off the cliff, rolls past our positions like a runaway truck, and roars out of sight.

The bombardment stops. Covered by the machine guns and mortars, two regiments, one of them ours, set out to assault the caves. There is so much noise that no one can hear the commands, however loud they're roared. Each man does about as he wants.

As usual, no rebel surrenders unless mortally wounded. The fighting is not literally hand-to-hand, but we are firing submachine guns at men who often do not show themselves till we are less than five yards from them.

The idea of modern war is a grand, impersonal, remorseless massacre. As for us, however, we still see very well whom we are killing and that they are men like us. Fortunately, in the heat of action, we soon stop thinking, except of killing, so as not to be killed first. And, though we kill each other sweating and clenching our teeth, we apparently do so without any malice.

On the way up to one of the caves, a dapper second lieutenant suddenly turns a tremendous somersault and lands flat. The muzzle of the rebel's gun is still smoking in one of the openings.

Someone shouts: "The lieutenant is dead!" and picks up his carbine. But we go right on. A dead man is the stretcher bearers' business, not ours. We hear shouts behind us: "Wait, wait for me!" We don't even turn around; it's better not to. Someone is running past us. It's he, our second lieutenant. "Give me back my gun," he shouts, pale and breathless, to the man who had taken it. The bullet had only creased the back of his neck. He had fallen from sheer astonishment.

Suffocated and exhausted, the last rebels come out almost everywhere. The ones who left their weapons inside are spared, at least for the moment. But those who come out gun in hand are shot down.

Back in the largest caves, we find corpses and even some

rebels wounded in the previous operation. An infirmary too, with cots and blankets. And, as last time, records, typewriters, propaganda leaflets, new clothing, food and water. All this is taken out, and a great bonfire closes the operation.

## 46

Contrary to what we thought, not all the rebels were caught this time either. Some of the caves had long passageways leading to valleys we weren't guarding. Among those who escape this way were probably the thirty-three legionnaires (including a lieutenant and an officer cadet) who deserted at Tebessa. We later learned that it was mainly against them that this whole operation was planned.

**57 mm Recoilless Gun**

The men of the "faithful Legion" are deserting too!

One evening, the platoon is asked for ten volunteers to lay an ambush in the ruins on the outskirts of Tebessa. We feel badly when we learn that the object is to intercept a group of rebels coming to meet two legionnaires. The latter are expected to desert tonight, bringing their automatic rifles with them.

We take position at ten o'clock and stay till morning. But the two legionnaires never do come to the rendezvous, nor the rebels either.

These two legionnaires didn't desert, but others had, in just that way, two at a time, and by previous arrangement—and not one has yet been caught. We learn that the Legion unit we relieved here was not transferred solely on account of the fire we were told about. More important was the fact that some of its men, in most cases Germans wanting to get home now that their country was prosperous, had let themselves be persuaded by unidentified civilians to join the army of "National Liberation" for a few months' service as officers, after which they would be free.

We have now reached our regulation percentage of dead and are to be relieved. But, before we go, we have to finish our interminable corporal-candidate training.

This is the home stretch. We are now handling all the weapons we don't yet know: the Rewbell machine gun, the 57-mm. recoilless rifle, the latest thing in flamethrowers, ultramodern rocket throwers, etc., etc. We are mounting 60- and 81-mm. mortars at infernal speed in all sorts of terrain, and are being more and more severely timed at it. We jump more than ever on the turfless Tebessa D.Z. As for T.N.T., we now handle it with the utmost familiarity. Grenades and booby traps have no more secrets for us. We know every one of the thirty-six ways to exterminate one's fellow men.

At dawn on July 1st, we leave Tebessa with a little farewell parade. It takes our convoy of overloaded trucks all of twenty-four hours to get to Duvivier, our new capital.

Duvivier is a big, mostly European town in the arrondissement of Bône. It is surrounded by immense tobacco fields, equally vast stretches of shoulder-high wheat, and a fringe of gray olive trees weighed down by their fruit. To us it seems like a land of Canaan. Like any little town in the south of France, Duvivier has its little white church surmounted by the Catholic cross, and its equally white little town hall, set amid flowers and adorned with a gigantic metal R.F.,[1] from which hangs a long tricolor flag. There is also a charming little prison, half hidden by cascades of wisteria, with bars so slender you would think it a railroad station.

Attracted by water, we instinctively pitch our tents in a pasture—as lush as those of Normandy—and then run down and soak ourselves in the lovely stream that runs along its edge.

There are hardly any Arabs in this region, but even so, it is not unusual nowadays for magnificent wheat fields suddenly to catch fire, right at the gates of villages, or for dozens of superb olive trees to be cut down in a single night.

The very next day after our arrival, we therefore leave for a large-scale operation in the surrounding djebel, for the mountains threaten the plain, here as everywhere else.

Unlike the Némencha, these mountains are so thickly wooded that one cannot even see the color of the soil. Sturdy cork oaks and laburnum and rosemary abound here in wild confusion among the prickly, fragrant herbs that ring the Mediterranean with green.

Being right on the Tunisian frontier, these heaths have been forbidden territory for months. Every village has been burned, either by the villagers themselves before leaving, or by passing soldiers, French or rebel. And, as in Kabylia, we have orders to shoot immediately any human being we encounter, man, woman or child, armed or not.

Around the tumbled-down dwellings, the once prosperous fields are going back to wilderness. The fruit is rotting in the heat, and the sun-baked vegetables in the ruined gardens are returning to their dwarfed and shriveled natural state. Whole herds of cattle roam the abandoned meadows. We catch the best calves and fattest heifers as we go by, and thereby greatly improve our rations.

Our first night is spent in pastures overlooking the sea. We lie in soft grass of the finest texture, in which grow thousands of tiny but extraordinarily beautiful flowers, very comfortable to our tired feet. The multitude of stars raining down on our faces keep us awake at first.

All we ever find of the rebels is their tracks, not very

[1]République Française.

clear, but everywhere. Once we even cross the frontier without knowing it and go twenty kilometers into Tunisian territory.

Return to Duvivier. There's a rumor that in the 9th R.P.C.,[2] the regiment that relieved us at Tebessa, two corporals and nine paratroopers have deserted to the enemy. Is this an epidemic? Everybody is amazed. But why? We have idealized combat and danger. What greater adventure than to become a rebel oneself after hunting them so hard? Where find greater risk than in the ranks of the fellaghas of 1956? What greater adventure than to spend the rest of one's life as a traitor under sentence of death?

July 13th. Airborne operation at Redjas. Twenty-four rebels killed. We've come a long way since wounding one rebel constituted an event. Deaths now come by the dozen.

The fellaghas are attacking Duvivier. That peaceful little town of Duvivier where they've never been seen before, as the terrified Europeans shout to us from their doorways. "It's you who attract them!" It must be true. Should we apologize? The rebels bombard the railroad station and its vicinity, spreading panic. In spite of the overpowering heat, our whole platoon is sent to counterattack. There are practically no other troops in the town.

The station is down in a hollow and is dominated by a high hill covered with olive trees. The rebels are on top. We start up the five hundred yard slope on the double. The shooting stops, and, when we get to the top, there's nothing there but hot empty shells. As usual, the rebels have gone.

We start off cross country on their tracks, running and falling in the high wheat that brushes roughly against our faces. But we soon have to give up. Pursuit is futile, because a man can make himself invisible in this wheat merely by sitting down. We were wearing ourselves out for nothing.

When we return, streaming sweat and wiping our faces with the backs of our hands, the townspeople watch us from their shaded windows with severe and disapproving eyes.

---

[2]Régiment Parachutiste Colonial.

They must have expected us to come back driving thirty rebels in chains ahead of us.

By truck from Duvivier to Bône. At one of the posts along the road, they tell us that only the day before, a convoy, headed for Bône just as we are, was machine-gunned on this same route. We sit back to back on our benches, facing both sides of the road, and with our weapons in our hands keep ceaseless watch on the crests of the slopes. However, we have an uneventful trip to Bône, formerly Hippone, the bishopric of St. Augustine. The barracks yard where we park our trucks is still full of Roman ruins: broken shafts of columns, capitals, wreckage of an amphitheater.

Leave: three hours of happiness in town. Along the Cours Bertagna, in the blue shadow of the trees, the young Creole girls parade their charming indolence before us like a smile. All the people are laughing and enjoying themselves. The rebels are there, however, side by side with them in the streets and scarcely disguised. A few days later, Colonel Bigeard, out in just his shorts for his morning jog along the harbor, gets a burst of submachine-gun fire, which only wounds him. He is said to have "baraka," divine protection. Wasn't he wounded this same way in the Némencha?

As we sit around laughing and singing in the restaurants, on the café terraces, and on garden benches, we forget the war for a few hours. So much so that on the way back we have to deposit the platoon sergeant on the floor of the truck to conceal, if not his condition, at least his stripes. As we drive along, he never stops shouting, to the syncopated rhythm of the jolts: "J'encule l'armée! J'encule la France! J'encule la terre entière! Je conchie le monde!"* We laugh, uneasily. The deep and scornful sadness of all this scurrility is too strong for us not to feel it.

During one of our combing operations, I was searching a mechta, and in obedience to orders was just poking my bayonet into a pile of multicolored clothing that might have concealed a weapon, when a man came up and, taking my hand with great solemnity, presented a very pretty little girl to me. At first I didn't understand and almost mechanically offered the child some candy. She took it without a word. But

---

*"Fuck the Army! Fuck France! Fuck the whole earth! I shit on the world!"

the man said, in perfect French: "She's a widow, sir . . . She's fourteen. Five thousand francs." He was selling me his daughter! "I should be very honored," replied I to the honorable papa, "and very interested, really, but . . . but, to begin with, I've no money with me." Any other explanation would have been wasted on him. There was complete silence. Then he went away, leading the little girl by the hand. She was still smiling.

During the night of the 21st to the 22nd of July we are assigned to guard a trainload of rebellious replacements in the Duvivier station, on their way to Tebessa. We are there with fixed bayonets till morning.

While we walk silently up and down along the cars, these draftees, who had already almost mutinied in Marseilles, never stop jeering at us bitterly: "Salauds! Vendus! Mercenaires!" Pleasant job for us!

Last operation of our corporal-candidate platoon: Chéria.

As we're now great experts on explosives, we prepare the three hundred pounds of T.N.T. required for blowing up the entrance to a gigantic cave where we expect to catch a whole band of rebels.

When the charge is in place, we silently advance about sixty yards into the pitch dark of the cave, one of the deepest we have seen. But, since the risk of being machine-gunned increases in proportion to the distance we cover, the captain orders us back. We don't wait to be told twice.

The cave is blown up a quarter of an hour later.

On the cliffs of several of the thalwegs we go through on our way back, we discover corpses of fellaghas, concealed by bits of brush or heaps of stones. They all seem to have been killed the same day. By whom? Why?

# 47

Final examination day has at last arrived for our interminable special training.

They assemble us out in the trampled tobacco fields. Some newly disembarked recruits are there watching us with astonishment and admiration as we begin, very excited ourselves. A platoon is turned over to us. In front of the colonel, who is stiffer and severer than ever, we have to take this heterogeneous mass of men and make of them a unit capable of maneuvering, pirouetting, and almost dancing, on a few square yards.

Having handled men, we next handle explosives. We pinch and sever the long black tubes of hypersensitive fulminate of mercury, we crumble the T.N.T. The problem is to shorten the brief time a grenade takes to go off, and throw it into a marked circle without blowing ourselves up.

In the evening, the results are officially announced. Contrary to usual procedure, the top four are straightway appointed chief corporals, and thus it was that on the 24th of July, 1956, Private Pierre Leulliette became Chief Corporal Leulliette in the Airborne Troops of the Colonial Infantry, and, what's more, had his miserable, merely nominal, monthly pay of 12,000 francs raised to 76,000.

With my pack on my back, I go and join the 1st Company, the best in the Regiment, which is camped in a wheat field on the bank of the Oued Mellah.

This river is overflowing with thick, yellow water, whereas everywhere else there's nothing left of the streams but white pebbles. The water, however, does not bring us luck. Two men, one right after the other, dive too deep in the same place, smash their heads against an invisible rock, and float off in the current, dead. Then a strange illness lays nearly half the company flat on their backs with a high fever. Blood specimens sent to Paris show some sort of poliomyelitis.

Another jump at Bône, a pretext for sauntering all afternoon in the city, which is turning out to be a charming place.

How incredibly kind the people are, and especially the young women. Our reputation has never been so good. Here we are just nice young men, irresponsible but brave, not very moral, of course, but not base or evil. So you see six-foot "paras" sipping sherbets under the trees and allowing themselves to be made much of.

In the cafés and restaurants, everybody wants to buy us a drink. Even retired veterans, with their long mustaches, though they've certainly lived long enough to know there's no one so boastful as a soldier on leave, listen with polite gravity to our outrageous yarns. Many of the shops refuse to take money, unless a civilian pays for us. We owe this popularity to Colonel Bigeard's regiment, the 3rd R.P.C., which has been here a long time and whose prestige is immense. We never see anything like this again.

We return to Duvivier and leave on an operation the following night.

---

## 48

---

We soon find that the mountains of our new hunting ground, though less hot, are no less formidable than the Némencha, for they are overgrown with thorny brush which lacerates our legs day after day, despite the new make of very high leggings which has been issued us.

Bad luck! I'm in charge of a mortar. Outside my responsibility for aiming the piece, all I officially have to carry is the sights, a complicated and very expensive device, in a metal box on my belt. This is light enough, but the mortar itself weighs forty-five pounds, and the firer, strong though he is, gets completely exhausted. Neither the ammunition bearers nor the loaders can possibly help, for they already have very heavy loads of shells. It is therefore up to me to pitch in and carry the mortar myself toward the end of the day. The first time he saw me throw the heavy metal tube up over my pack, my firer could hardly believe it. He looked at me and stammered: "Thank you, chief, thank you," in so sincerely grateful a tone that I have never forgotten it. Actually, it was the first time since I joined the army that I had heard the words "Thank you." And when I showed astonishment at such gratitude, he murmured: "Chief, even the cross of Christ must have been less heavy. At least, there can't have been this heat... And it wasn't so far."

This man had been an apprentice mason in Saint-Denis and had belonged to the Young Communists. What did he ever learn about Christ, except the matter of the cross?... He'd been carrying this mortar for three years. His back was bent by it, and his shoulders looked as if they had been branded.

Just as we start to return from this operation, a Piper drops a message on the colonel's jeep. Countercommand. About face. A new rebel band, bigger than the one we were looking for, was seen in our rear, barely half an hour ago.

With great difficulty, the whole convoy turns around on the narrow road, and, though without water or rations, and much in need of rest, we set off for the airfield, from which helicopters take us to the strategic points.

Through the Sikorsky's open hatch, I admire the deep valleys now turning to blue in the twilight... We land on the edge of the largest clearing in the Laverdure forest, hoping to find a village in which to take shelter, for it has suddenly begun to rain.

This operation lasts ten days and ten nights, all spent in these apparently boundless woods. The helicopters that bring us ammunition and cans of wine every three days are our only contact with the outside world. We quickly return to the natural state, devouring animals an hour after killing them. One day, to prevent the rebels' getting them, we slaughter an immense flock of sheep, one by one, with submachine guns.

"So what? We've shot women," remarks someone, "why not sheep?" The big eyes of dying week-old lambs seem to epitomize the world's naïve astonishment at pain.

Some extraordinarily beautiful horses have been cavorting for several days around this village which we have made into our advance base.

One quiet afternoon when the rebels allow us a little peace, a comrade and I crawl through the grass toward these magnificent animals. They have gone wild, but we know they are sometimes used as mounts by the rebel liaison agents. We make halters out of our "commando" ropes, finally succeed in mounting two of them, and off we go at a full gallop. What fun. What an easy, graceful, natural gait. We ride a long time in the deserted meadow, then make a triumphal entry into the village, in front of our comrades stretched lazily in the grass.

I keep my horse till the end of the operation. He soon becomes a pet and follows me about in the thick undergrowth like an enormous dog.

The last evening, I take him for a walk with orders to shoot him. But I can't! I slap him hard on the rump, fire my pistol in the air, and off he goes full speed through the brush. I never missed any creature so much, in all those three years.

We are going back. The helicopters set us down on the edge of a road.

Our convoy is joined by a truck load of rebels who have just been tortured in a neighborhing gendarmerie. The trip back is long. Several nights we camp out in the forest. Our exhausted prisoners have to follow us everywhere, tied hand and foot. At night, they have to sleep without blankets, not only manacled, but also all tied together by one rope, a very refined torture...

We return to Bône. Near the city, we cool off and relax on a beautiful beach of warm soft sand. This swim is hardly a luxury, if you consider that for ten days not a drop of water has touched our bodies. Led by the colonel, the entire regiment goes in and soaks voluptuously. In the evening, we stretch out on the sand in our sleeping bags, and everybody goes right to sleep. The sea breeze blows very gently till morning. The coast is deserted, and we sleep in complete security. The only sound is the soft tread of the sentinels pacing the sand in the clear night.

At eight o'clock next morning, the regiment, like a monster with eight hundred legs, bestirs its immense carcass in the early sunlight. We are emerging from one of the longest sleeps of the year, and the Nescafé mixed with our last remaining cup of cold water is not enough to wake us. We run down to the sea, stepping over comrades who are not yet up.

Ten minutes later, everybody is in the water.

Everybody except one: G.R. Why? He's no lazier than anyone else. Is he sick? He hasn't even put his head out of his sleeping bag.

An hour later, as we are about to leave, his platoon leader finally comes up in a rage and starts shaking him violently. We all laugh. "Oh, R.! What a loafer."

R. still doesn't move. "This is queer," declares his lieutenant. "Has he got a fever, or what?" A chief corporal starts to undo the tightly closed sleeping bag. He gives the zipper a pull: "Oh . . . God . . . He's dead, Lieutenant!" In the bag, a still face. Two bullet holes in the head, the hair sticky with blood.

The news spreads like wildfire. Men run up from all directions. Our comrade lies with his eyes closed as if he were asleep, but there are the two round black holes, and his face is old and yellow. The mouth is only half open. "Incredible!" "Do you see?" "But who did it? And why close the bag afterwards?" . . . "It must have been a fellagha . . ."

We have known bold rebels to come into our positions during operations and kill men sleeping among the rocks, under the noses of our sentinels. But the terrain was very different. Here, there's nothing but sand. A man crawling on his hands and knees would be obvious here, even to a very sleepy sentinel. And last night there was a moon, too. We don't understand . . . We don't dare understand.

The two empty shells are easily found, right near the dead man: 9-mm. Army caliber. Brand new. Of the same year as those issued us two weeks ago. This may well be murder, and the murderer one of the men now standing around the corpse.

The records will show that G.R. was killed by an outlaw, during an operation. The honor of the army. But here no one is fooled.

An investigation is begun; but in order not to make the murderer too wary, it is spread over several weeks and over the entire regiment. It accomplishes nothing. The sentinels all say the same thing. They saw nothing, heard nothing. Was the sound of the sea enough to cover the noise of the two shots? Some say they know who the murderer is, but that they aren't going to talk.

As this gruesome discovery has poisoned the sea for us, we leave the beach. Our orders, moreover, are changed: instead of returning to our base, we go back to the maquis, a long way from the city, so that no one will talk to civilians always eager to hear and spread army scandals.

We enter a forest of gigantic pines in which the only human signs we ever come across are very disquieting: two heavily fortified forestry centers that have been attacked and destroyed by the rebels. The steel-plated doors are dangling, and the concrete blockhouses are riddled with bullets.

The region is very unwholesome. At night, we have to climb to the highest hill tops to get any air. The atmosphere in the valleys is stifling, and to a height of thirty feet there are clouds of frantic mosquitoes, which even crawl all over the ground, a hideous sight.

The road we took yesterday morning to go to the forestry buildings was cut last night. The rebels blew up the bridge over the deepest oued, but the woods are so thick that we did not hear a thing.

So we can't go on. We have to wait till a convoy of engineers gets here and puts together a temporary metal bridge, which they will remove as soon as we are across.

We camp beside the wreckage of the first bridge, delighted at the unexpected rest. Some go to sleep under the trucks. The mosquitoes are not so bold in the daylight. They keep away from the smoke of our fires. It suffocates us as well as them, but nothing could be worse than having to scratch oneself the whole time.

The engineers arrive twenty-four hours behind schedule. The road had been cut in still another place lower down, and to get to us they first had to put a bridge across there. Stripped to the waist and blowing like oxen, the pontoniers work for hours lifting the steel girders into place. Tired as we are, watching them sweat makes us feel on vacation.

We return to Duvivier for the 14th of July, which, oddly enough, is observed by a mass, celebrated by the regimental chaplain under the olive trees. There is also the regulation drunken orgy, and, finally, swimming—not regulation—in the polluted water. The latter results in fever for almost everybody, but after so much marching it's not unpleasant to have a bed and clean sheets in a cool hospital, even an army one.

We are supposed to be "mopping up" the Souk-Ahras region. A million men would almost certainly not be enough to do the job properly. Our problem is with the climate, and with the terrain, even more than with the rebels. We are tired, tired of the whole thing: of these trees buzzing with heat, of being hungry and thirsty, of getting no sleep; tired of all this stupid marching, for nothing. Our whole philosophy is reduced to putting one blistered foot in front of the other.

The trucks are waiting for us in some village on the edge of the woods. We at last find them, get in, and go limp, happy at not having to drag ourselves any farther. The truck jolts and lurches, but we hardly feel it . . . And, then, crash! it turns over, and there we are, all mixed up together in the middle of the road, like crabs dumped out of a basket. We are so dim-witted that we don't even moan. We just get back in the truck. Why complain? Who'd hear?

Neither the exhortations at daily assemblies—about the eyes of France being on us (whatever that means)—nor wine itself are enough to restore our morale. Our officers finally notice, and we are given three days' vacation in Bône.

We are in a big school building by the sea, and we have three whole days, for relaxation and all the pleasures, including that of doing nothing. We even get a week's pay in advance. We drop our packs and weapons on the cool stone schoolroom floor and rush to the Cours Bertagna to look for our pretty friends of the last time we were here. We find them drinking iced tea under those little black trees with shiny leaves that no one can tell us the name of . . . Every morning, the corners of our lips hurt from having smiled so much the evening before.

How beautiful the sea is when you are free and happy. And how wonderful to stroll along with nothing on your back but a light shirt. To live becomes a privilege, and each day is better than the last.

Back to Duvivier, where we learn that a micheline[1] has just been blown up, at the very place where the rebels derailed a whole train of phosphates the day before we left. The people are all out in the streets and wild with worry. They give us wine as we go by, to induce us to stay. The bottles pass from hand to hand—but hurriedly: a marching column cannot stop.

The hot sirocco from the south is upon us. Even lying down, you feel streams of sweat oozing out of your skin and pouring off you. And, to make matters worse, we now have athlete's foot, in addition to poliomyelitis, of which there are sixty-three serious cases in the regiment. Our overworked feet puff up with foul blisters which suppurate and burst, starting new ones, and the skin between our toes breaks down and bleeds. The smell and the pain are horrible.

We finally leave for Castiglione, though the population does all it can to get us to stay and protect its threatened prosperity.

## 49

Castiglione is the prettiest sea resort on the North African coast. It is about fifty kilometers from Algiers and as yet untouched by recent events. The beach is so perfect that the rich colonists are still coming there in crowds for rest and relaxation.

Arriving August 2nd in the heat of the day, we stand up in the trucks as we come slowly down the main avenue, and in dress uniform, with nails cut and berets pressed, we feel pure in heart and light as bubbles.

---

[1] Railroad car, something like a Budd Highliner.

Parade of honor the whole length of the shore boulevard. Along the wide sidewalks, mingling with the oleander blossoms, the groves, the sand and the sea, fabulously elegant girls are strolling about in such abbreviated bathing costumes that they seem to us more than naked. "Que belles! Que belles!" murmurs one of our comrades. "Ah! Que belles!" This ration of beauty is so powerful that it makes us tremble.

"Djeniene El Afia," a red and white villa facing the calm sea, opens its doors to us. From the window of the room a comrade and I are sharing, we can see the whole dancing Mediterranean. We go down and stretch our great tired bodies on the sand close by the bronzed, smooth bodies of smiling little sirens. We rise every morning in love with everything, and, till midnight, the hour for the last swim, there is nothing but play and laughter, in complete relaxation and intense happiness.

The days go by. The air is blue and cool like a kiss. But why this long, unexpected vacation? That is the question we all sooner or later ask ourselves, with anxiety. Finally, the answer comes with a shock: beginning tonight, we are in a state of alert for Egypt.

End of the vacation? No. Like men whose death sentence has been postponed, we plunge back into the pleasures of the city at every opportunity between duties and details. We don't actually leave until October 27th, but we get up every morning, thinking: Will it be tonight? And the sun and the sea seem to shout to us: "Enjoy life while you can."

"Alligator" (LVT)

Meanwhile, we keep on with our operations. On August 17th, we are taken by helicopter up into the djebel of Marengo. The heat is fearful, even in the middle of the night. The woods are on fire all around us. Invisible fellaghas running in the smoke attack us. We suffer casualties, and three days later there are women weeping in the cemetery.

Maneuvers to prepare us for the operation in Egypt are our main occupation now. As it's not yet known whether we are going in by air or by sea, we are being trained for either eventuality. Every morning, at Koléa, we have instruction in mines, how to detect, how to disarm them, how to blast a path through them.

At Zéralda, off an abandoned peninsula, we have disembarkation maneuvers, A huge concourse of "Alligator" landing barges, combat ships and troop transports, crowds the sea all the way from Algiers. Over and over again, as many as twenty times, we attack the beaches, running in water to our waists. We spend several nights in old American ships, relics of the 1944 landing. The transshipping maneuvers are the most dangerous. At the risk of being squashed between them, for the sea is rough, we have to get from one vessel to the other, clinging to the ropes, fully armed. We also do a great deal of jumping. Never before were there so many broken legs and sprained ankles—it's true we'd never jumped in such a high wind before, but some insinuate that not all these accidents are involuntary.

Sentimental moonlight walks are few and far between now. Instead, we have all-night marches along the sea from Castiglione to Tipasa, or long circuits of the hills, through vineyards whose grapes have just ripened. As we return, it is a joy to catch sight of the Tombeau de la Chrétienne, whose gigantic pyramid casts its shadow far over the moonlit plain, and at sunrise is a flaming landmark for scattered paratroop squads.

New alert: the "ultras" are making trouble in Algiers. We are called together and told in case of intervention our mission will be to control the Europeans, who are very excited. We take the magazines out of our P.M.'s. You don't fire on Frenchmen. This is a police job.

*    *    *

In the evening, I often stand with a girl by the balustrade overlooking the beach. We entertain ourselves watching the people going by in the sunset. One evening there is a sound of slow, measured footsteps coming down the avenue. The patrol. Every evening, a group of fifteen men from the regiment parades through the town in full uniform and with submachine guns at the ready, supposedly to prevent crimes by the rebels, but actually to break up drunken brawls. We watch them. They look miserable. Three paces ahead of the others, comes Sergeant L., just promoted after eleven years as corporal, officiating with a severe though somewhat vacant eye, and puffing out his little chest as far as it will go.

He sees me and draws himself up even stiffer. The little man is now a sergeant, and I therefore owe him respect. The regulations are precise: any soldier meeting a patrol has to come to attention at six paces, click his heels and salute. "At six paces," say the regulations. Not at seven.

The patrol is coming by, at seven paces, and now the sergeant is right in front of me. I look at him, and don't budge. He looks at me. Around us, some of my comrades have instinctively come to a half ironical, half bored attention. I am still leaning on my balustrade, not moving a muscle. The civilians look first at the sergeant, then at me. I am miserable, but there's no way of backing out. The sergeant's expression changes from petty tyranny to fear, and back again.

". . . I . . . Give me your name," he finally stammers. He knows my name perfectly well, but I give it to him all the same. "Aren't you saluting patrols any more?"

I serenely quote him what the regulations say about salutes. ". . . At six paces," I tell him, "not at seven." Choking with rage, the little noncom turns his back to me. "We'll settle this later, chief corporal!" he yells in a squeaky voice, and the patrol departs amid general silence.

Sure enough, two days later, I am sent for by the captain. Charge: direct disobedience. Fortunately, the captain has a sense of humor and dismisses the case.

Chiffalo is a pretty little sardine-fishing port a few kilometers from Castiglione. There's no one living here but Italians, all of them extraordinarily kindly people, very different from the colonists, neither miserly nor greedy. Of the acts of terrorism since 1954, not a single one has taken place here.

I go there on Sundays and join in the night fishing. All along the spotless streets, paved in places with red flagstones, the people sit on straw chairs in front of their doors, talking and relaxing. Radiant young girls walk to mass, with gilt-bound books under their arms and white lace mantillas over their smooth black hair.

Families invite me to their noonday meal, and I sit at the round table between the father, a fisherman like all the men here, and the mother, beautiful as a madonna, and opposite the two or three young daughters of the family and a few dimpled babies. What a contrast to army meals, with noisy, half-naked ruffians round an ammunition crate stealing each other's meat and grabbing for the beans.

After the pleasant formalities of coffee, I go on Sunday afternoon walks along the beach with the whole family. Their life is simple, humble, poor even, yet happy and proud. How good it is.

We leave our first quarters for a farmhouse above the city, in a banana grove alive with chameleons. All about, on the slopes running down to the sea, thousands of tomatoes are reddening in the sun, protected from the salt wind by tilted hedges of rushes. They are taking us in hand, after these weeks of dangerous idleness in which we unconsciously were becoming the civilians we might have been. The guerrilla war is over. It's for a real war, in the grand European manner, that we are being trained now. Tanks and airborne divisions are engaged in war maneuvers from Douaouda to the Mazafran estuary.

"Visit Egypt—Health—Romance—Sunshine." We can still see those old posters that used to be in railroad stations when we were children. We make feverish preparations, send our valises back to France, write moving farewell letters—which we have to write all over again the following week. A few even draw up their wills, with three copies. Our vehicles are painted sand-yellow. Immense H's adorn their hoods. H, as in Hamilcar.

Three more days of waiting. And now goodbyes, final this time. In a touching little speech, the mayor thanks us—for what?—with tears in his voice. We have become more attached to these people of Castiglione in a few weeks than to all Algeria in two years. On Saturday, October 27th, we finally get aboard our planes. A light rain is falling.

Tunis, Malta, Crete, spots of light. Seven hours of flight at 20,000 feet. We land at Limassol, on Cyprus, as night is falling, in dry, hot air heavy with blowing sand.

---

# 50

---

Trucks are waiting for us, their motors purring in the dark. We drive through the Greek and Turkish villages, grassless and surrounded by black cypresses. The low houses have flat pink roofs.

At four in the morning, we arrive at a Franco-British camp, planned for several divisions. In the new tents, already faded by the sun, we find beds awaiting us, almost without legs, level with the ground. And there are sheets! Ah, the luxurious British! But the heat wakes us in the afternoon. The sun is merciless and everywhere—not one speck of vegetation.

For a whole week, we stay on these few acres of sand, penned in by barbed wire! All communication with the outside is absolutely forbidden. We're being held incommunicado, and can't even write our parents. The nights are as cold as the days are hot. From the time the sun goes down, even though we sleep with our clothes on, we shiver under our thin blankets, like beggars caught unprepared for winter. We suffer from hunger too, like neglected prisoners of war. All our food has to come in special planes. We get a half plate of lentils per man per meal. Little bread. Hardly any water.

To restore morale, the regimental commanders organize group singing, and there are masses, parades, and outdoor movies. Every morning, we go out bare-chested in the freezing dawn to enjoy a run around the camp, led by the captain.

Somebody finds a lot of colored chalk in one of the

supply crates, and in no time the tents are decorated with innumerable drawings. A good many of them are of "Nasser— drunken liar": a few days ago, he was talking about "perfumed little French soldiers."

There is more and more talk of a drop on Port Said, that is, an airborne attack on enemy territory. The old world war veterans, survivors of Narvik and Arnhem, are far from encouraging. "A jump in wartime," say they, "is a toss-up. Either you achieve complete surprise and get away with almost anything, or they know you're coming and everybody gets killed, from the colonel to the last ammo bearer...But fortune favors the brave. Isn't that the motto of this regiment?"

On Sunday night, November 4th, while we are all, as usual, only half sleeping, the officer on duty goes silently from tent to tent and pulls from their beds, one after another, the men whose names are on his list. It's eleven o'clock. The night is pitch-black.

We're forbidden to light even a candle, for Egyptian spies have been prowling about the camp for several days. In complete darkness, we equip and arm ourselves, with beating hearts. A war jump! The dream of every paratrooper. We treat each other with the respect people have for those about to die, and assemble with the utmost gravity.

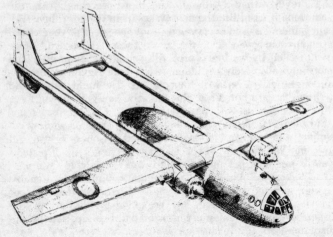

Nord 2501

In the dark, we each receive a printed sheet: General Orders No. 5 of General B., commanding Force A.

Officers, Noncommissioned Officers, Corporals, and Soldiers, we are going into Egypt with our Friends and Allies, the British.

France and the World will have their eyes fixed on You.

You can be proud of the important mission with which you are entrusted. I am sure you will be worthy of it. If need be, you will revive the exploits of our predecessors in this Land of Egypt. I have full confidence in your Valor and your Faith.

Nor shall you forget that Egypt has long been our friend. You will represent France. By your attitude and your behavior, you will strive to make known the greatness and the humanity of our Country!...

Too many capital letters!

At exactly midnight, we leave forever Camp Michel-Legrand. A quarter of an hour later, we board the Nord 2501's waiting for us wing to wing in perfect alignment. The checking and testing of parachutes has been rushed through so quickly in the half-light that one of my comrades will break a leg on reaching the ground tomorrow morning, because improperly strapped.

Our heavily loaded planes rise from the Cyprian soil. Four hundred kilometers separate us from Egypt. A three hour flight.

## 51

Except for the captain, an old corporal and two sergeants, the thirty men in this plane are hardly more than boys, for whom parachuting has never been anything but a game, often terrifying, but still a game. Tonight it's different. Our turn has come at last.

The plane reaches its altitude. We are alone in the world, in the half-light of the humming cockpit. As we huddle elbow to elbow on the narrow benches facing each other, each wonders: Am I going to pass this test?

"France and the whole world have their eyes fixed on you..." The sky is crystal-clear. The imminence of adventure lends pathetic majesty to our smallest act. We speak to each other almost with deference. What a mystery is fear, at first sly and secret, then a beast devouring one's vitals.

The engines run smoothly. The plane vibrates like a metronome, and our thirty hearts beat time. Empty minutes. Suddenly, a certitude, mad but absolute, confronts me as inescapably as the rising sun: I am going to die. I am going to die this morning. Our first objective is the water reservoirs of Port Said, which are defended by numerous machine guns and 30-mm. cannon. I think: thousands of bullets will fill the air, thicker and thicker as our green parachutes open like stars against the blue sky. One of those bullets is for me.

My brain is working hard; I try to imagine horrible tortures in comparison to which jumping would be nothing. In vain. I think of the Indian story in which the prince, wishing to know what will is, asks the sage, who replies: "You see that young banana tree? Take your sword, and, in one impulse of your will, sever it!" The tree falls, cut clean through. "Now, hold out your arm. And, if your will is still as pure, sever it likewise." Here in this dim cockpit, fear against which my will is powerless humiliates me as it did that prince.

Right near me sits the company corporal, like an old sick toad. In the faint light, with his mask gone, I see that our terrible "juteux" is after all just an old man, an old man who really doesn't love the army so very much, however much he may want the Legion of Honor.

The little red lamp has gone on. A bell starts to ring like an alarm clock. With one impulse, we're all on our feet, even those who appear sleepiest. "Stand up!" nevertheless shouts the instructor, as, in the courtroom, they shout: "Defendants, rise!" No more laughter, not even nervous laughter. Not the shadow of the palest smile. The faces, all terribly sad, are turned tensely toward the lamp.

Nervously, I hook my S.O.A. to the cable. I check the string which will tie my helmet to my chest. I run my hand over my weapon. I give a last little pat to the two parachutes to which in a moment I must entrust my life.

Ten more minutes.

The fear of the void is replaced by the fear of being afraid.

The instructor walks down between the two lines of us: we have to "spurt" from both hatches at once. The first men of each squad get into position. With one knee on the floor and body thrust forward like a thirsty dog, they are ready in one motion to spring into the void. Only their hands, which must be sticky with fear, are holding them now.

Only one minute more. In one hour, where shall I be? "Jumping into enemy territory...certain death...from the colonel to the last ammo bearer."

"In position...Go!"

In a gesture of the utmost violence, those two masses of flesh have simultaneously catapulted themselves into the vast and as yet silent void. An invisible chain binds us to them, and we follow with a rush over which the instructors no longer have control. From impulse, as if frantic at seeing the broad back of the man ahead suddenly drop away, each of us in turn goes through the door, his breath suddenly cut off. In fifteen seconds, the cockpit is empty.

Our eyes close. Our legs fold. Then the opening, the incredibly brutal wrench to the whole suffering body. The gigantic cupola fills the whole sky. No wind at all. And immense joy flows through every vein, like liquid gold.

The earth is now rushing toward us at constantly increasing speed. Only when I am down to fifty yards from the ground do I remember that today I am landing in foreign, unfamiliar country. Then the air is rent with terrifying uproar. To our right, to our left, in front of us and behind us, the machine guns are suddenly blazing away, and the air between us and the ground is vibrating with hundreds and hundreds of invisible bullets. The descent is nearing its end, and I recognize some of my comrades around me. They are gliding

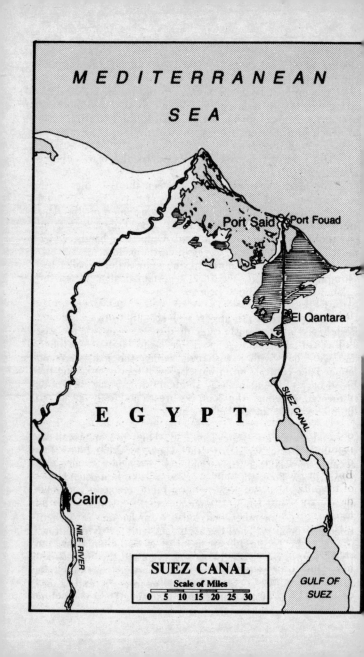

slowly down, apparently very relaxed. Again fear disappears, and a strange joy comes over me. This is war. Real war, at last.

Still thirty feet from the ground. The machine guns are singing very loud now. What's to be done about it? For the moment, nothing. Fifteen feet more...I flex my legs and gather myself together, ready to fall as correctly as possible. This is not the time to sprain a leg...And, wham!...Bounce. Here I am in Egypt.

## 52

The sand is a heavy gray paste, soft and warm. I have sunk in it to my knees. I stand up and look about for my mortar firer, but a bullet immediately whistles past my ears. Instinctively, I lower my head. Another. And still another. In front of me, I notice one of those ill-defined hollows so numerous in this sand. I plunge into it, but it is almost full of water. On the edge, with beating heart, I slip out of my harness and extricate myself from my two parachutes, now lying limp around me like great pieces of gauze.

Freed of my load, and submachine gun in hand, I rise out of the ground and see my companions springing in like manner from every hollow. Even topographically, the terrain doesn't seem very safe: pools, humps and holes everywhere. But over there, a few hundred yards ahead, is a green ribbon of magnificent palms. And behind them are great buildings, dazzlingly white: the reservoirs, our first objective. It is from those trees that the machine guns are firing on us; with field glasses, we can see the gun crews busy at their work.

We set out toward them on the run, leaping, falling and starting over again, wildly, with the captain in the lead. But how long a few hundred yards seem, on legs tired by the jump, under fire. From time to time, one of us falls face down in the warm sand. We can't tell if it's for good, but we can't stop.

Cannon in their turn begin to fire on us. We are not under one of those deluges of fire imagined by people who have seen war only in the movies. No, just here and there a bullet going by, a small shell bursting. No more than that. But it's enough to fill the atmosphere—though, as we run on, we begin to realize that all this noise is not stopping us, nor even scaring us any more, so great is our excitement.

Yet, in a flash, my brain records a picture I shall never forget: Sergeant B.'s body hanging by the ropes of his parachute from the top of a palm tree and slowly dripping blood into the sand. He must have been one of the first to die, before reaching the ground, shot in mid-flight. The tall body is still swinging a little among the razor-sharp fronds. Ten yards further on, in the shadow of the palm trees by the reservoirs, I see another body, lying among the broken stems of a rose hedge in full bloom: the small yellow-brown corpse of an Egyptian soldier. The contrast between the health of the flowers into which he has been crushed, and the deathly pallor of his face, stops my breath.

The F.M.'s set up on the edges of the reservoirs, and likewise the gun in the center of the D.Z., were very quickly put out of action with bazookas and mortars. Their crews died bravely: three or four bodies are lying around each battery. But at the entrance to the bridge connecting Port Fouad and Port Said there remains a formidable concentration of 30-mm. cannon and machine guns. You don't silence cannon with submachine guns, or even mortars. We have to wait.

The surprise was complete, and we are still nearly all of us alive. But this is only the beginning. The bridge, the essential objective, remains to be crossed.

The fighter aircraft have come to our support and are strafing eighty yards ahead of us. Their 20-mm. bullets pepper the enemy batteries, which, being partly underground, are quiet for a moment and then resume fire.

At the risk of our being spotted, I set up my mortar on the railroad embankment. There is nothing to use for cover and no possibility of digging in. Taking advantage of the air cover, we open fire immediately.

At last one of our shells lands on the crossing keeper's lodge, which is held by Egyptian riflemen. It bursts into flames, and we rush forward at least fifty yards.

An hour later, our first riflemen reach the bridge. We

still don't know what's happening anywhere else. Our company, the 1st of the 2nd R.P.C., is still alone in Egypt. Not till
afternoon, will another company, and then another, land on
our right. We have to hold out at least till three o'clock.

The moment we are in possession of the reservoirs, we
cut off the water. In an hour, all the inhabitants of Port Said
will be thirsty.

Virtually the whole Egyptian air force was destroyed
yesterday on the ground. There is nothing to fear from the
sky. Flying very low, our fighters machine-gun everybody still
alive in front of us. The planes come and go and come back
and turn again. Deluged with point-blank fire, the Egyptian
crews of the ultramodern 30-mm. cannon, the biggest of the
guns defending the bridge, finally take refuge in their trenches.
After a last bombardment with mortars, and still covered by
the fighters flying thirty feet above us, we make a combined
assault on guns and earthworks. Shots, confusion. The Egyptians
are hemmed in and surrender. They come out of their case-
mates one by one with their hands up. They are all wearing
fine red berets, just like us. These are Nasser's famous
"commandos of death."

But their comrades still hold the bridge, and won't
surrender. They are still firing, from under the great steel
girders that protect them from the planes. Steady fire. Losses
on both sides. Then they begin to fall slowly back.

While his comrades cover each other's retreat, one Egyptian
remains alone at the entrance of the bridge and, with nothing
but a rifle, furiously defends it against our whole company. A
real commando of death, this fellow. Finally a bullet hits him,
and he falls.

The bridge is free. We cross it on the run, as cautiously
as possible. The body of that last fedayin, with outstretched
arms, soaked with blood, still blocks our way. We take his
gun, his belt, his knife. A medic instinctively bends over
him, but he is really dead. The whole company goes by the
body, a little to one side, so as not to step on it. There is no
one to close his eyes: the war is not over. The flies, attracted
by the tears of death, are already at work, circling the eyes
with black rings.

The first objective has been reached—in barely an hour

and a half: we are ahead of schedule. We have to halt at the end of the bridge and wait till the other company arrives, in spite of our desire to continue the pursuit.

We dig foxholes—easy work, in the soft sand, till we are interrupted by violent Egyptian mortar fire. Where is it coming from? From those fedayin barracks on the plateau, a hundred yards ahead of us? The right thing would be to advance and find out. But orders are orders: we're to stay right where we are.

We accordingly protect ourselves as best we can by digging deep, firing only now and then, when an Egyptian puts his head up over a fold of ground to see if we're still here.

Early in the afternoon, the 2nd Company finallly arrives, none too soon, for the silence of this city of Port Fouad ever since noon was getting on our nerves. We imagined them making frantic preparations to resist.

Ninety of our comrades are jumping before our eyes. Egyptian tanks and machine guns, invisible from where we are, at once open fire, and keep on at ever-increasing tempo. Very slowly, the sky fills with parachutes, eight hundred yards to our right. All we can do is watch, and hold this bridge. The two companies join forces at four o'clock. At last we can assault the barracks.

The attack begins under heavy fire from the loopholes. We finally break in, but the defenders do not give up. They continue firing from behind overturned tables or piles of blankets. One by one, we at last slaughter this dozen or so of die-hards, probably all of them volunteers.

We take possession, breathing hard, as if we'd been running. Delightful place, these little barracks. They consist of small model houses arranged in a square, and are full of civilian and military supplies. Several tables are still set for this morning's breakfast, and the coffee is hardly cold. We drink it without ceremony. The comfortable beds tempt us very much. The usual pillaging begins. Everybody wants to take home his little souvenir of Egypt.

We climb up onto the flat roofs, with armfuls of blankets and mattresses. These will make our watch more comfortable tonight. Not that we can sleep: the sector we're responsible for is too important. A few hundred yards off, between gigantic oil tanks, begin the enemy lines.

Around the barracks are scattered a few small buildings, quite far apart. Patrols go out, covered by our automatic rifles. There is no one anywhere. Except in one of the buildings. Another lone sharpshooter! We try to neutralize him with grenades. The furniture hits the ceiling, the walls split. He goes right on shooting. Three of us get seriously wounded in his infernal shanty: two rooms, one behind the other. He is in the back, behind a heap of furniture and mattresses. We bring up a bazooka. We aim it. The rocket goes right through the house, which bursts into flames. The man staggers out, black with smoke and covered with blood. He is howling, but still shooting. Four or five bursts hit him at once. That's the end. Heroism is a lonely game. We salute this fellow. Enemy or not, we admire him. He died alone. All the more alone because everywhere the Egyptian army is retreating.

Night falls. Further operations are adjourned till tomorrow. We have quite enough to do to hold our positions till dawn, when we expect the British. We are very much alone tonight, and facing a whole city, filled with soldiers—and also with civilians, to whom the commandant is distributing weapons.

Immense fires break out at dusk. The dark red of the high flames brings out marvelously the exquisite blue of the sky, already inlaid with a few stars. The bombers are hurrying to finish their work before it gets completely dark.

The first half of the night is very quiet. The only sound is the heavy rumbling of the fires on the horizon. But at about three o'clock, when we are all quite drowsy, the sudden crackling of an automatic rifle makes us straighten up with a start, weapon in hand.

We scramble down from our roofs. I reach the entrance to the barracks—and see an enormous yellow and green truck crammed with Egyptian soldiers disappearing into the dark at more than a hundred kilometers an hour.

Too late! "The officer of the guard, where is the officer of the guard?" Here he is: Sergeant C. He's still all upset. What an experience!

With his finger he ejects an empty shell from the submachine gun he borrowed from a sentinel, and explains: "I was making my rounds and I was talking to R.—the sentinel who fired the F.M.—when suddenly I saw a truck full of men roaring up the road with its headlights on. It stopped right in front of us. I said to myself: Good. Here are the first elements of the 4th Company, ahead of time. I went up to welcome them. The officer next the driver got calmly off the truck and asked me some question. But I couldn't understand him. I got him to repeat it, and came still nearer. Then I noticed his flat cap, and was saying to myself: This is an Englishman . . . when I suddenly noticed Arabic letters on his jacket. An Egyptian. At last I understood, fired my pistol, and shouted: 'Call out the guard!' R. then fired his first burst. The Egyptians were just getting off the truck. They were so sleepy and so much in each other's way that they never had time to shoot. They scrambled back in. Two or three may have been wounded; I didn't go and count them! The driver started so suddenly that the officer almost got left behind...And they disappeared...They can't have known the barracks were taken. We'd better be careful. They might come back in force. There were at least thirty of them in that bus of theirs . . ."

"Too bad," remarks someone, "they didn't come right into the barracks . . ."

"Just as well they didn't," retorts another. "After all, we're only thirty ourselves. And practically all of us were asleep."

At dawn, more shots, mingled with reports of grenades.

Moored along the canal in front of the barracks, are a dozen old ships and a few feluccas. We didn't have time to attend to them yesterday, and it's from them that all this noise is coming. We run over, with our P.M.'s cocked. About a dozen fishermen have just been found hiding in their boats.

They have their hands up and are trying to convince us that they are noncombatants—which is quite likely. Suddenly finding themselves right in the middle of our position, they may well have had no choice but to hide to escape the shooting. But: "No useless prisoners! They're a nuisance, and they have to be fed."

We empty our magazines . . . And, one after another, the prisoners fall into the water. There are only two left, and they jump overboard in a desperate effort to hide along the hulls.

Private L. has never engaged in this sort of sport before, but, to show us that he's really tough, he gets on the last boat. Nobody in sight. He leans over the gunwale, and kneels, waiting for the moment when the two suffocating men have to put their heads out. After several minutes, a face emerges: "Ta...ta...ta...tatata...tata..." goes Private L.'s P.M. And the head disappears, mangled, blasted, at point-blank range. Three more minutes go by, and the head reappears, dribbling blood and water. Second burst of fire. The head sinks and does not come up again. A large round pink spot slowly widens on the surface, then grows more and more faint. The second head comes out of the water a little further off, with close-cropped hair like the first and the same wide open, terror-stricken eyes; and it shares the same fate, and there is the same widening ring of little scarlet waves.

Two days later, crossing the great canal, we see these two corpses again, all swollen, floating slowly toward the sea. We know them by their mangled faces.

The second day begins. We are surprised to hear artillery fire and at first think it must be ours, but the shells begin to land so close that we soon have to face the truth. Concealed Egyptian batteries are aiming right at our little barracks. Last night's phantom truck must have made its report.

The shells are now dropping all around the square of buildings. As we have no artillery but our little 60-mm. mortar, it would be ridiculous to try to return the fire. We have to retreat before it is too late. Seizing our packs and weapons, we run back across the bridge, under increasingly threatening fire. To judge from the spouts of water they send up from the canal, the shells are large caliber: 75, or 77. Splashes to our right, splashes to our left. A shell finally lands square on the courtyard we left seconds ago. "Good shot!" remarks somebody as we run. "It was about time! But what's become of our marvelous air force? Why don't they do something?"

We dig trenches under the palm trees at the entrance to the bridge. The shots get louder and louder. This is not so good. At ten o'clock, we finally learn where all these shells are coming from. Four Egyptian tanks—some of those left here by the British—sneaked in last night between the big oil tanks and slyly posted themselves right in front of them.

Since the oil belongs to some powerful Anglo-American company, what air force colonel would take the responsibility of setting it on fire?

This is a new experience for us. We are used enough to fighting rebels armed with submachine guns, like us, on their own ground, and with their own weapons. But this grubbing in the earth under the fire of tanks we can't even see is nearly driving us crazy. We've no choice, though. Some are cursing between their teeth... We had it so good. It couldn't last.

Toward eleven o'clock, the fighters finally appear, but without doing any machine-gunning. It seems they've not yet spotted the sand-colored tanks crouched like crabs beside the oil tanks. Then we're told they've made out one, then two, and that they're going to try to strafe them—without hitting the oil, of course.

The fighters come over our heads, in threes, with bombs under their bellies. I follow their evolutions through field glasses, standing on the edge of my hole.

The tanks are so taken by surprise that, before they can elevate, they are already being sprayed with machine-gun bullets. Almost immediately, there is a concert of enormous explosions, and huge red sheets of flame rise like walls against the blue sky! The oil reservoirs have been hit and are on fire. Tons of pitch-black smoke hide the landscape like a gigantic screen.

What's become of the four tanks in this furnace? Everything is blotted out by the smoke, which soon reaches us, though there's no wind, and covers us with flying coals and greasy soot. We shall be black as coal miners when we enter Port Fouad tomorrow. The tanks have stopped firing.

We run back across the bridge, with everybody sneezing his head off, and reoccupy our barracks.

There is still mopping up to do. Our patrols cautiously inspect the outlying buildings of the waterworks. They might be mined. But there's nothing in these great dusty sheds except here and there the body of an Egyptian soldier—who probably was wounded by the air force yesterday and came in here to die during the night.

The Egyptian lines, and, behind them, Port Fouad, are on the other side of a high dune, which completely bars the horizon. Ever since the fire started, furtive figures have been scurrying along the top of this ridge. Now a head appears.

Then the upper part of a body. We look at him through field glasses: a Negro! He is obviously a scout, trying to see exactly where we are, and seems unmindful of his danger. One bullet from a sniperscope Mas 51 is enough: the unfortunate black man drops his gun and rolls all the way down our side of the dune.

Then another raises his head, perhaps to see if his comrade is wounded, or to recover his gun. A second bullet hits him, and he falls just like the first one.

We fortify our positions, then go and recover our parachutes, which are still lying about in the sand. It is none too soon. The nylon they are made of, though very strong, is also very perishable. All this expensive equipment could be ruined in the wet sand and stagnant water.

There are enemy dead lying among the parachutes. Only our own have been taken away. But near the custodian's cottage in the reservoir gardens I come upon the bodies of two comrades killed yesterday. Why have they been left here? To protect them from the flies, they have been wrapped in their parachutes, and in accordance with tradition, they will be buried in them, without coffins. In their great white cocoons, they lie among the broken rosebushes like recumbent statues. Not far from them, two Egyptian soldiers—whom they killed, or who killed them—are also waiting to return to the dust, but they are wrapped only in torn old tent cloths and in their jackets burned by the bullets that killed them. Their heads are bare and their legs stick out from under the canvas. Wherever their skin is exposed, it is covered with little black insects, which are particularly thick about the eyes and mouth.

The artillery fire has momentarily stopped. Our colonel is parleying with the Port Said commandant. The population is without water and starving. Let the town surrender unconditionally, proposes the colonel, and the water will be turned on again. The city could not possibly hold out more than a few days, surrounded as it is on all sides. The British are arriving in force by sea, and we have already cut all the land communications.

But, in defiance of all logic, the commandant not only refuses to surrender, but swears he will distribute his large stock of new weapons to all the civilians in the city and its suburbs—and this he does, with a contribution from the Soviet ambassador. The British squadron resumes its bombardment, and we renew our advance.

That same evening, the British paratroops enter Port Said, and we, Port Fouad. The British Centurion tanks make contact with our company, and the whole city is surrounded and taken.

But it's not all over. We have to take over several kilometers along the canal, and make contact with the Israelis. We therefore start off at an infernal pace for El Qantara. There is practically nothing to stop us now. The Egyptians are in full retreat, leaving behind their weapons, their baggage, and even their shoes, so they can run faster. In less than two days, we have captured quantities of ultramodern equipment and several hundred prisoners. Passage through the canal has been restored to England and France. The victory is total.

We are only two kilometers from El Qantara, and in the excitement of our advance have even forgotten the time of day, when, suddenly, we are stopped dead by a general order, or rather countercommand, so incredible we at first think it a joke. "Stop! All further advance forbidden..."

"The captain's gone crazy," say we. And crazy he certainly is, but with rage. On all fronts, everybody comes to a halt. We even draw back a little, utterly bewildered. Politics has won. "Ambition for which one does not have capacity is a crime."

"...Advance, retreat, get up, lie down, get up, lie down!" So simple! "Go die, little soldiers, it's an order." The little soldiers go. "Orders canceled, come back..." Too late. The dead are dead, irrevocably. They will not come back. That's war, we say. What's done, is done. Life goes on—for the others.

Again, we dig holes in the sand for the night. But we no longer know which way to turn.

Whether this Egyptian affair was justified was not for us to judge, but it did fall to us to stomach the shame, the ridicule, the ignominy of retreating as if disgracefully beaten, after we had won.

So, here we are, stuck in the sand, forbidden to fire a single shot. Landing barges come and get us. We've barely time to destroy the fine new 30-mm. cannons we captured at the risk of our lives! They have to be left where they are. They're not transportable! On the other hand, we carry off armfuls of machine guns, bazookas, and Russian and Czecho-slovakian rifles.

Even so, we have conquered, not only the city, but a long strip of the canal, which we shall not give up until the arrival of the U.N. "troops." From the barges, we are able to estimate the magnitude of the battle. On both banks, there are many buildings still burning, and from time to time collapsing into the black water. At the mouth of the canal, several steamers, that the Egyptians scuttled in the hope of keeping out our fleets, point their dripping, broken hulls to the sky. In among them, float wreckage and dead bodies.

We land in Port Fouad. Our comrades, the "marines," are already there. Port Said proper, the parent and twin city, is reserved by the British for themselves. Everything is still burning. The air is as black as the water. A company of Bérets verts covers our disembarkation. The city is not yet entirely safe.

# 53

Port Fouad is a pretty town, mostly European. But the destruction is so complete that everything has taken on a tragic mask.

The first thing we see as we go ashore is a confused heap of Egyptian troop transport trucks, still burning, with ma-chine guns twisted and tires melted. From under one of the motors protrudes a half-incinerated body. All the streets are strewn with wreckage. A few dead too. But, above all, quantities of matériel, even on lawns, which have been ruined by tanks. Palm trees are blazing like torches. The whole city reeks of fire, grease, metal, gasoline, powder, and carrion.

Pineapple and crabmeat cans, some empty, some un-opened, are strewn about everywhere, among empty ammunition crates and all sorts of bottles. The huge American warehouses along the wharf had been broken into, first by the Egyptians, and then by us. They contained enormous supplies of luxury food and beverages, including frozen turkeys and cases of Scotch whisky. We pay no attention to the canned goods, but fill our packs with bottles. For several weeks, whisky and turkey are the staples of our diet.

A man in striped pajamas staggers toward us, held up by two fellow citizens also in pajamas—which are worn here like suits. We laugh. His friends let go of him and run away, but he keeps on, shouting and laughing, twitching like a jumping jack, threatening us with his fist. When he gets to the stacked rifles, the sentry beats him off and laughs in his face.

The man is crazy, and the confusion of this war is so like the confusion of his own mind that he is simply delighted. This is the biggest day of his life, and he has been making the most of it. We had just come out of our landing barge unshaved and armed to the teeth, like Hieronymus Bosch's madmen out of their ship. He took us for kindred spirits and, at the risk of being machine-gunned, came to enjoy our company. A little while before, the Bérets verts had seen him on the docks, drunk as a lord. Now, he is dragging himself along the ground, drooling. We don't know what to do with him, and soon forget him. He finally collapses on the scorched lawn, croaks a few times, kicks his legs, and fixes us with a ridiculous, horrible stare. A symbol.

The looting of the warehouses goes on for days, despite the sentinels. We find all sorts of strange objects, from Swiss cuckoo clocks to American ashtrays. Ships used to stock up here, before continuing around the world. There are quantities of gin and cognac. Tremendous all-day drinking parties. "Amid the worst misfortunes," said Bossuet, "we are still capable of joy."

We leave the warehouses. Protected by machine guns mounted on armored cars, we march in step across the whole of the devastated city to barracks on the other side of it: these barracks were built by the British for the crews of the two great 220-mm. naval guns—which they left pointed at the sea when they departed, and by which their own ships were bombarded yesterday. On our way, we cross the magnificent fairways of the golf course, so long lovingly kept up by the

British. The clubhouse has been wrecked by shells and no longer looks very distinguished. Tennis balls and broken hockey sticks are scattered all over the lawn, among fragments of glass and unexploded shells.

With fixed bayonets, we enter the abandoned barracks. Everything points to a hasty and disorderly retreat. Tons of ammunition, matériel, and rations have been left behind. For several days our company will be the only link between the city and the desert surrounding it on all sides, while the rest of the regiment is installed in the city's most luxurious palaces. Our captain is furious, for the second time. Why, when we were the first into Egypt, do we have to be quarantined like this? At the risk of serious trouble from the colonel, who has his own ideas of precedence, he has us assemble with weapons and baggage. An hour after arriving, in the midst of getting settled, we are leaving! At that moment, a messenger from the colonel arrives in a cloud of dust. The captain receives a paper, which he reads in evident exasperation. "Break ranks and go back into your barracks!" he shouts to us with fire in his eye.

The barracks are well furnished. Those whose instinct is always to "salvage" ("salvage" is a much used word here, and also the expression: "c'est normal!") whatever has, or hasn't, any value, are in the seventh heaven. There is endless booty here. With the Egyptian officers' feather mattresses, we make ourselves regal couches for the night, and even surround ourselves with the unheard-of luxury of furniture. We soon feel at home.

The two 220-mm. naval guns, over thirty feet long, weighing several tons, but so perfectly balanced on their electric pivots that they are easily moved by a mere touch of the hand, are magnificent monsters of fine steel. Several gigantic empty shells at their breaches indicate that at least a few shots were fired at our fleet, though so unskillfully and in such panic that they cannot have done much damage. Fascinated by the beauty of these formidable contrivances, from time to time one of us unconsciously pats the perfect curve of the long shining shells, so heavy that it takes two men to lift them. Others watch the Fleet in full force swaying idly before us.

We admire the very pretty electric firing system, which has only one drawback: the moment the current is cut off, there is nothing to do but retreat, through a shower of shells... On the breach of each gun is a trademark, engraved in fine English style: MADE IN BIRMINGHAM. From breach to muzzle, they shine as if sand-papered.

On the ground, among bullet-riddled sandbags and a few dead bodies, lies the sight of one of the guns, undamaged. "He who has the sight," they say in the artillery, "has the gun." So, not being able to take the gun, I take its sight instead. I keep this terribly complicated device for a long time, with its bubble levels and British graduations, study it in idle hours, and even try to take it apart. Eventually, however, its weight obliges me regretfully to part with it.

The food provided for the soldiers of the New Egypt makes us wonder. Their storerooms contain nothing but tons and tons of tiny packages of dried dates, preserved bananas, and white biscuits full of black insects. No vegetables of any sort, but heaps of cans of "Madagascar Beef," with genuine French labels on them. Nothing to drink but water, and what little there is of that is brackish. There are very few faucets—perhaps the British carried them off? Not a single shower. How do Egyptian soldiers wash?

The stocks of clothing are richer. Huge piles of combat uniforms just like the ones in the caves at Djeurf. This must be the main supply house. We also find fine English sneakers and immediately put them on instead of our old jump boots that are stiff with sweat and sand.

Not a blade of grass anywhere around the buildings, not even a cactus. Nothing but sand, littered with tin cans and rags.

Suddenly, a sound of footsteps behind one of the sheds. We cock our submachine guns. Could this be some Egyptian soldier left behind in the rout? No, a gigantic and very embarrassed camel. She refuses to have anything to do with us, and runs off, bleating, with her enormous legs flying in every direction. We catch up with her, talk to her, pat her on the back: "Take it easy, old girl! Take it easy!" How lovely she is, with her big flabby humps, her enormous nostrils, and her lips pendulous with boredom and disdain. "Are you hungry?" We gorge the noble animal with packages of preserved fruit, to which she seems very partial, and with bananas. We give her water, and get her to lie down. Her two humps shiver with contentment, ans she is unanimously adopted.

She is a quiet, unobtrusive mascot, though she likes to

rest her big head on our shoulders when she thinks we are forgetting her. She follows us everywhere, even into the corridors, though she has a terrible time getting her big body through, and she parades majestically through the dormitories, where she sleeps at night, curled up like an antediluvian cat. Rides on the beach astride her great back, at a walk, or a trot, or even at a gallop, become the 1st Company's greatest amusement.

Tucked away between the waves of sand surounding us, there are a few little shanties that the artillerymen overlooked. Ragged Egyptians, half civilians, half soldiers, are still wandering about among them. We catch several. We could easily take advantage of the disorder and just shoot them, as others wouldn't hesitate to do for sport. But what's the use? Haven't hostilities been suspended? We're content to bring them back to camp as prisoners and use them for chores. They're lucky: a few days earlier, a burst of submachine-gun fire would have laid them forever in the sand.

The handsome villas constructed by the Suez Canal Company for its resident personnel are unharmed, and most of the occupants have had time to move out their belongings. All are carefully locked. But there is talk that a few Egyptian soldiers who didn't have time to get away may still be hiding in them. Any private investigating is about to be forbidden, because there were quite a few women raped in the city, and even some very young girls, also a number of shops were looted and some European apartments wrecked. But today nothing is as yet settled, so we climb the brick garden walls, break in the glass doors, and inspect some of these villas. All are empty. How deeply sad is a house when there's nothing left alive in it but the marks on the walls where pictures used to be.

It will take us several weeks to fully realize that, though conquerors, we are also vanquished. Throughout this time, our generals, who at first bowed to the orders of their governments, attempt to retrieve the situation. One evening, we even make up our packs, draw ammunition, clean our weapons, and remain at order arms till morning, ready to move on El Qantara. A telephoned order stops us at the last moment.

The first casualty list indicates sixty of our regiment wounded. The hospital ship takes them on board. Our thirteen dead, we bury almost secretly in the sand, behind the barracks. A fourteenth, listed as missing, is found a few days later, riddled with bullets, behind what had been the enemy lines. On the morning of the jump, his parachute opened wrong and caught on the tail of the Nord 2501 that was carrying him. He hung there till the planes were heading back to Cyprus, then fell, long after all the others, into a group of Egyptian soldiers who were running away but found time to massacre him.

We are said to have killed several hundred Egyptians, and to have taken a still greater number of prisoners, who continue to come in from all directions. Most of ours are nice young fellows who threw down their fine new weapons without even being asked to, and surrendered right away. They seem quite pleased to have had the war end so well for them.

With fixed bayonets, but good-naturedly, our sentinels keep them busy on details around the camp. No one thinks of maltreating them. They have food and drink, and beds about like ours. In short, this isn't very different from the barracks life they had before.

Among these poor devils, there's an officer. Though he surrendered just as fast as the others did, he nevertheless has that haughty air characteristic of so many officers. You wonder why he hasn't got a swagger stick—probably lost it running away. He's just as much a prisoner as his men, but he continually scolds and bullies them, staring scornfully at the French sentinel, who couldn't care less.

Unfortunately for him, there comes a moment when the sentinel is D.R. There is nothing mean about this D.R., but he doesn't like officers' putting on airs, whatever army they're in. He therefore definitely wants to humiliate this officer before his men. As there's still a room left to clean, he holds the broom out to him. The man doesn't move. The Egyptian soldiers look on with interest, and with some amusement and satisfaction: everybody is having his turn!

R. gets tired of holding that broom in one hand and his gun in the other, and he finally throws the broom at the officer. It lands on the floor. The Egyptian hesitates a second, bends down, picks up the broom, and throws it in R.'s face, on which he lands a resounding slap at the same time.

R. goes white, but doesn't move. The officer waits, probably for us to fall on him and tie him, but R. beckons us to stand back. Very pale, without a word, he pumps a cartridge into the barrel of his Mas 36, clac, clac. The regulations are explicit: slapping a sentinel in wartime is aggravated rebellion, and the penalty is death. I have full right to shoot this filthy "boukak" on the spot, in fact it's my duty! says R. to himself. The officer is leaning against the wall, still not making the slightest move: R. lowers the barrel of his rifle—whereupon the captain, who, unnoticed, had seen the whole thing, puts his hand on R.'s shoulder, and, with a tense look on his face, stops him. "Follow me with that individual!"

He turns on his heel and heads for the sea, across the dunes, followed by two of us, with the prisoner in between. The latter's scorn is withering. He doesn't condescend to look at anybody, even the captain. He is still thinking: The war is over. Tomorrow I'll be free, and my men will be telling about my courage. The group stops on the shore. The captain gives a brief order. Someone cocks his submachine gun. The haughty face turns from bronze to gray. He opens his mouth to speak: "I . . . I . . . "—but the bullets are on the way. The man falls in a heap. "That's that," says the captain. "Good job . . . A prisoner is sacred, but so's a sentinel. Get him buried in a hurry, after the last bullet."

Sergeant S., a good Alsatian with infinite respect for army regulations, resented that slap as if it had been on his own cheek. He asks for a rifle and fixes the bayonet, the long slender bayonet of the Mas 36, sharp and round like a rat's tail, but with four grooves, for the blood. And, bending over the man, who may be not yet dead, instead of giving him the usual coup de grâce with a pistol, he pierces his chest twice, with two precise little motions. The two round holes do not make one drop of blood. We bury the body in three minutes, in the soft, watery sand. The sea is near and will soon carry it off.

In the afternoon, we go crabbing on one of the Zodiacs the Navy commandos left here when they landed, then we lie about, almost naked, in the sun. In the evening, we do a little private exploring in some desolate territory where there are still quite a few fishermen's cabins to look over. Most of them are tucked away behind sand dunes and practically invisible. We find food, chickens to carry off, sometimes the corpse of a civilian lying in front of a cupboard. All the cabins have already been looted, but so superficially that there's still lots to do. From time to time, we are assailed by a pestilential smell, and discover a group of dead Egyptian soldiers behind a cabin, among the ammunition crates, at the bottom of a caved-in trench.

Despite the cease-fire, boatloads of French and British troops are endlessly pouring in to support us. In anticipation of a possible surprise attack by the Egyptian army, which has had time to recover and would have little trouble provoking us, we are starting to regroup. One morning, we leave our sand-blown barracks for the comfortable Canal Company villas in the heart of the city, where many of our comrades are billeted. From the balcony of our new residence, we can admire the white minaret on the edge of the wide blue canal and, near at hand, an elegant palm that lifts its head above the spotless walls.

The war is indeed over. The marks of street fighting disappear. A few civilians and even a few Egyptian policemen—first without their guns, then with them, but without car-tridges or bayonets—begin to animate the streets. As an exceptional favor, we even get a few leaves to visit Port Said. The ferryboat is resuming service. Mingling, always in pairs, with the most mixed population on earth, we once again play tourists, our favorite game.

The city has been badly hit by the war. Many houses were split open from top to bottom by the long-range guns of the Royal Navy. A section of the Arab city—the poorest, made up entirely of five- and six-story wooden buildings—was burned. Some accuse the British, others the Egyptians themselves. Anyway, there's nothing left but ashes, very dirty ones too. Where can the people who lived here have taken refuge?

In this city where everyone, from the youngest to the oldest, from the richest to the poorest, is a seller of something, they speak every language: Greek, French, English, Yiddish, Spanish, Turkish, Arabic. As we go by, the merchants, like earthworms after a storm, emerge from the cellars where they were hiding. They appear furtively in doorways, lay hold of us with a mixture of timidity and impudence, and try to get us to pay high prices for worthless objects that, three days ago, we wouldn't have stooped to pick up.

Food is scarcer than ever. British troops are guarding a warehouse containing flour in sacks that have been burst open and are crawling with vermin the size of a finger. People had been stealing it, in spite of the risk of poisoning.

We are scattered about, a half squad of five or six men to a villa, with nothing to do but pace up and down in the silent rooms. As there have been several more incidents in town, we can get practically no more leaves. We are just waiting, without even knowing what for, and so bored we can't speak.

To combat the depression, we try no matter what. Even reading. But all we can get to read is the anemic, sentimental publications distributed by the Red Cross. These "novels" are so dismally silly that one can't possibly read three pages of them without being more bored than before. As for the cloak and dagger adventures of the Paul Févals and the Michel Zevacos, we outgrew them years ago. We spend whole afternoons sitting on our folded blankets with our heads in our hands.

Shooting practice with the captured weapons has been organized in the sand fields surrounding the city. But these Czechoslovakian bazookas have muzzles so much like their breaches that one of our comrades nearly burns one of his arms off.

One Sunday, a comrade and I wander into some sort of Coptic church. They are having a mass, all full of incense and salaams and big fraternal kisses. We're soon noticed and put out, after being sprinkled with holy water.

A week after the burial of our regiment's dead, a great ceremony to honor all the dead of Force H brings out a few generals and some sort of cabinet minister. As there are no amusements any more, many come to it as to a party. While the list of dead—much longer than we'd thought—is being read before the eight hundred men at attention, I have the

sad honor of responding, after each name, with the traditional
"mort pour la France." It takes so long that at the end no one
is listening.

The Arab Quarter, in which Egyptian commandos are
said to be still circulating, is strictly forbidden to soldiers. A
British lieutenant is later murdered there and found folded
up in the trunk of a car. I go in often, however, curious to
learn more about this miserably poor population I see walking about barefoot, in ragged pajamas, in the dreary sunlight.
The sordid wooden buildings have quantities of multicolored
wash hanging from their balconies. These narrow streets with
their foul open drains belong to the Middle Ages, and are full
of ill-tempered quarreling children, whose faces are already
old. Nobody ever smiles. And I can't even get the eye of a
single one of these terrifyingly thin men who walk tottering
with hunger along the walls. Some look so weary of this war
that one feels they would like to bite.

As I make my way through all this, the people observe
me with disapproval. They all know, even though their radios
have been confiscated, that the U.N. troops are about to
replace us, and many eyes express insolence as well as fear.

While photographing some little girls running about
barefood in the mud, I suddenly sense hostile vibrations
behind me. I immediately turn around. Five or six men,
barefoot too, and unshaved, are staring at me in a semicircle.
One shouts something at me, threateningly. His companions
are rousing the neighborhood. They are making signs to each
other. Are they about to leap on my back like enraged cats
and tear off my insignia, before joyfully hacking me to pieces?

Not a soldier anywhere. A crowd is gathering. I take my
photograph all the same, very quickly. The man who first
shouted at me leaves the others and comes toward me with
an ugly look. This time, my boy, say I to myself, you're like a
rat in a trap. The others are also coming up fast. Almost
instinctively, I draw the big black 9-mm. pistol that hangs at
my belt, cock it with a sharp click, and brandish it in front of
me, very level, barrel outstretched. One instant of carelessness,
and I am done for.

Growling, rather like animals, they slowly break their
circle. And I pass through, very slowly.

*  *  *

**M 1950 Cal. 9 mm.**

Whole shiploads of blue-helmeted U.N. troops are beginning to land. They go about Port Fouad in pairs with their
big shiny wooden rifles on their backs. Their gingerbread
complexion proves pretty clearly that they've come straight
from South America. And, to hear them chatter, you'd think
they were macaws. These elegent pygmies have probably
never used their rifles. We don't have anything to do with
them. To us, they look futile.

Our last few nights in Egypt are enlivened by some
pretty brisk skirmishing. To show it is they who are putting
us out, Egyptian irregulars infiltrate our lines, disguised as
fellahs. Relying on the protection of the little U.N. soldiers,
they "bump off" a few of our sentries, both in Port Said and
in Port Fouad. Our captains feel this would be a sufficient
*casus belli* for a resumption of hostilities. But the staff plays
dead. Usually, it is the British who are attacked, for Egypt
hates them with an incredible hatred. Moreover, they're not
content to return tit for tat like bored players, the way we do.
They "raise the ante" every time, and with a vengeance.

One night, under mysterious circumstances, there is a

second big fire in the Arab city. A whole section of it bursts into flames amid a pandemonium of gunfire. In the morning, thirty-three dead civilians are picked up, some of them possibly soldiers out of uniform. The high flames of war dance till dawn in the waters of the gleaming canal.

Two days later, it's goodbye. In a ceremony at which everybody is uncomfortable, our colonel transfers his powers to a colonel of the international forces. That's the end. Except for the military installations, we leave Port Fouad intact. The British, though, carry off everything, even the doorknobs.

Under the protection of naval guns trained on the shore, we march in step, singing, down to the landing craft, and they take us to the *Athos II*, which is waiting offshore. We were the first to arrive in Egypt, and the last to leave it.

The old ship moves slowly out of the devastated port and glides on past the perfect line of the warships. The flagship pays us honors, with her entire crew drawn up at attention on deck. And, as the officers salute us and the sailors present arms, the band strikes up the marine infantry hymn. All this is very moving, no doubt about it. But we are not deceived. The discouragement is general.

# 54

We have a rough seven-day voyage on our old ship. She used to ply to the Far East, but is now fit only for Middle Eastern runs—till she winds up on the Marseilles–Algiers crossing, or the bottom. They say that all that keeps the water out of her now is her innumerable coats of paint: underneath there's nothing but rust.

The voyage does not diminish our boredom. In more than one heart, it overflows, and the least talkative will tell his life story to anybody, for instance Sergeant V., whose hammock is next to mine.

"I wanted to be a hero," he says. "As a civilian, I couldn't be one. Everything irritated me. How can a man be a hero in the subway at eight in the morning, jammed in a crowd of white-collar coolies? I know, I know, the hero is the man who does what he can. I wanted to do more, no matter what, but more, right away. So I volunteered at eighteen, like so many others. For adventure, mainly. I'm too fond of liberty to really like the army. Adventure! That was the only thing that made sense to me. I craved it.

"I've been to Indochina three times. I was wounded five times, but I always went back—for adventure! I never found it, either among the Moïs, or in the jungle, where the leaves are like hands and the vines like women's bodies. I said to myself: 'Keep on! You'll find it some day, and the more you have suffered, the more beautiful it will be!' But I never did. Even the death of comrades seemed insignificant. Even the suffering—mosquitoes, thorns, blood—was meaningless. Even my wounds...Look."

He shows me his chest, furrowed and sewn together from shoulder to shoulder. I ask: "Shrapnel?"

"Yes. And that," he points to a badly scarred leg, "a grenade. Even Dien Bien Phu...The Viets captured me there, gun in hand, among the last ones. Even that was of no real interest. Now they've made fools of us again in Egypt. Seven years in Indo, two years in Algeria, three weeks in Egypt. Total: zero! I feel empty and dried up, useless. I don't want to be useful any more. I don't want to be used! I don't want to die! And I'm alone. Twenty-eight, paratroop sergeant, unmarried, médaille militaire, croix de guerre, seven citations. I don't exist! No hope, nor even despair. Adventure doesn't exist!

"Oh, I could get out and settle down, tired of waiting for the impossible. My parents are rich. I could marry, and have my glass of brandy, my car, my cigar, my Sunday afternoon walk, with a bank account, television, respectability, office, slippers, little woman, and all the rest of it—especially as I've been able to save quite a nest egg during my ten years in the service! But I don't want any of that, and I never will. Not because I believe in 'bagarre' and all the movie nonsense about the war. No. But I'd rather be fooled. Even if death is ugly, stupid, dirty, it's better than a life you lead because you can't do anything else. So, I'll be 'brave,' till a bullet in the face ends the whole business. If there could only be some adventure besides getting killed—which certainly is horrible, but no worse than being a civilian and beginning the daily grind over and over again every morning—how I would throw myself into it. But it's too late. I know more about death than about life!"

Having got that off his chest, he rolls over in his hammock and says not another word for the rest of the day. I know that all my comrades, or nearly all, have said these same things to themselves, and that this whole ship is thinking them tonight.

The only observance of Christmas is an abbreviated mass, sung without conviction in the ship's storeroom. We are too used to doing everything on an order to be able to put our heart into anything. We lie in our dirty gray hammocks, down in the smelly, creaking hold, and talk only in whispers, as if we were dying.

When his fit of depression is over, Sergeant V. takes several little typewritten notebooks out of his pack and begins looking through them. Noticing my surprise, he explains that, having never gone beyond primary school, he decided last year to study for the baccalauréat, which he has to have if he is ever to be an officer. These notebooks were sent him by the correspondence courses of one of the big Paris schools. He intends to study as regularly as he can. And he certainly does, with unbelievable determination and courage.

I will often watch him in the days to come when, just back from the most exhausting operations, the rest of us will collapse limply on our beds with no thought but sleep, while he will quietly take out his notebooks and doggedly set to work. And he will do this as he has done everything else in his life, with enormous—maybe even with an excess of—willpower. But it is his way, without his knowing it, of trying to attain a manner of perfection.

When it finally gets dark, the men come up one by one from the bowels of the ship to take a few breaths of sea air. Shivering with cold, groups of them walk up and down the deck, very slowly, with lowered heads, silently thinking about this failure of a war and, very often, the failure of their lives. All the suffering accumulated in the holds has risen to the surface.

\* \* \*

Algiers. We are gliding into the harbor, which is veiled in dirty gray fog. The Egyptian War is over.

Despite the December rain which really pours just as we dock, there is a large crowd on the pier. We had been expected since morning. An army band, lined up in the deluge and lashed by the cold wind, salutes us, and then, notwithstanding the water in the brasses, strikes up a terrific "Marseillaise." The crowd, attracted by the noise, closes up and cheers us wildly. "Héros!... héros!" they shout. "Et ron! Et ron!" jeers Bernard, who loathes demonstrations like this, especially in the rain. "Et ron, ron, ron, petit patapon!" he roars, putting to his lips the bottle of beer that is handed to him.

For, besides a little crowd of generals and "officials," there is a whole bevy of Red Cross ladies, in the front rank of the crowd and practically holding out their arms to us. They are crowded around the foot of the gangplank that we are going down one by one, and smilingly jostling each other for a chance to offer us cookies, and bottles. We are so encumbered by our packs and weapons that we are quite unable to take hold of all these things. But they slip their offerings into the wide pockets of our jackets. Hurray for France, hurray for Algeria, hurray for them, hurray for us! Wild excitement... Poor people! Women are crying with emotion. For the past three years our path has been strewn with women in tears. There's an enormous amount of weeping, south of the Loire.

## 55

Slightly drunk, we climb into the wet trucks that have been waiting for us since dawn. One by one, the companies are dropped off in the villages around Algiers.

We are assigned to Bou Haroun, a village of Italian fishermen, and we set down our packs on the floor of a fish factory that nearly chokes us with its smell of sardines.

The fishermen of Bou Haroun have noticed that in their quiet streets we sometimes laugh, but never smile, and they have divined our low spirits. With that infinite delicacy so rarely found except among the "lower classes"—because in place of money they have room for a heart—on the 1st of January they individually invite us all to come and celebrate the New Year *en famille*.

The whole family is standing about the round table, waiting for me. They are standing in my honor. A soldier comes to have a horror of honors, which often conceal ingratitude or indifference, but this evening they touch me. The best seat has been saved for me, a chair decorated with a red cushion covered with an embroidered doily. I ought to smile. But, on seeing it, I become sad, terribly sad...

... I love the young girl sitting on my right. She has the unbelievable beauty of all very young Italian girls. I love her, though she will never know it, and I love her father, the fisherman on my left, who, again in my honor, has put on an extraordinary black suit, suggestive both of a first communion costume and of an undertaker's. And I also love my young friend's mother, that woman with the chignon of gray hair. And I love all those little brothers of hers, whose chins hardly reach the edge of the table. I am forgetting that I'm a soldier. And I am seized with a wild desire never to go back to Paris, to rid myself of all the nonsense of my soldier's life, to get out of this uniform that cuts me off from the world of people who are really alive, to become a man among these free, quiet men. And to spend my life here, in uneventful happiness... A happiness into which would creep neither guile nor ugliness, nor luxury even...

I imagine that this pretty girl here beside me, so sweet and so perceptive, always smiling as if smiles were her only language, is my wife, my young wife. And that my whole life is still intact and in my hands. And that I am giving it to her. And that we are entering this small white house. That it is our home. And that we are free, because no one in this village can pretend to be our superior, and because we have no inferiors either. And that we love each other! And that... And that...

The temptation of happiness is strong. I forget to make replies. I only smile. The hours go by. Time doesn't matter. This really is happiness. How easy it was.

In the evening, I go out fishing with the father and all the other men of the village. I get back in the early dawn, not a bit tired after hauling well-filled nets all night long. Never has the Algerian night been so beautiful.

But now the company is moving. We are leaving Bou Haroun for Castiglione. Though no one was told about it, the entire village is out to see us off. The trucks start noisily, drowning out our goodbyes. And no one feels like laughing at the white handkerchiefs being waved in our honor along the road.

At Castiglione, we go back to the Villa Djeniene El Afia where we spent a month of our wandering life before leaving for Egypt.

It will soon be three years. The captain calls us together. He wants to know whether we are going to re-enlist, for two or five years. On his table is a long statement to sign. Most of my comrades sign it without reading a word, just as when they first volunteered. Even the worst grumblers. They sign absentmindedly, without thinking: in fact, it's a long time since they've thought of anything really important. Nor do I read this long contract that is handed to me. But I don't sign it. The captain's good-natured smile vanishes. I see the corners of his mouth go down. He knows me, but, all the same, he wouldn't have believed it. "So?" he says, ironically. "Back to the soft life? Adventure, excitement, service . . . over for good? . . ." I wait for him to finish. I salute. About face. And out I go.

We have a few more easy days, and resume life here just where we left off. While the staff overhauls the regiments damaged in the Egyptian affair, we renew our idylls along the beach, which winter has nearly depopulated. Once more the moonlit sands are crossed by shadows that embrace every ten steps, tottering with love.

I use the time for a bit of sightseeing. Every afternoon I thumb rides along the coast, to Bérard, Chiffalo, Tipasa, Zéralda, Koléa—as far as Cherchell to the left, and Algiers to the right. All these little Algerian towns are charming, provided they are right on the sea and inhabited by fishermen. Here the Europeans and Arabs live together like brothers, fishing for the same fish, and getting the same price. But the differences separating natives and colonists begin on the other side of the coast road, and increase the farther you go into the interior, as does the hatred in the unsmiling faces.

Algiers has taken on the aspect of war. There are as many soldiers now as civilians. The tension has obviously increased during our absence. You cannot go two hundred yards without meeting a patrol, moving silently and rapidly through the streets. The Arabs hardly ever come out of the Casbah any more, and the pockets of most civilians are bulging with weapons.

The 2nd R.P.C. continues its château life in Castiglione. It seems that we were heroes in Egypt, and we are only too willing to be told so. We can't be heroes without hero worshipers. One family invites me to lunch, and even to dinner, as many times as there are days in the week. I am gradually resuming civilian ways I had thought forever lost. I begin to regard my uniform as an incongruity. We are enjoying the advantages of civilian life—without any of its disadvantages.

Our commanders see the danger. We're off again. But where? This time, no one knows—till we suddenly find out to our astonishment that it's only Algiers. But we're going with weapons and packs and the whole baggage train, followed by quartermasters, secretaries and all the rest. This couldn't be for a parade. Could we be going home?

Far from it. The battle of Algiers is beginning.

## 56

Algiers has become a battlefield. In the name of liberty, the dignity of man, and a few other things, terrorists and counterterrorists are spreading bloodshed and confusion, slaughtering each other night and day, in buildings and in the open street, with grenades, bombs and guns. The police are swamped; sometimes they just hide. Our turn to join the party.

For three months, our life will be ugly. We shall be doing the hard and thankless job of policemen. A few will enjoy it, others will be miserable, some won't be affected one way or the other, but the majority will regret the mountains, where they were only asked to fight an enemy capable of self-defense. Here it will be all street-corner ambushes, secret arrests, foul play, and murder—with a pistol in your pocket, or a grenade, and sometimes even handcuffs.

We arrive in Algiers at dusk and camp the first night in the street, under old rotten tents, as if we were out in the bush. The next day we camp (though it's January) in the courtyard of the Hussein Dey barracks. From their dormitory windows, the astonished recruits watch us pitch our tents in the driving rain on muddy soil full of old paving stones. The old tents leak, the guy ropes are rotten, and we're short of tent pegs. Lovely day.

The very night we arrive, we have our first patrol in town. We shall wear out more shoes in three months of this patrolling than in a year of campaigns. Night and day, every half hour, from every one of our bases (which are scattered all over Algiers), commandos of from four to twelve men will set forth silently into the city to make a tireless check of avenues, streets, alleys, even the stairways in buildings. The mission of these teams will be to ferret everywhere and to spy on everybody.

We shall be responsible for surveillance of the entire population. And, as we have to watch everything, we shall soon have practically full license to arrest anybody without explanation, without even a warrant, simply by the authority of our submachine guns. We shall give orders to the regular police—in fact, we will soon be the only police. Men, women and children—at first only the Arabs, but later the Europeans too—all will be under our unlimited power. No building, public or private, will be closed to us, and many a time we shall do what has never been permitted the Paris police, enter people's houses at night without just cause. No one will be secure against our investigations.

For some of us, this new work will be a veritable revelation. Several are so enthusiastic about it that, instead of re-enlisting in the "paras," they go to the C.R.S.[1] School, so as to be able to do all their lives what as paratroopers they could only hope to do occasionally: kill people in the streets with the authorization of their government.

---

[1] Compagnies Républicaines de Sécurité.

What a pleasure to grasp the shoulder of a passerby, read the terror in his eyes, and press the muzzle of a submachine gun against his stomach. And what a delight to search a trembling woman from head to foot in the street. And what an ecstasy if she is young, supple, and naked under her dress. What a joy to humiliate people. Just the life for a no-account who as a civilian would not be worthy to shine the shoes of the man he's now seizing by the collar!

The F.L.N. is preparing a general strike of all Arab workers. It is to be political and insurrectionary, and its essential point is to enable the rebels to count their numbers. For us, the danger is very great. All Arabs are, of course, already under suspicion as such, but still only vaguely so. As we can't arrest and kill everybody, we must at all costs prevent this strike. We've got to beat them, no matter how, before they get ahead of us. We must search systematically, everywhere, everybody, take the initiative, not wait, strike blindly, but strike. Nine unjust blows, if necessary, to one that's just.

As the most dangerous outlaws have sometimes taken refuge in the most private establishments, we very secretly organize an expedition one evening to the most taboo building of all, more closed to Europeans than the most sacred mosque—the Arab baths.

We go in at dusk, two by two, through all the doors. The doorkeepers don't have time to give the alarm. They're made to stand quietly, close to the wall, with their hands up and a submachine gun in their back. We move on into the corridors. Nothing but laundry and steam, the acrid steam that comes from washtubs. Empty room after empty room. This building is immense. Suddenly, we hear vague murmuring. "Behind that door, perhaps?" We give it a push.

We are on the threshold of an enormous room full of heavy white steam. These aren't rebels we're looking at, but about thirty completely naked young women. They are scrubbing themselves, playing under the water, or standing motionless like voluptuous statues and letting the warm steam caress their pale gleaming bodies. They've not seen us, for we have learned to open doors noiselessly. Here and there about the room, a few women are lying on couches, and others, just as naked as they, are massaging them with slow, lascivious gestures. The scene arouses sensuality to the point of pain.

Then, one of the women comes toward us. Her supple body dances softly as she walks. Not till she almost bumps into us does she notice our presence. She gives a fearful shriek and instinctively tries to cover herself with her hands. The scene changes. The chamber of delights becomes a battlefield. The women on the couches get up in horror. The four smooth walls of blue tile, are as bare as they are. There's only one door, and we're blocking that. They run wildly all over the room like caged animals, screaming and bumping into the walls. In their ever increasing terror, they hurt each other, or slip and fall on the wet floors. Their faces are distorted. Finally they just stand in front of us, shaking from head to foot, too frightened to move. One of them faints.

Standing there in the steam, with our submachine guns in our hands, we feel ridiculous and ignoble. We pick up the unconscious woman . . . But other comrades of ours burst into the room, and soon there is total confusion . . .

We never found out whether this was all a monstrous joke, or a mistake, or an authentic mission. The affair caused much comment. But the Arab women made no complaint, perhaps because ashamed that French soldiers had caught them with nothing on. The matter went no further.

Later there were other "pacifications" of Arab baths. But perpetrators and victims alike always kept very quiet about them.

The bars and cafés are favorite places to investigate. Patrols rarely leave till the proprietor "treats" them to coffee or liquor. The fashion is for all to go in together, like cowboys entering a saloon in the Far West.

Maltreated by everybody, searched every five minutes— and half, if not wholly, stripped—by the patrols, who bat them back and forth to each other like tennis balls, the Arabs don't dare go out any more, except for indispensable provisions. They never know if they'll get home.

Because of too scandalous abuses, we received an order a week after the "Battle of Algiers" began. It set limits beyond which we were not to go, but it was so phrased that we could ignore it. We must not search women—except in special cases. We must not arrest Europeans, or enter people's houses at night—except when necessary. In fact, every patrol leader, in connivance with his men, does just about as he pleases. After several rebel leaders are caught in women's clothes, we make a point of searching Arab women. Despite their lamentations, they are inspected from head to foot, more meticulously than the men—it's not hard to imagine in what manner. A few naïve civilians complain to the police, but the latter are too concerned about their promotion to dare transmit complaints to us.

In Castiglione, a grenade is thrown the day after our departure—the first since 1954. Driven from the capital, the fellaghas scatter to the outskirts. Two days later, the Algiers–Koléa bus, "my" bus when I was touring in the direction of Algiers, is burned only two kilometers from a barracks. The bodies of six Europeans are found around the overturned vehicle, the Arabs who were in it having managed to get back to their villages on foot. The people in Castiglione feel that they are being singled out for having harbored us so long. They are very worried and ask to have us sent back, but we can't leave Algiers now without imperiling a great number of Europeans and Arabs who have been acting as our auxiliaries and informers. As it is, our presence does not prevent increasing numbers of individual and mass outrages in the capital.

Mixed with the F.L.N. terrorism, there are now more and more acts of violence by the as yet secret counterterrorist organizations, which give us a great deal of trouble because, some days, they succeed in killing more Arabs than the latter do Europeans. Some even set up secret interrogation chambers for "their" suspects, who are not always ours, and very few of those they "question" survive.

We soon have to arrest some of these "patriots," and before long we have as many enemies among them as among the Arabs. Even little clerks in offices and polite old gentlemen in retirement reproach us bitterly for "not killing enough rats."

I seize the first opportunity between two patrols to get to Castiglione, disguised as a civilian. The territorials shivering in the rain finally recognize me and let me through their barriers. In less than an hour, I pass from the ferocious imbecility of the army to the sweet life along one of the loveliest seas in the world.

Some of our comrades are disguised as civilians because so ordered. In flannel trousers and open collar shirt like the colonials, they are assigned to mingle in cafés with Europeans suspected of communism and get them to talk. Such is now the noble profession of arms.

We seldom sleep except in the daytime. Almost every night there are secret expeditions into the Casbah or the suburban slums. We prowl through them like wolves, drag from their beds those whose names are on our list, and return in the morning, always followed by prisoners half crazy with worry and hatred.

# 57

Algiers is now being terrorized by three armies, the F.L.N.'s, the European extremists', and ours.

At the Villa Susini, torture has become the routine method of investigation. Being mostly Germans, the Legion Bérets verts encamped there merely resume the old methods of the Gestapo. Several, who claim to be Alsatians, are in fact former S.S. men. The captain commanding the villa personally arranged and fitted out its rooms for an interrogation center.

In a fine spirit of emulation, the Bérets bleus billeted next door adopt their neighbors' methods of procedure—at first somewhat reluctantly, but soon with enthusiasm. At their "re-education camp of the Bouzaréah subsector," they operate in a big unfinished concrete building near the Place d'El-Biar, with a fine view of the beautiful Bay of Algiers. And we, the Bérets rouges, not only have our own center, in a villa overlooking the city, but each company also has its own little torture room.

I shall speak of the torture room of the 1st Company of the 2nd R.P.C., my company.

We were billeted in the big abandoned Hussein Dey candy factory. On the ground floor, besides a vast hall that was always cool—a rare thing in Algiers—there was a large, rather dark back room, full of equipment left behind by the owners. As the factory was between two adjoining buildings, this room was invisible from the street. It was also surrounded by several little dusty rooms, which made it practically soundproof—in short, an ideal torture chamber.

Every day the lieutenant on duty, assisted by Sergeant T., of the Signal Corps, and another sergeant, a very muscular Alsatian, spends several hours there. They have plenty to do. Their specially selected three-man teams operate in shifts under the benevolent eye of the captain. With interrogation for a pretext, their work really amounts to torturing naked, bound prisoners, one after another, from morning to night.

The room is well equipped. Besides the long zinc tables that had been used for making sugarplums and on which the prisoners are laid out naked when they arrive, there are a few workbench vices which prove very effective for crushing the most vulnerable parts of the human body, most frequently the sexual parts.

On the floor, big pails of water take the place of the usual bath tub. The big Alsatian loves these. With a grip that would bulldoze an ox, he slowly immerses the shaved heads of his victims, who are often suffocating with anguish before they even touch the water.

At first, they used the heavy "commando" ropes for whipping the groins or eyes of obstinate suspects, but these ropes made too many marks. Clubs, well handled, get the same results with less apparent damage.

The basic torture still is slaps, and the slaps that our Alsatian sergeant delivers at the slightest provocation on an already bruised face can drive a man crazy in less than an hour, no matter how vigorous he is. The grooved soles of his heavy jump boots also crush many trembling bare feet. The idea is to daze them with pain.

Our principal implement did not, however, exist in the Middle Ages. This refinement of civilization presents at first glance a quite innocuous appearance: simply an electric wire attached to a floor plug. Its role is to "pleasure" the most important suspects. No need for the "gégenne" familiar to so many Algerians interrogated during operations. Here there is all the electric current we could wish for. Torture by electricity, first looked upon as useful, then as indispensable, has finally come to be considered matter-of-course, just as normal and proper as any other. Besides being efficacious, it has the added advantage of leaving no marks.

The wire is very carefully installed by a Signal Corps sergeant. The end of it is perfectly bare and furnished with an insulated handle. To the bare end is added a plywood tube which is always kept wet so that the maximum of electricity will accumulate as it goes through. Two slender, pointed wires extend beyond the tube, like feelers, quivering at the slightest movement.

These little antennae are brought in direct contact with the bare skin. Generally on the sexual organs. They are also moved over the whole body, stopping for a long time on the chest, where the thoracic cavity barely protects the heart, which goes wild, causing the sufferer to bound like a wounded cat.

A refinement used by the experts on the more stubborn captives is to hold their noses till they open their mouths, and then push the antennae all the way down their throats. Sometimes, however, the man being questioned reacts to the pain with such a violent closing of his jaws that he severs the wires in one bite. We change to heavier wire.

Even if the great majority of those we interrogate are criminals of the most evil sort, there are also among them men only suspected—of, for example, harboring members of the F.L.N., or of collecting money for them; and there are some completely innocent, who, like most innocent people, cannot possibly prove it.

The ceiling of the room has an opening, through which a rope could be let down in the days of the candy factory. This hole enables us to hear the screams; and, on particularly interesting days, some of us take turns looking through it. There is talk of sealing it up, but this proves unnecessary, because, after a while everybody loses interest.

Other forms of amusement are discovered. One day, a sergeant got a bit high and then scoured the neighborhood in a truck, picking up all the Arabs he came across wearing good European clothes—without even bothering to ask for their papers. He came back with his truck completely full. After assembling his captives in the muddy courtyard, he first made them do a few squats and pushups. Then, because he saw they were trying not to get their clothes dirty, he continued with more and more strenuous exercises. "Stand up! Lie down! On your back! On your stomach! Move your legs, your arms, your head, etc." When one would collapse, completely out of breath, a good jab with a bayonet brought him to order again. We were at the windows, laughing, jostling to get a better view.

Since then, it has become an unwritten rule to make a particular search for well-dressed Arabs. Heaven help the suspect caught with a necktie on and with his shoes shined. What began as a drunken noncom's foolery is now a new measure of discrimination.

After interrogation the stubbornest suspects are taken, if interesting, to a re-education center, where they are interrogated all over again. But we keep certain prisoners more than a month: some, simply because we expect orders to transfer, or, more rarely, to free them; others, because we are investigating the effects of nervous strain. Many talk better after a week of solitary confinement than under torture by electricity.

When in solitary confinement, they are indeed isolated. All along the wall of the big front room is a row of gray coffinlike boxes. These are voting booths loaned by the city government. At least ten are in constant use, with their openings to the wall, sealing the prisoner in. He not only can't escape, he can't even sit down. When he collapses from fatigue he has to remain cramped against the wooden wall, as in those medieval dungeons where one lived diagonally.

Sentinels with loaded guns walk up and down this row of boxes night and day. Every two hours they are required to order their invisible prisoners to put their hands out over the upper edge, to make sure they're still alive. Two yellow hands emerge as out of a well. Most of the sentries, annoyed at losing sleep to guard these "filthy boukaks," take this opportunity to strike the tensed fingers with the metal butt of their Mas 36, once, twice, three times. If he doesn't want this little game to go on indefinitely, the victim must keep both outstretched hands up there under the blows.

I have seen young men of twenty amusing themselves at this game.

* * *

It is so cold in this month of February that we always put on our sweaters before going out at six o'clock for our morning exercise in the streets.

This is the hour they take the prisoners out of their coffins. They've not slept, and their faces are swollen from the blows received the day before—and the days before that.

While we drink our hot coffee, one of the guards picks up a length of garden hose and turns on a faucet. After making sure the pipe's not frozen, he attaches the hose and calls the first prisoner. The latter has to come of his own accord. Stark naked, shivering with cold and humiliation, he leaves his box, and is immediately hit by the water. The poor wretch dances and howls in the freezing spray, which plasters him like a fly against the wall.

This lasts for several minutes... Next! It's now another prisoner's turn. The game is first to turn the water on the cramped feet, then to make the whole body writhe under the slowly rising stream. The stomach turns blue, yellow. You hold the stream for a while on the genitals. The man gets covered with purplish blotches that turn to black. He screams, and his face is convulsed with pain, and also with mortification. This is officially known as bathing, hygiene. It's not counted as a supplement to interrogation.

Some of our prisoners risk everything to escape. A few succeed, but only to be caught next day—and to pay for their few hours of freedom. All one day, their hoarse yells are audible through the ceiling, as of animals being slaughtered, very slowly. Sometimes I think I still hear them. I saw one brought out of the interrogation room with both wrists broken and unskillfully tied in handkerchiefs—the work of the Alsatian sergeant and his workbench vices.

One day, we ceased to hear the cries. Handkerchiefs had been stuffed into the prisoners' mouths.

The scale and frequency of these interrogations astonish us. My comrades discuss them with considerable fervor. Some are amused, others scandalized. The cynics think it all perfectly "normal," and that "there ought to be lots more." The "humanists" think we should just shoot them. Very few seem to think that some of the victims might be innocent men.

* * *

The prisoners keep accumulating. Little though we feed them, they do cost something. We therefore set up a system of rotation. Whether they've talked or not, we almost automatically get rid of the old ones as soon as the new ones arrive. G.M.C.'s take them away to the re-education center—unless they are in such hopeless condition that they're not wanted there either. In that case they're assigned to the much talked-of "wood detail," off somewhere in the outskirts of Algiers, from which none returns.

The Alsatian sergeant confides to me one day, I don't know why, that he's just working mechanically now. He's lost interest. All these rats yell the same way—"just vermin you get tired of exterminating." He'd like to interrogate Europeans. But there aren't many of them.

One morning, as we are leaving for daily exercise with the captain, someone is naïvely surprised to find a corpse in one of the gray boxes. Two hours later, at reports, the captain announces that "one of the *salopards* hanged himself last night." It doesn't occur to anyone to wonder how you could hang yourself in one of those boxes when they'd taken away your belt, necktie, and shoelaces.

---

## 58

---

General Massu has thought up a ruse to prevent the great strike that the F.L.N. has ordered. A propaganda sheet, printed in the utmost secrecy, is dropped one night by commandos into the letterboxes of all the Arabs that have them.

FRONT OF ALGERIAN NATIONAL LIBERATION
ARMY OF ALGERIAN NATIONAL LIBERATION

### ALGERIAN PEOPLE!

How right we were to urge you to be vigilant, and to beware the trickery of the unscrupulous colonialists! At this very moment, MASSU, the general driven from Port Said by the glorious Egyptian Army, is turning his rage and spite against the starving population of the national capital.

Being bolder against defenseless civilians than against the valiant troops of Gamal Abdel NASSER, MASSU is preparing a sinister trick to establish a pretext for massacring the population. Emissaries in the pay of the colonists are distributing leaflets urging the people to begin a general strike.

Unable to silence the Voice of Fighting Algeria, Radio Lacoste is spreading the same orders.

Algerian People! This is transparent! Having failed to overcome the will to national independence by force and oppression, MASSU is resorting to lies.

He is preparing a false excuse for the pitiless massacre of innocent people. He is trying to lure the commandos of death into the open in order to shoot them down.

But the trick is too crude to deceive a clear-sighted people!

If a general strike is to be the natural culmination of the great armed struggle that has been carried on for more than two years by our valiant Army of National Liberation, the hour for its beginning will be decided by the Front of National Liberation and not by General Massu!

Algerian People! In the face of this colonialist incitement, the F.L.N. directs you to keep calm and to continue to go about your business.

The F.L.N., as sole lawful representative of your aspirations, will choose the hour in which you shall rise as one to end the shame, the humiliation, and the ignominy with which colonialism covers Algeria.

LONG LIVE THE INDEPENDENCE OF ALGERIA!
LONG LIVE THE FRONT OF NATIONAL LIBERATION!
LONG LIVE THE ARMY OF NATIONAL LIBERATION!

Obviously a bit crude. But, even though they aren't deceived, some Arab tradespeople may take this excuse not to join the strike—or so we hope.

The strike takes place anyway, and is virtually total. On the appointed day, which the F.L.N. put off twice to throw us off balance, not a shop opens its doors and all the factories remain silent.

The Arabs' wages being what they are, we thought the strikers couldn't hold out more than two days. But they do. We are therefore sent out in trucks in the early morning to get the workers out of their beds. Many of them come along quite good-humoredly. They explain to us: "If I go to work of my own accord, my neighbors will see me, and, when you've gone, I shall be in trouble! I have a wife and five children, sir. Oh, I'd rather work. There's no more bread in the house, and the last to get to the factory will be fired. I wasn't the only one threatened. My wife and children were too. One of my neighbors had his house burned, though we never knew who did it—as a warning. You must understand, messieurs les soldats."

Thus threatened on the one hand by the paratroopers and by their employers (who are taking this chance to discharge hundreds of them), and on the other hand by the F.L.N., which will never forgive them if they go to work, even under compulsion, the unfortunate Arab factory workers go through some very painful weeks.

At dawn, our commandos surround their cabins, submachine gun in hand, and break down all doors that do not immediately open. And, in front of their wives in nightgowns and their weeping children, the men have to dress and follow us, without even time for coffee.

Some say they are sick, having taken the precaution to get a medical certificate before the strike. This was not hard to do, in many cases, for, out of ten supposedly healthy workers, five are actually tubercular. There are also some who have cut off a finger.

At first, the sick are exempted. But as we find more and more of them, we finally stop paying any attention to what they say. Whether they have a certificate or not, they all have to go to work. Men who have long been too sick to work are caught in our dragnet and pulled from their beds like the rest in spite of their protestations and certificates, which nobody bothers to read any more. Even if they are at the point of death, they have to set out, clutching the sideboards of the truck and coughing their lungs out in the early morning fog, to go back to factories they have not set foot in for years.

The artisans and the little tradespeople shut their doors. On the first day, some streets do not have a single shop open. The army reacts immediately. G.M.C. trucks, armored cars, and a multitude of little tanks overrun the city, pushing in the metal shutters one after another. As the houses are often nothing but big mud huts, quite a few completely collapse. While shop windows are giving way in a shower of glass, we are sent to look for the proprietors, who are usually hiding on the second floor. The shops of owners who cannot be found are thoroughly looted by other Arabs.

This was a time of tumult and confusion, very favorable for the settling of private scores; many men disappeared without the army's having anything to do with it. Murders and reprisals continued at a furious rate. Bombs, grenades, shells, mysterious packages, kept exploding in every part of the city. It did no good to search all parcels, all pockets, all people using public transportation or entering public buildings. Explosives continued to circulate as never before, and the F.L.N. continued to counterattack without pity for women and children, numbers of whom we picked up every day with heads or legs blown off, or riddled by machine-gun fire.

One night, the city is waked by a terrific explosion that destroys a block of at least a dozen houses in the Casbah. Thirty corpses, men, women, children. We're told it was an F.L.N. bomb factory that blew up. While the dead are being picked up and the firemen are trying to put out the spreading fire, we make the first arrests, enough to fill several large trucks. We are praised for our zeal. But we learn later, from the perpetrators themselves—who are very proud of it!—that what caused the explosion was a bomb thrown by counter-terrorists of the extreme right.

In the long run, we find just about everything in the Casbah, even authentic terrorists who not infrequently greet us with submachine-gun fire through the door, or killers just about to start down the rue d'Isly with their package of bombs in their hand. For weeks on end, we pursue elusive rebel leaders through endless labyrinths, we break down dozens of doors, and, if most of the time there is nothing behind them but dust and rats, we do sometimes surprise men who get up pale when we arrive, and flee, putting out all lights, amid brief orders and the first shots.

Whatever the outcome of this Algerian war, it is certain that fifty, a hundred, years from now, the Algerians will still remember, and will still be telling their children, about this year 1957: when the Casbah, the symbol of all they had most deeply in common, was day and night in a state of siege, when terror was absolute master, when every one of its inhabitants could every moment say to himself: "Within an hour, men will perhaps be knocking at my door to take me away forever."

# 59

We are leaving Hussein Dey for Birmandreis, a residential suburb with luxurious villas overlooking the Bay. A white palace hidden away among palms has been reserved for us.

This house has been deserted for several months. Its owners went back to France when terrorism broke out again in the city. In emulation of the idle rich who used to live here, we install ourselves like pashas. I have my own bed-room, with private bath (no water, it's true), and in front of my window are plants with huge swaying leaves. Terraces everywhere, and patios paved with cool tiles, pleasant to walk on with bare feet.

Nothing but board fences separates these exotic palaces from the thousands of grocery crate shacks that have been patiently built on the edges of the city. That may be why most of the planters have fled. We are protecting the rest.

Opposite our pretty dwelling, the owners had dug deep mushroom pits in a small cliff, just the place to keep our prisoners, of whom we now have at least two dozen that have been sent to us for interrogation.

This is a great responsibility, and our platoon leader, a
pallid officer-cadet, is almost losing his head over it. Here he
is, master under God over the lives and deaths of two dozen
men, and a long way from his captain, who has remained in
Algiers. From the very beginning, he takes on as a matter of
self-discipline the duty of personally giving at least one slap
in the face to every suspect brought from the mushroom pits
to the interrogation room.

From time to time, two "French" policemen come out
in plain clothes from Algiers to help our officer-cadet in his
interrogations. They help him so much that one night we
have to go and get a suspect that just died in their hands,
and bury him in the quicklime at the foot of the garden.
There will be others.

This possibility was provided for. An enormous common
grave, big enough for an entire company, was prepared as
soon as we arrived. The prisoners dug it themselves in the
dark shade of the orange trees.

Despite strict orders, I escape to Algiers as often as I
possibly can. I have been silent among jailers so long I feel
myself becoming vile, and what is more serious, I feel that in
my mind the scandal of all these crimes that make up our
day-to-day war is daily losing a little of its virulence.

To civilians capable of talking calmly about the army—
there aren't many, but they do exist even in Algiers in
1957—I tell about what I see every day. They have always
had a lofty idea of the greatness of France. They listen
politely. But I sense their disbelief. They are thinking: "This
isn't possible. We'd have known about it." Will they ever
know about it? The German people, after the war, never
stopped saying, and it was probably true: "We didn't know . . ."
Have they ever really believed in the crimes of Dachau and
of Auschwitz? Have they ever realized that not knowing is
also a way of being guilty?

Friday, March 22nd. A second suspect has died in the
villa. He had not talked—whether because he did not want
to, or knew nothing, we shall never know. In either case, like
the first one, he died of the blows he had received.

Burial, or rather discreet disposal, of the corpse, which
is placed by the other one in the big grave. It is covered with

a thick layer of quicklime, and, on top of that, a little more earth.

As the prisoners have to go about the garden on their various chores, and might discover the graves, we always have the garbage thrown into this same hole. The combination of swill and bodies will gradually raise the level of the ground.

My superiors are beginning to look on me with suspicion. In spite of reiterated warnings, my absences have become more and more frequent, by day a well as by night. Then a little altercation I had during a patrol brings matters to a head. And I am transferred. I leave my pretty villa, its palm trees and its graveyard, for the 1st Platoon.

I am no longer wanted anywhere near the interrogation rooms. The platoon leaders are competing with each other for the privilege of not having me. I take this opportunity to apply for a month's leave in France. It's granted immediately. Very unusual, that. No doubt about it, they've seen enough of me—or I've seen too much of them.

Thirty days in Paris. It is already May when I return to Algiers, on a Sunday magnificent with blue sky and sun. I find that one short month of contact with the happiness of Paris is enough to make me forget the suffering that lies so deep over unhappy Algeria. And I am ashamed. Ashamed of having been so happy.

The regiment has moved. Algiers being momentarily "pacified," the companies have left and dispersed among the farms. But not to rest. The day I arrive, there's no one in camp but the chronically lame and the storekeeper: the whole regiment is out on an operation. The war's not ending tomorrow.

## 60

We go back to our rainy old Kabyle mountains, to hunt rebels once again. But what a far cry from the three hundred rifles

of November 1954, less than three years ago. Today, the men
we seek, and who seek us, are hundreds of thousands,
forming a network over mountain and plain. Neither their
losses nor ours have changed matters, except for the worse.

In a rain beating like a hundred thousand drums, we
leave l'Arba for Rivet, and from there, soaked to the skin, we
march to the Palestro gorges, which are still a valley of death,
notwithstanding the line of concrete posts bristling with
machine guns that have been constructed at regular intervals.
But today the valley is white with flying paper. The
leaflet war is on with a vengeance. We are reminded of those
bilingual sheets in 1955, when we were still trying persuasion
to bring the population back to the right ideas. The model for
this sort of literature was at that time a declaration by a
certain Mohamed Ben Hamadi El Aziz, several hundred
thousand copies of which were printed. He was an officer in
the military school in Baghdad, a lieutenant of Abd El Krim,
and had been wounded and taken prisoner while fighting in
Kabylia. Under what circumstances was his declaration obtained?
That's not the question. He said, in the two languages: "I
address my brothers of Algeria and I say to them: it is better
for you to keep calm, abandon your weapons, and return to
your homes, that these may prosper, and that your hearts
may be at peace..." There followed a long discourse on the
ineffectiveness of the "Army of Liberation," "a mere handful
of men," and on "the indecisive action of Ben Bella"... "The
action you are executing is not an organized military action. It
is more an individual action, and you must realize that
individual action always has a criminal character..." The
psychological war was still in its infancy.
Now, in 1957, persuasion has given way to force, and
what's being dropped on the mountains, that have become
saturated with rebels, is simply aggressive summonses—in
one language, French. If the recipients don't understand,
that's too bad.
In accord with the military authorities, says one of the
new leaflets, the Prefect of Grande Kabylie has decided "to
chastise in examplary fashion those who have most compromised
themselves... You, the inhabitants of Ouled Ikhfigher, Ouled
D'okkane, Ouled Djerreh, etc., must leave your houses
before June 30, 1957. You who have continued to supply the

rebels with food, you who harbor them and assure their protection, you who have so many times cut the Beni–Khelifa road, you whose husbands, sons or brothers have taken arms against France, will now be punished... You will leave your villages, with your families, your flocks and your baggage, before sunset, June 30, 1957. You are to seek shelter among your relatives of Sohana, of the Ouleds Bensalah, of the Ouleds Oula, of le Figuier, or of Palestro... After June 30, 1957, it will be forbidden to anyone, man or beast, to remain in the evacuated zone. The army will use your fields and pastures as target ranges, and all persons found in this zone will be shot without summons... Understand this and tell it to those about you: you cannot appeal to us for pardon until you have made up your minds to denounce the criminals and to punish them with us... Palestro, 11 June. By the Subprefect, etc."

We are entering a country stripped of all life. Most of the villages have been burned and bombed. The roofs are gone, and there is nothing left but fragments of walls crumbling in the cold sunlight. We find nobody around them except now and then a few rebel irregulars among the rocks, shod in espadrilles and supple as snakes. We do not take a single one alive. From time to time, helicopters pick us up on one hilltop and drop us on another. But we seldom achieve surprise. The rebels have dotted the whole region with little huts made of straw and branches, from which they see and hear everything within a dozen miles.

With terrifying uproar, the fighter planes begin machine-gunning before we get to the scene of operations. The terrain is so chaotic that you get a dozen tumultuous echoes criss-crossing each other like cannon balls and endlessly prolonging every sound. As it gets dark, the cold returns and stops the rain, which has covered us with mud. The latter stiffens. As there are no mechtas we can get to, we have to sleep in the open.

In a spirit of efficiency, we have permanently adopted the "commando" system of not carrying anything not indispensable. No packs, or even clothes—except those we have on, combat jackets and rough sweaters next the skin. Almost no food. Just our weapons. The air is icy cold. How we regret our good old packs out of which at just this time we used to get at least a hunk of coarse bread and a tent cloth. Taking turns, we sleep three hours while others are out in the wet rocks, waiting with fingers on their triggers for rebels who might come by.

For several dozen kilometers, we follow a oued that is an inferno of concentrated heat. It is as hot by day down in this river of red and white stones as it was cold by night up above. We trudge along like convicts over this lonely trail, incapable of thought.

Suddenly, with a strange vacant look and saying not a word, one of our comrades lies down on the pebbles of the dry riverbed. It's a long time since such a thing has happened. We think the man has fainted. But he lies there with his eyes wide open, looking at the men bending over him, and on his lips is just the suggestion of a smile.

We lift him to his feet. He starts off again without complaint, goes fifty yards, and lies down again. We relieve him of his weapons, and of everything else he was carrying. And again he gets under way. But, like an animal that feels it's going to die, once more he lies down, still without saying anything. Whether we beseech him or insult him, he makes no reply. He is completely apathetic, free perhaps.

The medic doesn't know what to give this peculiar patient. But as he loosens the man's belt, he notices that his pockets contain two red Maxiton boxes, each emptied of its forty tablets. We have to get a helicopter to come and pick the man up.

Maxiton was introduced into the army in little eight-tablet boxes for the "commando" kit. Then they decided to take them away from us—and found thousands had disappeared, and that at least one soldier in five had developed such a taste for this psychotonic that he had been drugging himself for several months, buying it wherever he could in such quantities as he could afford.

They later arrested one of our medics, who had appropriated a large quantity of our boxes at the time of an inventory and was selling them on the black market. He confessed to the policeman: "I could always spot my future customers, just by glancing at the men seated at mess. They all had the same symptoms: thinness, abnormal sweating, pimples, a haggard, wild look." This medic had also made several millions selling morphine he stole from commando kits.

Back in Castiglione, shaved, and after an eight hours' sleep, the heavy, surly grenadiers who yesterday were slogging through the mud are changed to dapper light cavalry. With smiling lips, and beret over one eye, they invade the beach restaurants and bars in joyous bands. Others rush off in jeeps for a spree in Algiers. One night, a sergeant of ours is captured like a wild mustang by the military police. He was driving his jeep a hundred kilometers an hour through the city and firing his revolver at the crowd as he went along.

June 2nd. New operation. It's Sunday. Noon. Our convoy of trucks goes through Castiglione, now full of holidaymakers happy to be alive. With our big automatic rifles and our old mortars between our knees, and rather in need of a shave, we pass women on their way to their swim and men in shirt sleeves going fishing. Our glances are ugly and full of jealousy. Some singing begins in the trucks. The civilians cheer us. They don't know that we despise them as much as we envy them.

Night is falling as we reach the foothills. Halt, and a few hours' sleep in the cold grass of Akbou, protected by the artillerymen who have a post there. Their faces are almost out of sight in their woolen helmets.

Before daybreak, we are back in the trucks and on our way to Birtouta, one of the most dangerous defiles in the Haute Kabylie. There the road ends, and we invest the Djurdjura again, as a month ago, three months ago, a year ago. Only, this time, thousands have come with us, from every arm of the service. All France is here this morning.

The rebel companies, regrouping as they draw back, are soon forced to the summits, which we rapidly surround. They will have to stay and fight, or be killed. The first skirmish starts at about noon, in violent wind and rain. Four dead and two wounded on our side and some on theirs. The fighter planes prowling above us rush up at the first shooting. But all they can do is observe. We are much too mixed up with the rebels for the machine gunners to tell which is which.

For seven hours on end, we hardly move at all from the positions we took at the start. Until dusk, there is continuous heavy fire through the wet brush. When it gets dark, the French on one side and the rebels on the other by tacit agreement all open their cans of corned beef.

The rebels occupy a curved line of brambly ledges facing us. There would be no sense in trying to drive them out before daylight. The first squad fortunately managed to reach the bottom of a little thalweg, right on the line of fire. In it runs an infinitesimal stream, and we can slake our thirst. We've no more food, though, and no blankets, nothing but our sweaters next our skin under our wet jackets. Our feet are already freezing cold.

The wet ground is strewn with sharp stones and so steep we have to dig little ledges to lie on. Our best protection against the cold is those dry thorns that grow in round clumps between the rocks. We pile as many as we can around us and curl up till it's time for our watch.

About one o'clock, as before at Djeurf, a few fellaghas try to get through our lines. But the first two are given away by their light-colored burnouses. They are hit and fall into the stream, where, dead or alive, they remain all night. Their comrades run back. From then till dawn there is only sporadic and confused firing.

On waking, I notice several comrades talking to one of the recruits. He is sitting on a stone, apparently in despair, giving vague answers to questions. Two months ago at this hour, he would have been sound asleep in a warm white bed. This morning, he has just killed his sergeant by mistake. His face is like a collapsing wall.

This sergeant was a Eurasian. He had come into France with the expeditionary force. He moved and looked somewhat like the mountain Arabs: dark skin, wide nose, very black hair. He was known for his bad habit of trying to improve on the strict rules governing NCO's on watch. When you make your rounds and approach a sentinel, you are under orders to warn him, by some sign or password, and to avoid getting in his line of fire. But, that night, our unfortunate NCO thought it would be smarter to surprise our comrade, and perhaps disarm him—just to see. He'd already

caught several men this way. Unfortunately, the recruit didn't
know this. He later gave me the details of the tragedy.

"I was so tired I was almost asleep, but with my eyes
wide open. Suddenly, I saw a shadow rise in front of me. It
was about one in the morning, the darkest time. Ten years
ago, I'd have thought it was a ghost, the way it seemed to rise
out of the ground. At first, I stood stock-still and stared. He
came forward with a strange half-smile on his lips. I was
guarding the entrance to a little path among the rocks. It
could have been a hallucination due to fatigue. I said to
myself: 'It's a rock, a funny rock, white.' But the rock moved,
slowly, never stopping, still looking at me as if it wanted to
hypnotize me. I almost fainted with terror...

"I suddenly realized it was a man. A fellagha. Those
black eyes, that dark skin, those thick lips white with cold—a
rebel trying to get through. Right away I was less scared. I
cocked my P.M. I braced it on my hip, as on the range, very
fast. I shouted the password—I don't know why, either. He
muttered something, smiling. But I wasn't even listening. He
probably hadn't time to finish. I was pulling the trigger. To
the last moment, he must have thought I'd entered into his
little game and that I was kidding, with my submachine gun!
He was two yards from me, maybe less.

"When he fell, his head almost touched my boots. I was
pleased, and said to myself: 'Ah, I got one! I've killed a rebel
on my first operation, with my first shot!' It was only when I
started to take the pistol out of his belt that the truth hit me.
'The sergeant, God!' I didn't call. I wanted to kill myself, I
was so afraid of the disgrace. But I was even more afraid of
dying! I didn't do anything, just waited till I was relieved."

A helicopter has come to get our unfortunate NCO. We
have carefully wrapped and tied him in his tent cloth, still
dirty with last night's mud. It's too short. His big feet in his
worn old pataugas stick out at one end, and at the other you
see all the upper part of his face, his nose, his swollen
eyelids, his short thick black hair.

The killer is not sentenced. Just an investigation. No
reprimand. Not his fault. C'est la guerre.

We set out again in the early morning, minus one
sergeant. Everything goes pretty well all day, but toward

evening we begin to feel the lack of sleep, and, rather than spend another night in the open, we do a forced march to the Birtouta Pass, where a transport company is waiting for us, shivering around their fires. We leave behind the dead and the seriously wounded. The Sikorskys will take care of them.

Thirty-one rebels, they say, were killed, and many weapons were captured. It seems we did very well. I still think a little about the dead sergeant, but I know that in a few days I shall have forgotten him for good.

We've had at least two full years of service. We're tired, worn out. Yet it's the draftees—they now outnumber us in the regiment—who have done the most to spread discouragement. Every three months, they see their release postponed without explanation to a later date. Except for a few regular officers and NCO's for whom this everlasting police operation means double pay, we are all utterly sick of the war and never expect to see the end of it.

We now always have from two to ten comrades to bury, on our returns from operations, and what some call the "cemetery fatigue" is having a deplorable effect on the newcomers. Kabylia, the unconquerable battlefield, is being extended by an ever widening graveyard.

# 61

To make matters worse, we get for platoon leader a little second lieutenant fresh from Reserve Officers' School and totally ignorant of the "art of war," and especially of the Algerian war.

You can't despise everything. But I've not forgotten this little sneak. He would have made a privy cleaner vomit. He has some sort of certificate for the first part of the baccalauréat, and he's proud as Punch because he has a gold stripe on his shoulders. His dwarfish eyes exactly mirror his soul, perpetually passing from small tyranny to fear. Though he cringes before the captain, who's amused but a bit nauseated, he's capable of odious ferocity toward "his men," and especially toward prisoners. Some of my comrades seriously considered shooting him like a dog.

# 62

An assemblage of rebels is reported to be taking place at Maillot, near Palestro. Here, thinks the staff, is work for the paratroops. We repack, get into the trucks, and take the old night convoy road.

It all begins like an ordinary operation: fine weather, the usual terrain, the normal number of troops. We arrive at Thiers at six in the evening and camp for a few hours in the open. We eat a little, sleep a little, and are waked at 12:30 A.M.

At six we're in Maillot, the end of the road. We leave the trucks to hide themselves as best they can among the low houses, and walk to the windy D.Z., where the helicopters are waiting for us among the cannon. We are always amused at the sight of these beetlelike aircraft. There is lots of coffee, and everybody is in a good humor.

To our disappointment, we do not get into the planes right away. The companies group themselves around the thin tree trunks, for the sun is already hot. Here we stay till noon, as isolated as on an island. Many go to sleep.

At ten o'clock, the artillerymen aim their 75- and 105-mm. howitzers toward the wine-colored mountains rising almost vertical in the hard light, at the end of the plateau. Their objective is one of the highest summits of the Djurdjura, so high that for months several rebel bands have been based there. All the villages on its slopes are about to be shelled one after another, so they cannot be used as fortresses when we arrive. The firing begins. Ten or fifteen shells are discharged almost simultaneously with deafening uproar. The men who were laying down sit up. From under the trees, they watch through field glasses, as people watch a game from a grandstand.

As always, the shells first fall all around the douars, surrounding them with white plumes. Then they slowly draw nearer, and soon the roofs of the mechtas are breaking like tight-stretched paper. Finally the shells fall so thick that the villages, that had stood out sharply in the sunlight, disappear in masses of yellow, white and black smoke, mixed with flames. Through our field glasses, we see small figures running toward the woods and rocks.

Generals in stiffly creased combat uniforms are very busy around the campaign radios, and very important.

At two o'clock, the preliminaries being over, our company has the honor to be the first to take off. In squads of ten, we climb into our Sikorskys. The artillerymen are cleaning their guns. They look at us enviously. And we are proud!

We rise almost vertically. At the level of the summits, the helicopters disperse and, with roaring motors, thread their way into deep valleys, thickly overgrown with bushy, spreading live oaks, and obviously capable of sheltering large numbers of people. But where can we land? No level place anywhere. We have to jump from the helicopters about six feet into the brush.

When the planes have gone, there is utter silence. Enormous pale pink flowers grow in thousands under the brush, in spite of the heat. We move very slowly into the dark undergrowth, whispering our passwords as if in a cathedral. The vast forest is teeming with insects of all sizes, barely perceptible, or as big as a finger.

Here and there on the slopes, we see enormous heaps of white boulders. Little groves of tall cedars grow among them and spot them with their dense shade. At first we inspect these rocky excrescences with great care, for every one of them could conceal an entire company. Then we tire of that; it is so hot. And we continue on down into the valley, kilometer after kilometer, among the umbrella-shaped trees and the strange flowers. We are paying attention mainly to dodging branches and keeping our feet when, suddenly, a rifleman, glancing at the ground, notices something at the foot of an oak and picks it up in astonishment. A book. *The*

*Hospital Attendant's Campaign Manual,* big as a small dictionary and brand-new.

It might have been forgotten by one of our comrades. But it is more than six months since any of them have been here. And the book is quite undamaged. The enemy must be here.

We begin to search very carefully and slowly. We go round and round the tree where the book was discovered. We check every boulder individually, imagining invisible enemies behind it.

Ah! A second discovery: a cabin, built against a tree trunk and so well camouflaged that without the very closest attention we would have taken it for an ordinary clump of bushes. One of us starts toward it out of curiosity. Suddenly there is a shot, a man rushes out, fires and misses again, and runs away. This is the first fellagha of the day.

Then I see the second rebel, as near as across a street. He has a shotgun like the first. Like a flushed quail, he goes up from behind a boulder directly in front of me. He probably thought I'd spotted him. He runs up the slope without firing, no doubt to warn his comrades. I fire a burst at him, and another, and another. I absolutely must hit this man before he reaches the boulders he is heading for. At the fourth burst, right after the last bullet, he whirls around and lets me have both barrels. I am astonished not to feel the least pain. We are not more than five or ten yards apart, but between us there are several big tree trunks as well as the rocks, and a slug is a very small thing in space.

My outlaw squats down behind the biggest rock, and all I can see of him is the double barrel of his big black gun, which is momentarily empty. I mustn't give him time to reload, or it's sure death. I go for him on the run, determined to fire my fifth burst into him point-blank. He's about to take aim. I fire—just one bullet. My magazine is empty. While I am reloading, he runs away full speed among the rocks. This time, I really have lost him. Total failure. No, not quite. Another rebel, whom I hadn't seen, has been flushed to my right by Sergeant Sh., who is driving him toward me. This fellagha apparently doesn't see me, though I have a full view of him, and rushes straight at me, completely exposed. Behind him, the sergeant makes me a signal. I understand:

this is my shot. Without hesitating, for the man has his gun at the ready, I fire first. He drops and rolls on the ground, killed outright. I pick up his gun, a big boukala that fires enormous slugs. I draw from its holster the pistol he has at his belt. Then, without knowing why, I throw my handkerchief over his face, which is in very bad shape.

And I start up the slope again, with the fusillade continuing on either side of me.

Though very dispersed, the shooting is all of it very near; but I still don't see anything and am able only vaguely to locate the shots. They seem to come especially from a gigantic heap of gray rocks that we had not particularly noticed when we went by it an hour ago. In fact we had gone around, rather than over it, to save our feet. It was the nest, though, the big rebel nest we were looking for. The rebels, from their hiding places among the rocks, couldn't help seeing us, but they kept quiet and let us go by. Nothing would have happened if a forgotten book had not given them away.

In a small cabin wedged between two huge boulders, we find two women. Two young Arab women with very short black hair, tinted with red. They are wearing some sort of aviator's outfit, and have the green and white F.L.N. badge pinned on their chests. One of them had lost the fateful book.

While we get them out of their hut, with their hands up, one of our comrades, ferreting about behind them in the straw on the floor, discovers a loose board over the entrance to a small cave. Before venturing into it, we take all the medical supplies out of the cabin and set it afire. This will make a good landmark for the helicopters that have been circling around without seeing us.

Interrogation. The Arab interpreter doesn't like women in men's clothes. He searches them brutally, with an ugly look, rips their pockets, almost tears off their blouses. But they have no papers on them, not a thing. The interpreter is furious. He starts all over again, practically strips the two women naked in front of us. Still nothing, nor is there anything feminine about them now but their bodies, so hard have their faces become.

There begins a furious dialogue in Arab. But the two prisoners are not "talking." They have recovered all their presence of mind and they are speaking haughtily to the man, even insolently. He translates: "They say they're prisoners of war, and that they won't say a thing, and that they will complain." But they are actually saying a good deal more than that. To these women, the interpreter is an abject traitor. They would kill him like a dog if they could, and he knows it, and shows that he knows it. They even revile him in French: "Traitor, coward, traitor!" The wretched man's face darkens, fills with the black blood of mingled rage and shame.

Our little second lieutenant doesn't know what to do. He would like to take this chance to show himself a leader. But how... An idea! He goes up to the two women who have been ignoring him, and drawing himself up very straight, he slaps them both in the face, first one and then the other. Just like that. To show who's boss.

We look at each other in astonishment, horribly embarrassed. The two women have turned to statues, petrified with hate. Their pale faces go from grayish yellow to ghastly white. Two round red spots slowly grow on their tense cheeks. Fury, shame and fury. Finally, one of them, with perfect naturalness, walks straight forward into tragedy. She seizes by the collar the man who has slapped her and who, she well knows, holds her life in his hands. She seizes him, and she slaps him, as he has slapped her. The interpreter tries to intervene, but too late. A woman's hand is printed in red on the lieutenant's cheek... Silence.

"Tuez-la! Mais tuez-la donc!" our officer finally screams at the Arab in a choking voice. Why can't he kill her himself? But the interpreter doesn't hesitate. He throws the woman to the ground and holds her down with his foot. The little lieutenant, red with rage, never stops shouting: "Tuez-la! Mais tuez-la donc!" He seems to have lost his mind. Without batting an eye, the interpreter cocks his rifle, and fires five bullets one right after the other into the woman's body that lies crushed under his boot. First two bullets in the breast and then three in the stomach. She dies without a cry. We are dumfounded. Then, gun in hand, the man starts toward the other woman, standing silent, motionless, with closed eyes. Again he cocks his rifle, which is still hot. But now it's he that's seized round the waist—by us, determined, this time, to prevent him. The lieutenant, who's waiting without saying anything, doesn't dare insist. He gives vague orders: "Get on up there. There are more rebels..."

Three hours later, when the engagement is over, I go back to see the woman again. Her features, that were convulsed by terrible anger, are now relaxed. Her round, slightly plump face has turned to pale, dull wax. I pass in front of the lieutenant. I now know why I hated him. All that night, and often after that, I shall think of this woman, more than of the best of my comrades who, like her, died in vain. She will haunt me, as if I myself had killed her. And if it were true that each is responsible for all?

Is it because she was a woman? I don't know. But war, for me now, is her full breast, bloodstained like crushed grapes, her short, slightly frizzled black hair in disorder around her pale face. War is that body I am still ashamed not to have defended, that young Algerian woman who might have been loved by a fine young man. She was beautiful, I remember, even in that slightly ridiculous attitude of those who die astonished. War is that woman torn and mangled for refusing to believe that men are always vile when they have power. The fixed gaze of her dark eyes that we forgot to close tormented me a long time.

Meanwhile, up above us, one fellagha is still shooting. But as all the others have died, here and there and everywhere, we don't expect this one to resist much longer.

However, he's so well sheltered that we soon find we can't do anything to him. For a long time, we try submachine guns, incendiary grenades, rocket throwers. He never stops firing. But he is so outnumbered that in the end he is hit. Dead? No, there he is, sliding out from his hiding place. We see his two grayish-yellow hands waving to signify surrender. But careful! Is he alone? This may be a ruse. The interpreter shouts: "Hold your hands out in front of you, if you want to live!" He is half paralyzed. A bullet must have hit his spinal column. He gets halfway out, says a few words, disappears again. "He wants to surrender," explains the interpreter, "but he can't get out of his hole. He can't move his legs." We finally seize the man around the waist and pull him out, dying. He has great holes in his back.

We search him roughly, turn him over on his back like a corpse. Not a thing on him. He must have left everything in his hole. We have a look. But suppose another man had stayed in there, very much alive, ready to shoot?

I bend way forward, pointing my P.M. out in front of my

head to protect it, and slide into the opening. Nobody here. He really was alone. How hard his last hours must have been. I pick up the gun he dropped when hit. Beside it lies a belt, a genuine French gendarme's belt. Some previous crime? He must have unbuckled it to be able to breathe. A fine army pistol is still smoking near its red leather holster, loaded, with two empty shells, still hot, in the cylinder. Concealed under some stones, I find a pack, and in it the usual can of milk, a few rags for wrapping hidden weapons, some bread, and several packages of razor blades. No letters and no photographs. Finally, carefully folded in the very bottom, two pairs of socks, one brand-new. Pale blue socks, startlingly blue against the stones on which I lay them. It is socks like these that the rebels wear when, after a good shave, they go down into the towns, looking like any French citizen.

A dark area in the back of the hole makes me fear some final trap. Thinking of anti-personnel mines, I grope my way in. No, not a thing. This is too easy. I become wildly imprudent, and, after creeping stealthily into this hole that might well have been my grave, I go out with my head high. And Death appears once more, this time for me. A bullet passes within a very few centimeters of my body.

"Well?" is all I think of to say. And that might have been my last word! I judge that the shot came from the left, from behind and to my left, to be exact. I suddenly feel very much alone. I do have a comrade within ten yards of me, and another within seven. But ten yards, in this case, is too far. I crouch down. Another bullet comes, as if with regret at having given me time to take cover. And some beast locked up in me begins to moan, with fear, I think.

The shots come from a rock over which we walked at least ten times this afternoon, an enormous natural flagstone—like those in cathedrals of the Middle Ages above dead who lie with folded hands. Under this stone, a man lies hidden. He has fired without reflecting, convinced no doubt that I saw him when I came out of my hole. He lost his head. If he had kept quiet till dark, he might then have saved his life.

I now see the long black double barrel of his gun. It barely protrudes from under the stone, but danger gives you the eyes of a cat. The double black steel hole moves ever so slightly, searching in my direction. Like a guilty schoolboy, I can't help thinking: Why pick on me? I'm not the only one... But I am the nearest. So I fire three bursts at the threatening hole. Silence. Then a third shot comes from the rock, followed by another. The two big slugs smack against the boulder protecting me. As it is taller than I am, I can stand up, a great advantage if you want to take careful aim. My comrades cannot be of any help from where they are. This rebel and I have to fight it out alone.

I fire a fourth burst. This time my fear is entirely gone. I'm not even thinking of it. Only my head shows above the rock, but this shield is my prison too. If I show myself to right or left, the rebel, who saw me take cover, could hardly miss me, even if he's a poor shot. I'm just as trapped as he is.

I shoot and shoot and shoot. Not angrily but tranquilly, the way one performs some easy, boring task. I fire another three, four, five, six, seven bursts at the two black eyes of that double-barreled gun, which are still patiently following me. That gun has got to disappear from under that rock. All I have eyes for now is those little black eyes. They literally fascinate me. Were the general himself to grab my sleeve to make me fall back, I would not even turn around.

My bullets ricochet, scatter and fall (like black dragées) on the rebel's stone. He fires only from time to time, and then in dead earnest, straight at me. Does he plan to spend the night in that hole of his? Might there not be two of them taking turns with the gun? Have I wounded one? No. I should have heard. How slow this is.

A long silence. For a moment I think my sharpshooter is wounded, perhaps dead. The noise of the shooting might have covered his cries of agony. His gun's not moving. But soon the double barrel lifts and hesitatingly resumes its little gyrations. I reload. And I fire, fire, fire—desperately, to kill Death.

"Leulliette!" A sergeant very skillfully tosses me a grenade. I am the only one who can get it to the target. This new type of grenade, a little round green box you carry hooked to your belt, is theoretically only for automatic rifle or mortar men. It enables them, if worst comes to worst, to destroy their weapons before surrendering. We use it to burn anything we want to burn in a hurry. It is actually just a lump of phosphorus.

"Let him have it!" they all shout to me, now that I have the grenade in my hand. " Hurry up, or he'll get you!"

The rebel had just coolly fired both barrels at me again, while I was catching the grenade. I therefore prepare my "incendiary," without letting go of my P.M. Though not required to do so, I shout: "Surrender! The game's up! You haven't a chance! Throw your gun ahead of you and come out!" The interpreter translates. But from under the rock come only angry roars. "He won't surrender! never, he says. He won't be taken alive," explains the translator.

I pull the safety. I raise my arm. Perhaps a little too slowly, for just as I do so, there comes a shot from ten yards behind me. This is a different rebel, so well hidden nobody'd discovered him. I almost drop my grenade. But I'm not hit. Another wasted bullet! Tomorrow, I shall laugh a long time over my incredible luck.

But now I feel a sharp pain in my leg. Just as I was thinking I was all right. I instinctively scratch myself, with my grenade still in my hand. Halfway down my trouser leg, I find a little black hole with frayed edges. It must be a very small pellet! Anyway, I can move my leg as well as ever. I reassure myself as best I can.

One thing is sure: I'm not well placed, since I can be shot from behind. I'd better move right away. But first I've got to attend to this lunatic who refuses to die. And while my comrades deal with the man who just fired at me from behind, perhaps to save his squad mate, I poise my grenade in the hollow of my hand. To make a better throw, I expose my head. The rebel's barrel lifts, but is deflected by the grenade, which lands square on it and rolls like a ball into the narrow opening.

And that ends it. Instantly, an inferno of red, white and black flames bursts from under the stone. And one horrible cry! Just one, but terrible. The rebel crawls out of the hole, writhing with pain, his face burned to the quick. He tries to escape the devouring flames. But he is on fire himself, and his eyes are dissolving, drowned in blood. He still clutches his gun, and, blind though he is, fires one last shot. Then the gun slips from his burned hands. His eyes are not only bleeding, they seem absorbed by their sockets in a flood of corrosive tears. His last bullet goes up into the sky. The man sways, hesitates, more dead than alive. One final burst. And now he is stretched forever in the death he chose. I am soaked with sweat.

We search him, turn him over. He may be the leader of the band: he is older than the others, a little bald. No stripes, but magnificent weapons: a splendid gun, worth at least a hundred thousand francs, of shining damask steel; at his belt, an ultramodern automatic pistol of British make. And in his jacket pockets, half consumed by fire, a sheaf of French official maps and some bank notes of the Bank of Algeria.

The phosphorus on him is still burning. The face becomes a stewing mess of flesh and dirty ash. We watch. At last a black sergeant puts out the fire and out of decency covers the unrecognizable face with his big handkerchief. As my excitement cools, my awareness of the tragedy of this horror grows.

It will soon be dark. We have to hurry if we are to search the rest of the potential hiding places—but it's impossible: we'd have to turn the whole mountain inside out.

We scatter in pairs among the rocks, ready to leap on any hiding creature. Carelessly bending over an insignificant looking crack, I suddenly see a pair of eyes looking up at me from the dark. I leap back as if scorched by a jet of flame. I point my P.M. at the hole. And suppose it is some real wild animal, some jackal or wild boar awakened by the shooting?

With beating heart, I call softly to my teammate. "There's someone in here," I whisper to him. "Get up above the hole." Then I return cautiously to the entrance of the tiny cave, and shout: "Come out, or I'll shoot!"

I don't have to repeat. "Yes, yes," replies a voice from the bottom of the hole, "yes, yes, comrade, yes, yes..." The voice is that of a very frightened man. This one doesn't want to die. Out comes the long black barrel of a rifle, slowly and trembling. "Stock first!" yells my comrade, for prisoners have been known to give their

**Mauser Mod 98**

triggers a convulsive, involuntary squeeze. The gun disappears. It comes out again, and this time we are presented with the dusty butt plate of an old Mauser. "Good! Now come out. But first throw your gun ahead of you." Out pops the gun. I catch it on the fly. "Now you, with both hands out in front of you!" Two very dirty hands appear, and hesitate. The man doesn't dare come out. Does he know that one false move on his part, one wrong gesture, means sudden death? With great difficulty, he finally extricates himself from the hole and immediately puts both hands on his shaved head. He is trembling. If we had come upon him in the morning, perhaps he would never have surrendered. But an afternoon of suspense seems to have drained him of all courage. He is very young.

While we are carefully searching the man on the edge of the hole, up comes another gun, stock first. We hastily seize this new weapon, also a Mauser. There were two in there. We hear shouts: "Yes, yes, labès, labès . . . Yes, yes!" This one too wants to surrender before he's drenched with phosphorus. But he's so young that he hasn't the strength to pull himself through the rocky funnel that seems to have swallowed him. We help him out. He's almost a child, fifteen or sixteen. Probably one of those messengers who run at night from one band to another. He must have been here by chance, and been given a gun—did he even know how to use it?

In their cave, which is bigger than it looked, we also find two pistols in very good condition. What a contrast to the first rebels in the Aurès, who had only their old shotguns and a few cartridges. At the end of the hole is a narrow passageway, so narrow that no one could get into it. Let's not bother with this! A grenade will fix everything. It explodes in a tremendous cloud of dust, and hollow rumbling. The rocks heave and sway, blocking the entrance. No man will ever get in here again, or out, either. We can leave with a clear conscience. The two men, with their hands tied, are led in triumph to the command post, which has been set up under a tree. They are the last prisoners of the day.

My leg hurts. The medic seizes it with his big fingers. "Well!" says he. And with a single deft motion of his forceps he pulls out a big pointed fragment, the size of a bullet. This interests him at first, but he's disappointed to find that it's only a splinter of hard rock, broken off by a ricocheting bullet. Nonetheless, he makes me a fine bandage for consolation. I do feel ridiculous to have a pebble wound, after such an afternoon.

Near the dead lie the prisoners, with their pockets turned inside out, on their stomachs, their bound hands under them, piled one on top of another. This is the old method. If a prisoner tries to escape, you have plenty of time to shoot him before he can get up. Perhaps they now regret not having died on their feet?

Under all these trees, the heap of boulders we fought on all afternoon looks just like millions of similar piles of giant stones all over Algeria. From a helicopter, it would seem just a rocky hummock. And to think that for two years, as we shall learn this evening, regularly and in plain sight of all the surrounding villages, rebels have been calmly making themselves at home among these rocks. They held their councils in the open above their caves, and even in the village square, a few kilometers below. They brought their wounded here, hence the two nurses—who, according to the villagers, also looked after certain rebels in the best of health . . . Be that as it may, the day after the fight we find three underground surgical wards, all of them primitive but clean. No wounded, though, anywhere, except those we ourselves had shot that afternoon. Had the others fled? Were they in some secret hiding place?

We soon discover other passages, leading to other chambers. One of my comrades strikes the floor. There is a hollow sound, and we find this is just a thin layer of wattled branches and stones, with another chamber below. But from outside, the lieutenant is calling us. We shout to him that there is room in here for a whole company, that the rebels we were fighting were perhaps just lookouts, that others may be waiting in the darkness and silence for us to go away. But he isn't interested. He's been told to go back, and we're going back. Is he afraid? The captain would have sent us right into that cave with fixed bayonets. The little imbecile!

Night is falling. On the road back, we come across a small detachment of riflemen, all of them draftees, that I hadn't seen since noon and that I supposed wounded and evacuated. As we arrive they get up from the stones on which they were resting. They were holding the road, they say. In other words, while we did the fighting, they calmly waited for the battle to end. They are eating. They won't even have to clean their guns. I am astonished. Who posted them here, out of sight, even out of range, when, only a few hundred yards away, men were killing each other?

We go on. The village down below seems perfectly calm. The people are eager to help us and bring us food and water. But there's something very unnatural. We search a few mechtas, tired though we are of the old routine. And in one wretched little cabin we find an immense white and green F.L.N. flag made out of magnificent silk and stamped with the red star and crescent. Fifteen minutes later, all the surrounding mechtas are in ashes. All the males left in the village run off in all directions. We catch them. More prisoners. We can't wait, so they can come as they are, barefoot. As for the women, we leave them to solve their own problems in the smoke, with their swarms of children.

We reach the base, with our prisoners, after a long night march. Helicopters have dropped a few crates of rations for us but there are no trucks. We shall have to march another whole day.

As a reward for its good conduct, the platoon gets three bales of straw for the night—a real luxury. We go quietly to bed under the envious eyes of the other companies.

Next morning, everybody is scrambling over the mountains again. The fellaghas are just about everywhere, but few and far between, one here, one there, hidden in caves or hollow trees. Our platoon takes four prisoners, of no interest and more trouble than they're worth. At noon, after they have convinced us that they really have nothing to tell, they dig their own graves in the bottom of a oued, and we shoot them and cover them with pebbles. Next winter, the water will wash them out.

Not till evening do we finally reach headquarters on the plain. There have been changes while we were away. They have built a big hut of straw and tent canvas, and at least a dozen officers are walking feverishly up and down in front of it, and going in and out, carrying bottles of beer and maps, accompanied by Signal Corps men. Everybody seems nervous and tired. I ask a few questions. These officers have been up all night interrogating yesterday's prisoners. And, since more are continually arriving, they have much to do and no time to lose.

No one is allowed to come near. Nevertheless I go forward a little, and then I notice what seem to be big sacks hanging from the barren trees surrounding the hut—long, black sacks, perfectly motionless. Could it be possible? I take my field glasses. Yes, those are bodies, human bodies, hanging there. Are they alive? I go nearer. They do seem to be alive, yes, all of them, still. But for how much longer? Their faces are black. They have been hung by their feet, and all the blood in their bodies has been slowly going down to into their heads. They were strung up yesterday evening. They've been hanging like this for a night and a day. Two of them will live another twenty-four hours. But most will die tonight. Many will talk to escape the horror of this slow death. For reward, they will be shot and not have to wait.

My comrades are going to bed, unconcerned about the unusual neighbors.

Next morning, we get ready to leave. The hut is burned. The hanged prisoners are taken down. The officers get into their helicopters. We burn the old papers. In single file we go down on foot, like wandering ants, through the valleys to Bouïra. We have "pacified" one more square on the map.

The artillerymen are waiting for us down below, with their cannons still pointed at the mountain. They are all draftees. As we silently cross their camp, they look at us as we look at them, without friendliness, almost with hate, lips curled in disgust. We despise them, and they know it.

Joyfully, we climb into the trucks that are to take us back to the sea. "Start the motors!" The engines turn over, start, roar. Then, one by one, they subside like pricked balloons. A shout goes from truck to truck: "We're not leaving!" Something's wrong. "Nobody get off! Stand by!" The youngest among us had already collapsed on the packs and weapons, worn out.

An hour goes by. Many are asleep. Finally, at nine o'clock, what we all feared is confirmed. We're not leaving. "Get down! Packs on the ground!" shout the sergeants. The operation's not over, that's all.

We jump heavily down onto the road, and start off again,

not thinking, not seeing, completely taken up with our aching bodies, our sad old bodies that have not learned to lie.

The valley we are going up apparently has no life in it at all. No trees. Not even stones. Nothing but occasional waves of gray and white dunes. All of a sudden, at about two in the morning, we are ordered to turn around. Why? They don't deign to tell us.

We go through the artillerymen's camp a second time. They are all asleep, of course. Again, we get back into the trucks, like the obedient dogs we are. And this time we set out for Castiglione.

The dawn over the sea wakes us. At noon, we are home; that is, in the sheds the planters of Castiglione have been so kind as to leave us. Cleaning of weapons and of bodies, sleep, letters: the routine of return absorbs us till evening. At eight o'clock, I am at the house of some city friends, at a table loaded with flowers.

It is already July. As last year, the beach is covered with lovely girls, and once more the "paras" receive kind treatment. Even in the Casino de la Corniche, they are warmly welcomed (in return for cash), though in their cups they are more like bears than gentlemen. A bear is always amusing, if he is well brushed. There is laughter and drinking and singing everywhere along the shore. The sun is perfect. The sea is warm. How can one not forget in such an atmosphere?

The girls go about the sun-drenched streets. They smile. At life? At the idea they have of it? Theirs is the joy of contented hearts, of comfort and pleasure, the joy of those who dream, who dream of happiness. What luxury. I too dream—of men who died hanged by their feet.

## 63

July 3rd, we set out at night, this time toward the east, for the Chenoua, that huge dark blue mountain that from

Castiglione one sees tumbling into the sea. The Chenoua, once so peaceful, has become the main resting-place for migrating rebels and in a few months has been turned into an almost permanent battlefield. War is tightening its vice.

New stones. Perpetual newness of dawn. I signed my repatriation paper yesterday, and this is my last operation. I should like to behave as in some rare and solemn ceremony, with deep seriousness. But the heat is intense. When it is ninety in the shade, one forgets everything else.

By noon, even the helicopters are immobilized. Unable to get any purchase on the nonexistent air, they laboriously move their great useless blades for a while, then fall silent, and remain pinned to the ground like insects. We set out on foot for the summit. The heat burns like a flame. We march the whole day. But next morning, before sunrise, new helicopters pick us up and drop us squarely on the rebels, not near them, on them.

They are in camp, calmly lighting their morning fires. We think the victory ours. But they not only are less affected by the heat than we, they turn it to good advantage. In seconds, they have the brush on fire. Choking and blinded, we soon lose contact.

We are crying with thirst. By nine o'clock, all the canteens are empty. In the shade of the underbrush, a medic finds that the temperature is 106°. That's in the shade. But we have to do our running in the sun.

As we stumble forward among the rocks, half blinded by sweat, fellaghas crouched in some bushes take careful aim at our three lead riflemen. Three shots ring out. The three men fall. All three killed.

More shooting—now from behind us. We have just time to fling ourselves on the ground. This is serious. A quarter of an hour goes by. The rebels seem more numerous than we. Are there thirty, or forty, or more? We are one platoon, at two-thirds normal strength. For the first time, I think: We are done for!

Three rebels rush up and seize our dead comrades by the legs. They drag them out of sight behind the rocks before we can do a thing. In spite of all the shooting, a few of us want to get up. But there are shouts not to move. Three dead are enough for now. Our orders are to stay in our positions.

The radioman is calling desperately for reinforcements, but can't get the command post. This is bad.

Twenty minutes later a helicopter happens to fly over, and we make contact. The rebels stop advancing when they see it. None too soon. Five more minutes, and we should probably have been completely wiped out.

In exasperation, the captain, though usually far from excitable, seizes the submachine gun of a slightly bewildered recruit, stands up, and blazes away like a young man. The radioman had just told him orders were to hold out another half hour. That's impossible. We've got to take advantage of the rebels' hesitation and fight our way through. At the risk of a few more deaths, the whole platoon gets up and follows. The helicopter circles above us, and the co-pilot drops grenade after grenade on the fellaghas. (We learn later that this Sikorsky had been about to drop a load of mail somewhere else, but came over to us because of the shooting.)

Other helicopters arrive from all directions. Several dozens of our comrades drop in among us. The rebels haven't stopped shooting, but they are obviously retreating. Soon they disappear, leaving nothing on the field except two of their comrades we didn't know we'd killed. We look in vain for our three dead.

Not till we have gone another two hundred yards do we finally discover them behind some bushes, out in the sun and already swarming with flies. The outlaws had taken not only their weapons, their packs and their cartridges, but also their camouflage uniforms, their jungle boots, and even their socks. Hurriedly, like thieves, we wrap the three naked bloodstained corpses in our tent cloths. On their lips, those lips which prevent one man from ever being like another, is an unbearable little sad smile (what dies last in a face is the mouth) and in their eyes the stern wild pain of sudden death. We carry the bodies on our rifles, for there are no stretchers. The red and black holes that the bullets have made in their sweating flesh begin to ooze again through the canvas.

In the evening, the whole mountain is in flames. To halt our pursuit, the rebels lit brushfires everywhere. Smoke blots out the horizon, and the air is perfumed with burning rosemary. For a while, there is still sporadic skirmishing in the hot clouds, then the last rebels vanish in the darkness.

We suffocate up there for another twenty-four hours. The fires take forever to go out. Then, after helicopters have taken away our dead, we set out with hanging heads, and we march another entire night, raising clouds of hot ashes at every step.

With a deep sense of relief, I sit down on a water can in the truck. I am leaving these dead, and these living who forever trail death behind them. The convoy starts violently as though tearing itself from the road. Already my spirit is on the wing, on the wing toward France.

We reach Castiglione at two in the afternoon. We shave, then are immediately to go and bury our comrades. The hospital refrigerators are very full. I am to help carry a coffin and, just as I am tying my black tie, my marching orders arrive.

I rush to the supply room to turn in my uniform. When I return, I find my comrades back from the cemetery and I shake a few hands. They are leaving tonight for Palestro. Then I depart, almost on the run, with the papers in my pocket. The captain, who seems brokenhearted, makes a little speech, to which I can only respond by a great inner laugh. How can he praise the army right after a military funeral. Though I have no words, I do try to express the esteem which I still feel for him, by making the most correct salute of my military career. For he is a man, a rare thing. Perhaps he understands. An almost imperceptible smile of complicity passes over his severe lips, a smile which I return, I think, in just the same way. That was all, and it was much.

I jump into a car. Tonight I shall sleep in white sheets.

Not till morning do I feel really a civilian again. I am waking from a three years' dream.

"I shall come back!" I had said to the people in Castiglione and Algiers, knowing I would not, as they did too. This lie was to trouble me for some time. Yet what had my life been for three years if not a long lie?

I had promised to write, but what good are words?

Besides the landscapes, which to me meant much, I regret many comrades whose tastes I often did not share, and who did not share my distastes, but whose courage I have not ceased to admire, that courage without which there can be no virtue in man.

* * *

An hour before I left, I drank with them the "wine of farewells." In our old black cups, that wine had the deep red color of blood. I noticed it for the first time—this also was the first time I had drunk wine as a soldier. So I drank with them my cup of army wine, and, without their knowing it, it was like a communion.

"Good luck!" they all said to me. I dared not say the same to them. It was in part their blood, mixed with that of others, that I saw in their cups. "And long live France!" one of them shouted, half serious, half joking.

Yes, may France live! But may that not mean more deaths.

Two weeks later, one of them wrote to me:

> On the Chenoua, our last engagement was very hard. G.R., J.V., R.M., and P.E. were killed. They were burned alive. They were surrounded a second time near the thalweg where three riflemen were killed in your last operation. They could not escape, and the flames got to them while they were still living. Fellaghas in the rocks saw it, and watched their agony for a long time. One of them that we took prisoner boasted about it. As for me, I was wounded...

Georges R., Jean V., Robert M., Pierre E., with whom I drank that "wine of farewells"!

On the boat my joy is so great that all night long I whistle and sing—I who never whistle and sing. And I laugh and laugh and laugh... It's easy to forget how hard the world is. All you have to do is escape from it.

So far in my life I have done little but dream. The three years in Algeria haven't changed that. Am I now going to live my dreams? I have sworn to believe in them. I staked my life. I might have lost everything. And now everything has been given back to me.

The *Ville d'Oran* comes into Marseilles and my excited joy suddenly dissolves. For there on the dock several hundred soldiers are waiting to leave, just as I was three years ago. I am afraid, afraid for them, afraid for my thousands of comrades, known or unknown, enemies or friends. For I now know that they risk more than death.

They risk the loss of everything that could make them men.